Sports and K–12 Education

Sports and K–12 Education

Insights for Teachers, Coaches, and School Leaders

Edited by Ian Parker Renga and Christopher Benedetti

ROWMAN & LITTLEFIELD
Lanham • Boulder • New York • London

Published by Rowman & Littlefield
An imprint of The Rowman & Littlefield Publishing Group, Inc.
4501 Forbes Boulevard, Suite 200, Lanham, Maryland 20706
www.rowman.com

Unit A, Whitacre Mews, 26-34 Stannary Street, London SE11 4AB

British Library Cataloguing in Publication Information Available

Library of Congress Cataloging-in-Publication Data Available
Library of Congress Control Number: 2018942608

ISBN 978-1-4758-4139-8 (cloth : alk. paper)
ISBN 978-1-4758-4143-5 (pbk. : alk. paper)
ISBN 978-1-4758-4144-2 (electronic)

∞ ™ The paper used in this publication meets the minimum requirements of American
National Standard for Information Sciences Permanence of Paper for Printed Library
Materials, ANSI/NISO Z39.48-1992.

Printed in the United States of America

To Thomas and Caroline—IPR
To Davis and Sophia—CB

Contents

Foreword   ix
   Paul Wright

Preface   xv

Introduction: Kicking Off an Inquiry into Sports and K–12
   Education   1
   Ian Parker Renga and Christopher Benedetti

Part I: Sports and Classroom Success   9

1   Developing a Classroom Playbook: From the Locker Room
    to the Classroom   11
    Megan M. Buning and K. Jamil Northcutt

2   The Point of Missed Shots: Pursuing Greatness in the Urban
    Classroom   27
    Halley Gruber

3   Climbing the Pyramid of Success in a High-Stakes
    Environment   35
    Heather Rogers Haverback

4   Examining the Professional Identities of Academic Teachers
    and Athletic Coaches: A Case Study of a First-Year Teacher-
    Coach   49
    Alan Brown

Part II: Sports and Identity   65

5   Toward an Expansive View of Student-Athletes beyond the
    Court: 67
    Robert D. Greim

6   Student-Athlete Identity Formation and the Relationship
    between an Athletic Subculture and Academic Success: 77
    De'Andre L. Shepard

7   The Language of Teammates and Coaches in Action:
    Perspectives on Urban Girls' Volleyball and Basketball
    Teams   89
    Antonio E. Naula-Rodríguez

8   Race, Affect, and Running: A Decolonial Reflection on
     School Athletics   101
     Michael Domínguez

Part III: Sports, Media, and Schools   **117**

9   Sporty Girls and Tomboys: Negotiating the Rhetoric
     Surrounding Female Athletes   119
     Crystal L. Beach and Katie S. Dredger

10 Between Being and Becoming: The Adolescent-Athlete in
     Young Adult Fiction   135
     Mark A. Lewis and Luke Rodesiler

11 Beautiful Quarterback Passes, Golf Swings, and . . .
     Teaching Moves?   151
     Ian Parker Renga

About the Editors   161
About the Contributors   163

Foreword

Paul Wright

I was honored to be invited to write a foreword for this edited collection and I was intrigued by the topic for three main reasons. First, I am an educational researcher who specializes in youth sport and physical education. Second, as a professor, I prepare future teachers and coaches. Third, I am the father of three children who are all school age and have participated in a variety of sports in school and community settings. Through each of these lenses, I see the relevance and need for an ongoing conversation about sports and K–12 education.

The editors of this collection have brought together a team of talented and insightful authors. Because the experiences and points made by the authors vary, their work combines to illustrate the complex web of inter-actions between sport and K–12 education. At the same time, the collection of writings is well organized to represent the ways sport relates to the following three broad topics: (a) classroom success, (b) identity, and (c) media and schools.

The editors and the authors strike a balance between optimism about the positive contributions sport can make in K–12 education and a critical eye for the places it falls short, or, worse yet, does harm. I see no reason to summarize the contents of this collection in the remainder of this fore-word. Instead, I highlight some of its overarching strengths and contribu-tions as well as some of the questions it raises for me.

It may be useful for me to share a little about my background, because it shapes my interpretations and reactions to this collection. I specialize in physical education and sport pedagogy. As a professor, I have done re-search and prepared professionals in this area for sixteen years. I have published several dozen research articles and chapters on sport-based youth development and a particular instructional model called Teaching Personal and Social Responsibility.[1] I have received grants and awards from the U.S. Fulbright Commission, the U.S. Department of State, the Robert Wood Johnson Foundation, and the National Association for Sport and Physical Education, as well as the European Union's Commis-sion on International Exchange.

However, in writing this foreword, what probably is more important is the fact that for twenty years I have taught and directed sport and physical activity programs in K–12 settings. Most of my action research has been done in after-school and physical education settings, but I actively consult and collaborate with community-based youth sport organizations. The majority of my work has been done in underserved and marginalized communities (i.e., inner-city communities with high concentrations of racial segregation, poverty, and crime).

I emphasize the use of sport as a vehicle to promote holistic development and teach transferable life skills that students can use in other parts of their lives to thrive and reach their potential. Because I spend so much time working with students, teachers, and administrators in schools and the communities they serve, the practical insights and stories shared by the authors resonated deeply with me.

Relating to the needs of real-world communities and schools, I appreciate the fact that this collection so naturally blends theory and practice. Many of the authors are teachers, coaches, and school administrators. Who would know better than they do about the current state of affairs around sport in our educational system? As reflective practitioners, such individuals have a great deal of craft knowledge and situational insights to share.[2]

Make no mistake; these authors are deep thinkers who connect their work to theory and social issues. What stands out the most to me is that they do this in a very grounded and practical way. The noted psychologist Kurt Lewin once said, "There is nothing so practical as a good theory." This collection, by and large, has illustrated that. The insights and reflections shared are not only relevant to theory and practice, but they illustrate how the two should be working together as we continue to ask important questions about the role of sport in K–12 education.

My own work is based in the principles of democratic education, social justice, and holistic development. Therefore, I applaud the authors in this collection for their willingness to ask critical questions about the aims of education, access, and the ways we label and compartmentalize individuals. This occurs in sport and in K–12 education separately and where they intersect. Our current emphasis on meritocracy and achievement tends to reduce athletes to their free-throw percentage or their fastest time. In the same way, students often are reduced to their grade point average or ACT score.

In my view, any adult who is in a position of power and influence over students has a moral obligation to support their overall development and do what is best for them—this goes for principals, teachers, and coaches alike. This obligation includes a commitment to address systematic discrimination or inequity based on race, gender, ability, sexual identity, and other personal characteristics. Responsible adults should be aware of these issues and do what they can to address them and advocate for all of their students' rights to holistic development and sport participation as well as the right to be protected from bias and discrimination. I applaud the authors for taking such a stance as they discuss issues of educational equity, race and gender bias, as well as inclusion of LGBTQ students.

A major theme in my research is the notion of teaching life skills through sports.[3] To clarify what I mean by this, a sport-specific skill is one that can be taught and developed through practice but is only used in the sport (e.g., the free throw in basketball). A life skill can also be taught and developed in the sport setting, but it is not restricted to that setting (e.g., goal setting). Life lessons about perseverance, leadership, conflict resolution, communication, teamwork, and a host of other skills can be developed in sport and applied in other contexts such as the classroom, work, and home.[4]

An awareness and belief in this process undergirds common expressions such as "sport builds character." However, I would argue that this does not happen automatically; and, in fact, sport can teach negative lessons and develop poor character.[5] Consider the life lessons taught by a coach who encourages players to bend the rules, be overly aggressive, and win at all costs. What lessons does this teach about fair play, ethics, the rights and feelings of others, and so forth?

It is clear that the editors and authors recognize that educators often make the connection between their own sport experience and what they do in the school or the classroom. They sometimes discuss passing on these life skills to the next generation of players through their work. I applaud this but add one admonition: This aspect of sport should not be left to chance. In the context of an educational system, this is one of the most compelling reasons to integrate sport. Beyond psychomotor development, sport experiences at the team, school, and even district levels should have a clear commitment and intentional approach to teaching positive values and life skills.

Recently, I have been using the framework of Social and Emotional Learning as a bridge between the education system and sport programs (see www.casel.org). This framework identifies competencies related to self-awareness, self-management, social awareness, relationship skills, and responsible decision making. These competencies have been shown to help students do better in school, steer clear of trouble, and enjoy better life outcomes.[6] Social and emotional learning competencies are highly relevant in K–12 education and have been adopted as standards in some states. At the same time, they represent the sort of life skills that we know sport has the potential to develop.[7] The current collection certainly opens the door for a conversation about ways the aims and experiences of sport can be aligned with instead of separate from the educational mission.

No single collection can address every possible aspect of a topic as broad as sport and K–12 education. Yet, if done well, one can stimulate reflection and create a space for ongoing dialogue. With that in mind, I offer a few examples of questions that came to me while reading this collection. Although not all students are athletes, all are exposed to sport culture through the media, the daily life of the school, and so on. Those who do not participate often perceive athletes as receiving special attention and favoritism. We know that athletes often suffer from undue stress and pressure while trying to balance these competing roles of student and athlete.

It is also acknowledged in the collection that coach-teachers wrestle with a parallel role conflict. Is it possible we are getting diminishing returns? If the role of sport in K–12 education is to enhance and complement the overall educational mission, have we gone too far? Is it in some ways hindering the educational mission? As we wrestle with issues like this, it sometimes helps to take an international perspective. Our system of interscholastic sport is not the only way to involve youth in sport.

In many countries, competitive sport and pathways to the elite levels are based in communities and leagues. Children and adolescents who have these aspirations can pursue them but in a way that has little influence on their schooling experience. I am not proposing that one approach is better than another, but I do think we should follow the lead of the authors in this collection and not be afraid to ask big questions and look at sport's role in K–12 education with fresh eyes.

I explained earlier that pedagogy is my focus, and much of the work I do relates to physical education. Physical education is mentioned in this collection; I do hope it becomes a larger part of this growing conversation. Not all students elect (or are able) to participate in interscholastic sport, but virtually all students participate in physical education. Some scholars have argued that a major role of physical education in K–12 education should be to give all students exposure to a variety of sports and experience with sport culture. An ill-defined mission and marginalization within the curriculum have brought the quality of physical education into question in recent decades; a number of research-based best-practice models are relevant to this conversation.[8]

The sport education model, for example, was developed with the express purpose of providing students with a deeper and more authentic sport experience than they typically receive in a multi-activity program with six-week units. For example, in sport education, students might spend an entire semester on baseball that would be organized with a preseason, regular season, and postseason tournament.[9] Students would have genuine team affiliations, celebrations, and responsible roles in running their team (e.g., fitness instructor, equipment manager, journalist, and statistician).

Another instructional model that is well known for deepening the quality of sport instruction is Teaching Games for Understanding.[10] The objective of this model is to push students' understanding of tactics and strategies. Instead of focusing on isolated skills, a teacher using this approach would throw students into game play sooner, with minimal instruction, and then stop to see what questions emerge. Students become active learners in figuring out what they need to practice, what tactics work best, and so forth. I also mentioned the Teaching Personal and Social Responsibility[11] model above. This is an approach that places special emphasis on those positive values and life skills that can be developed through sport. I mention these various models because they represent best practice in the field of physical education currently and serve as examples of how a high-quality physical education program within K–12 education is an equitable approach to promoting sport culture.[12]

In their introduction, Ian Parker Renga and Christopher Benedetti position this collection as a conversation starter about ways sport culture can foster just and inclusive communities in K–12 education. However, they also acknowledge the subject introduces as many problems as possibilities and introduce some core questions the authors address, including:

- What practical insights on the challenges of K–12 teaching and leadership can be gleaned from coaches', athletes', and authors' own sport experiences?
- What dilemmas do teachers, coaches, and students face in navigating the multiple roles and identities associated with athletic participation?
- How do sports inform cultural understandings of students, teachers, and schooling?

These questions and more are addressed in a reflective, insightful, and practical way throughout this collection. For those interested in the topic of K–12 education and sport, this is an important piece of work. I am not aware of another book that addresses this intersection so seriously and comprehensively. This collection does an excellent job kicking off a conversation that should be had at many levels and by numerous stakeholders. I have no doubt that the ideas presented here will provide a great springboard for reflection and hopefully improved practice in sport and K–12 education.

Paul Wright
Lane/Zimmerman Endowed Professor
Department of Kinesiology and Physical Education
Northern Illinois University

NOTES

1. Donald R. Hellison, *Teaching Personal and Social Responsibility through Physical Activity* (Champaign, IL: Human Kinetics, 2011).

2. Donald A. Schön, ed., *The Reflective Turn: Case Studies In and On Educational Practice* (New York: Teachers College Press, 1991).

3. See Barrie Gordon, Jenn M. Jacobs, and Paul M. Wright, "Social and Emotional Learning through a Teaching Personal and Social Responsibility Based After-School Program for Disengaged Middle-School Boys," *Journal of Teaching in Physical Education* 35, no. 4 (2016): 358–69; Paul M. Wright, Weidong Li, Sheng Ding, and Molly Pickering, "Integrating a Personal and Social Responsibility Program into a Wellness Course for Urban High School Students: Assessing Implementation and Educational Outcomes," *Sport, Education and Society* 15, no. 3 (2010): 277–98; Paul M. Wright, Jenn M. Jacobs, James D. Ressler, and Jinhong Jung, "Teaching for Transformative Educational Experience in a Sport for Development Program," *Sport, Education and Society* 21, no. 4 (2016): 531–48.

4. Daniel Gould and Sarah Carson, "Life Skills Development through Sport: Current Status and Future Directions," *International Review of Sport and Exercise Psychology* 1, no. 1 (2008): 58–78.

5. Also see Albert J. Petitpas, Allen E. Cornelius, Judy L. Van Raalte, and Tiffany Jones, "A Framework for Planning Youth Sport Programs That Foster Psychosocial Development," *Sport Psychologist* 19, no. 1 (2005): 63–80.

6. Joseph A. Durlak, Roger P. Weissberg, Allison B. Dymnicki, Rebecca D. Taylor, and Kriston B. Schellinger, "The Impact of Enhancing Students' Social and Emotional Learning: A Meta-Analysis of School-Based Universal Interventions," *Child Development* 82, no. 1 (2011): 405–32.

7. See first reference in note 3; also see Jenn Jacobs and Paul Wright, "Social and Emotional Learning Policies and Physical Education: Column Editor: K. Andrew R. Richards," *Strategies* 27, no. 6 (2014): 42–44.

8. Paul M. Wright and David S. Walsh, "Subject Matters of Physical Education," in Ming Fang, Brian D. Schultz, and William H. Schubert, eds., *The SAGE Guide to Curriculum in Education* (Thousand Oaks, CA: Sage, 2015).

9. Daryl Siedentop, "What Is Sport Education and How Does It Work?" *Journal of Physical Education, Recreation & Dance* 69, no. 4 (1998): 18–20.

10. Linda L. Griffin and Joy Butler, *Teaching Games for Understanding: Theory, Research, and Practice* (Champaign, IL: Human Kinetics, 2005).

11. See note 1 for reference.

12. David Kirk, "Educational Value and Models-Based Practice in Physical Education," *Educational Philosophy and Theory* 45, no. 9 (2013): 973–86.

Preface

This book emerged, as collaborative projects often do, from a conversation between colleagues. Though neither of us identifies as an athlete, our personal histories are interwoven with sports in numerous ways. Ian Parker Renga can mark the passage of time by memories of watching big games and marquee sporting events such as the Olympics with his family. He played baseball, basketball, and soccer, and rowed crew for several years. Christopher Benedetti was raised in a sports-oriented family and supported the home baseball, basketball, and football teams while also competing in those sports as an outfielder, point guard, and safety through high school.

We also have encountered and continue encountering sports in our professional work. We find that many of our teacher and principal candidates are athletic coaches or plan to coach. Many of them played sports or, like us, continue to follow favorite sports teams. The impact of this athletic knowledge and experience seems relatively unexplored by practitioners and overlooked in preparation courses and K–12 professional development. *Sports and K–12 Education* is an effort to remedy this situation.

The book took shape one afternoon as we began chatting about how sports knowledge might be tapped to engage candidates in critical reflection of professional practice. Benedetti is a golfer and had been pondering the use of a golfing metaphor to help educators further understand the individual physical and mental challenges of teaching. Inspired by Benedetti's line of thinking, Renga found himself thinking about intriguing parallels between teaching and fly fishing while standing in a bend of the Gunnison River.

Benedetti's initial concept eventually transformed into something broader in scope. The selected authors, with their range of backgrounds, voices, and perspectives, aided in this transformation. As teachers and learners we find immense value in a liberal education that approaches topics from multiple angles, setting the stage for deeper scholarly investigation and critical reflections of one's practice. The book is best viewed as an entry point into a rich curriculum comprising a constellation of articles, books, and Web resources, many of which are highlighted in the authors' endnotes.

Of course, the curriculum also includes readers' own sports experiences along with the experiences of other stakeholders. Such experiences are easy to take for granted in schools, where physical education and sports typically are cordoned off from academics as extracurricular additions to the "core" curriculum. Readers are invited to foreground those sports experiences and view them against the theories, concepts, and ideas put forth in the chapters. We also recommend expanding the inquiry to include one's students and colleagues in a larger dialogue over sports and its presence, impact, and role in K–12 settings.

Sports and K–12 Education is a small contribution to a growing field. We are indebted to individuals within that field who provided insight, direction, and encouragement as the project got off the ground, notably Jennifer Hoffman and Alan Brown. We are grateful for Naomi Silverman's guidance and the invaluable feedback of several reviewers on early versions of the text. Our collaboration was enabled by the supportive faculty in the education department at Western State Colorado University (where Benedetti worked at the project's outset). Likewise, we are fortunate to have concerned partners championing our scholarly efforts—an enormous thanks to Katie Renga and Gillian Benedetti. Lastly, we couldn't have produced the book without the passion and commitment of our authors. It was truly a team effort.

Introduction

Kicking Off an Inquiry into Sports and K–12 Education

Ian Parker Renga and Christopher Benedetti

It is curious though not surprising that so much of the K–12 landscape is infused with sports. The evidence is everywhere: teachers and school leaders frequently say things such as "She really is a team player," "He hit a homerun on that project," "She goes to the mat for her students," or "That school barely cleared the bar on state tests"; school walls are festooned with the visages and insights of famous athletes; faculty and staff support their students by attending games; teaching teams tailor curricular calendars around sports schedules; coaches pipe in over the loudspeaker to announce Friday night's big game; and teachers try making content relevant by infusing lesson plans with sports examples. Educators also bring to their work the lessons of personal experiences as participants and observers of a wide range of athletic activities.

If the imprint of sports is everywhere in education, it is arguably because sports are everywhere in contemporary society. Major sporting events command prime-time television slots, while commercials peddle the latest athletic shoes and sports beverages. Children's participation in organized sports has become a staple of modern family life, and athletics are an entrenched feature of school culture.

In the United States, nearly 8 million of the almost 16.5 million public and private high school students played some form of organized sport during the 2016–2017 academic year.[1] Likewise, in 2012–2013, nearly half of British schoolchildren age eleven to fifteen participated in some form of organized competitive sports.[2] The number of children who play sports is almost certainly higher if elementary participation is included, and the impact of athletics is likely enormous when informal activity — that is, pick-up games, bike rides, playing catch, and so on — and the preponderance of sports products such as jerseys, T-shirts, bumper stickers, and mugs are taken into account. Therefore, it is reasonable to assume that sports have an outsized influence on the cultural fabric of twenty-first-century society;[3] what this means for educators — how it affects their work and might benefit their practice — is worth unpacking.

To frame the inquiry, readers are invited to adopt a cultural perspective on sports as it lives within and shapes K–12 schools. Especially useful is Clifford Geertz's notion of culture as "webs of significance"[4] that humans spin for themselves, discernible in practices, accumulated stories, and fragmented behaviors. These cultural threads are public in the sense that they form between people as they work together to develop common understandings of the world, which in turn serves to forge and renew bonds of kinship. The resulting webs thus provide a sense of coherence for communities and offer key resources for assembling meaningful identities.[5]

Significantly, accessing such resources can be difficult for individuals positioned as outsiders. Student-athletes of color, for example, often struggle to construct an academic or "student" identity given the frequent failure of teachers to tap the reservoir of knowledge they bring to the classroom, including rich conceptual understandings formed on the court.[6]

Furthermore, it is worth keeping in mind that threads of culture are not givens but constructions of the imagination. Talk of imagination can evoke associations with fantasy, or unreality.[7] But this undermines the powerful role played by a social, historical imaginary that shapes reality as humans convert the grist of lived experience into stories, myths, and narratives of special significance to themselves and their communities. These stories are ubiquitous and evolving as people communicate their preferred ideals and visions of the good life through simple conversation, scholarly exchanges, television, film, and social media, to name a few.

Charles Taylor suggests that stories within the imaginary of modern, Western culture often contain a common thread traceable to a theory of individual liberty that presumes each of us to be wholly autonomous and inherently competitive.[8] He observes that this theory signified an important break from the conferral of privilege and power based on a perceived cosmic order to a view that anybody, regardless of background, should have the right to make something of himself through hard work, ingenuity, and persistence. The central significance of the individual thus emerged; and merit, or earned achievement, took hold in the public imagination as the basis of fairness.

This theory of individual merit is readily seen in the mythologizing of modern sports culture. Take, for example, the following quote from Dick Vitale, the iconic and highly quotable college basketball commentator: "I learned from my mom and dad, who didn't have a formal education but had doctorates of love. They told me that if you gave 110 percent all the time, a lot of beautiful things will happen."[9] In his folksy way, Vitale offers a reminder that good things come to those who work hard at what they love.

For many, this is a commonsense recipe for success. Practice hard; give it more than you've got; keep getting up; and leave it all on the court: these are often highlighted as the core lessons of athletic pursuit and form the basis of a common understanding of merit. Leaders aiming to connect with the general public can safely make reference to this recipe given its hold on the social imaginary, as President Obama did while confronting the outcome of the 2016 U.S. presidential election. After using a relay-race analogy to frame the presidential hand-off of power, he added:

> And then if we lose, we learn from our mistakes, we do some reflection. We lick our wounds, we brush ourselves off. We get back in the arena. We go at it. We try even harder the next time. [10]

Such lines could have been lifted directly from a popular sports movie. For the hardened cynic the sentiment may ring hollow, and for the critical theorist understandably wary of neoliberalism's love affair with merit, it may seem misguided.

Indeed, the prevailing meritocratic storyline is troublesome given its tight association with individualism. Unchallenged, this storyline can breed blindness to difference and a belief that individual grit and gumption matter more than markers of group affiliation. Seen from this vantage, efforts to address systemic oppression based on race, class, gender, sexuality, or ethnicity are interpreted as attempts to "rig the game" against the winners and excuse the losers from assuming personal responsibility for their failures.

Critics of this view are quick to point out that "the game" of succeeding in U.S. society is, and always has been, rigged in favor of the dominant group—whites,[11] and white men especially—who nonetheless persist in seeing themselves as downtrodden.[12] This holds true for K–12 schools, where the privileges of race and class continue to benefit wealthier white students, whose parents often construct self-serving narratives that ignore the role played by their unearned advantages.[13] A swimming metaphor by Shankar Vedantam aptly illustrates the problem of an unchallenged story of individual merit in an unjust society: "Those who travel with the current will always feel they are good swimmers; those who swim against the current may never realize they are better swimmers than they imagine." [14]

These concerns would seem to indict merit as an inherently flawed concept, though such a dismissal might be hasty. The real culprit is arguably the overemphasis on the individual and the impoverished view of community it engenders. It seems possible for merit and a valuing of community to be compatible. In the aforementioned quote, for example, Obama uses "we" to co-opt the meritocratic narrative not for individual but collective gain—as a call for cooperation among fellow progressives who face long odds in the fight to keep the arc of history bending toward social justice. This is not to downplay the efforts of individuals in such a project; rather, it encourages an expansive view of success that assesses individual achievement by its production of mutual gains and shared benefits. This is a view of merit that seems lacking in public discourse on the value of schooling.

As readers strive to gain insight into sports and K–12 education, they are advised to proceed cautiously when handling the meritocratic narrative. It is important to remember that the powerful and seductive theory of individual merit is not rigid; following Geertz, it is comprised of many cultural threads under constant construction and renewal as individuals interpret their experiences to make sense of them, extract the key lessons, and share them with others.

The recipe for success can thus be changed. At the very least, in the short term it can be framed in insightful ways, debated, or put into conversation with novel perspectives that can redefine it in the social imaginary. Sports provide an entry point into such work, and the relationship of sports and K–12 education could benefit from a multifaceted investigation under the guidance of scholars and practitioners.

Although notable precedents exist in the literature for such an investigation,[15] many scholar-educators prefer to police the line between their aims, values, and practices and those of sports culture. To this point, Mark Edmundson notes how "most scholars don't see much symmetry between what they do and what runners and jumpers and (especially) blockers and tacklers attempt."[16] Comparing his days as a high school football player to his scholarly career, Edmundson sees parallels in how successful athletes and academics learn to confront failure. Being an athlete, he suggests, builds resilience as players learn to get up off the turf, brush away the dirt, and try again. He notes that good scholars become accustomed to transforming the sting of painful feedback into opportunities for growth.

This should sound familiar to K–12 teachers, coaches, and school leaders, who work daily to develop resiliency within those they serve. Educators may thus support the argument that sport has value for the healthy work mindset it instills. But there are significant downsides to sport that must be reckoned with by its supporters.

Edmundson contends that sport is a simulacrum of war, which sounds harsh until one considers the alternative: actual war. Invoking Plato, he maintains that everyone possesses a desire for glory (*thymos*) that is satisfied by playing sports or watching our favorite athletes. A major part of the competitive pageantry is the triumph of reason over *thymos*, which can be seen in players' displays of sportsmanship and respect for the rules. For Edmundson, the exemplar of this ideal is Hector, the famed Trojan warrior of Homer's *The Iliad*. On the battlefield he is fierce and nearly unmatched; off it, he is a loving father, devoted husband, and loyal son. He honors the rule of law and shows compassion for his enemies.

Not so for his Greek counterpart, Achilles, who is so consumed by *thymos* that he wears the warrior's mantle wherever he goes, being quick to temper, untrustworthy, and self-absorbed. As a competitor he knows no fear. The terrible cost, however, is Achilles's constant rage and dissatisfaction.

Contemporary society still arguably aspires to the Hector ideal but struggles with the Achilles reality. Edmundson observes how many of the best athletes are as violent and reckless outside the stadium as they are within it. These gods among mortals present a tricky dilemma as their selfish, shameful behavior evokes disgust even as their athletic prowess evokes adulation. Too often their indiscretions are overlooked, especially if they carry one's favorite team to victory.

Indeed, the best athletes can also be bullies who enforce a rigid social hierarchy based on oppressive social norms. Edmundson recapitulates the frequent observation that misogyny and homophobia are common problems among athletes as players vie for power and status by terrorizing the vulnerable. As many K–12 teachers and school leaders can attest to, this jockeying tends to carry over from the locker room into the halls and classrooms, poisoning school culture and establishing a hostile environment for LGBTQ students, students of color, women, and immigrants.

To this point, a number of scholars have provided compelling evidence of how sports can act as a barrier to progressive social change by normalizing harmful discourses around race.[17] Scholars of physical culture also have shown how the construction of body image through athletic activity poses a number of pedagogical challenges for educators.[18] Media representations of the body are especially troublesome in how they convey racialized and gendered norms of physicality that can have negative consequences on young people's health.[19] Reifying sports thus risks perpetuating a hegemonic status quo that manufactures desired ideals of beauty, strength, and success for the benefit of those in power to the detriment of the powerless, such as children.

So are the trade-offs worth it? Edmundson warns against viewing sports as an either-or proposition. Instead, he recommends foregrounding ideals of compassion and cooperation to enrich the athletic ideal so it can support a more holistic, democratic conception of citizenship.

This balanced approach is evident in recent efforts to develop students' sport literacy in school. Advocates of this movement lament the poor standing of physical education as compared to "core" subjects such as math, science, and language arts. Most teachers and the general public, they note, view physical education as a brain break — a way of supporting "real" academic learning.[20] They argue that physical activity, when treated as a social benefit, can produce individuals who are critical consumers of sport, come to understand themselves better, and support sports initiatives that build community.[21] In this way, the Hectorian ideal of the concerned athlete who strives to achieve greatness fairly and humanely is merged with the democratic ideal of the thoughtful citizen who strives to better society. This vision of merit directed toward the fulfillment of just and inclusive communities is what sports culture can offer K–12 education.

The book's authors are exemplars of the athlete-citizen ideal. Many of them were collegiate athletes, several of them served as coaches or work in athletic administration, and all of them are committed educators who seek to understand sports as it informs and influences their work. Though they address a range of topics, collectively they convey the message that a culture permeated by sports presents educators with possibilities and problems, both of which require thoughtful engagement to best serve K–12 students. Questions addressed by the authors include:

- What practical insights on the challenges of K–12 teaching and leadership can be gleaned from coaches', athletes', and authors' own sport experiences?
- What dilemmas are faced by teachers, coaches, and students in navigating the multiple roles and identities associated with athletic participation? How might educators support such navigation?
- How do sports inform cultural understandings of students, teachers, and schooling? How might those understandings be problematized and changed?

The book tackles (pun intended) these questions through three sections. The authors in the first section, *Sports and Classroom Success*, make connections between the insights of sports experience and various theories and strategies of teaching to stimulate thinking about classroom practice. These authors consider the parallels and challenges between teaching and coaching (Buning and Northcutt, Brown) and how attitudes that result in success on the court bear resemblance to what it takes to succeed in the classroom (Haverback, Gruber).

In the second section, *Sports and Identity*, several different theoretical perspectives are employed to examine the relationship of sports and identity construction in K–12 environments. Readers are asked to consider the challenges faced by student-athletes in constructing healthy and sustainable identities (Greim, Shepard), as well as the nuances and systemic headwinds complicating efforts to support young athletes of color (Domínguez, Naula-Rodríguez).

Finally, the book's third section, *Sports, Media, and Schools*, invites an examination of representations of athletes and athleticism in popular media to consider how they inform our cultural understandings of students, teachers, and schools. Authors unpack the framings of adolescent athletes in young adult fiction (Lewis and Rodesiler), as well as the educational implications of media portrayals of female athletes (Beach and Dredger) and beautiful athletic performances (Renga). Taken together, this diverse body of work offers a liberal education on sports as it informs the work of teachers, coaches, school leaders, and those who support them.

One thing about good coaches is that they linger well beyond the grueling practices and pep talks. They tend to "live on in the ear," as Edmundson puts it,[22] haranguing us to push ourselves to improve. The authors in this text achieve something similar by leaving a lasting impression that should reverberate in practice. Readers who knowingly and willingly are immersed in the world of sports and athleticism—who coach soccer, play on the faculty softball team, visit the cross-fit gym, or simply get the chores done before the games start—will find kindred spirits in many of the book's authors. These readers will take pleasure in the accessible languages and frameworks for making sense of their teaching and leadership experiences. Readers on the fringe of sports culture will be treated to unique perspectives on their work. In the authors' capable hands, they will find fruitful paths for engaging athletically inclined students, teachers, and colleagues around issues of common concern in schools.

Collectively, the chapters should nurture further understanding of the numerous intersecting strands of a rather large cultural web. Hopefully, this work will incite the telling of more stories so that, in Dick Vitale's vibrant phrasing, *beautiful things can happen* in the space where sports and K–12 education converge.

NOTES

1. Numbers acquired from "Participation Statistics," *National Federation of State High School Associations*, accessed August 8, 2017, http://www.nfhs.org/Participation-Statistics/ParticipationStatistics; and from "Digest of Education Statistics," *National Center for Educational Statistics*, accessed August 15, 2017, https://nces.ed.gov/programs/digest/current_tables.asp.

2. Nick Townsend, Kremlin Wickramasinghe, Julianne Williams, Prachi Bhatnagar, and Mike Rayner, "Physical Activity Statistics" (London: British Heart Foundation, 2015).

3. Readers interested in exploring this influence are encouraged to read Barrie Houlihan and Dominic Malcolm's comprehensive *Sport and Society: A Student Introduction* (London: Sage, 2015).

4. Clifford Geertz, "Thick Description: Toward an Interpretive Theory of Culture," in *The Interpretation of Cultures: Selected Essays*, edited by Clifford Geertz (New York: Basic Books, 1973), 39.

5. A number of scholars have richly theorized the sociocultural dimensions of community and the construction of identity within the community, notably Etienne Wenger in his seminal book, *Communities of Practice: Learning, Meaning, and Identity* (Cambridge, UK: Cambridge University Press, 1998).

6. Na'ilah Suad Nasir and Victoria Hand, "From the Court to the Classroom: Opportunities for Engagement, Learning, and Identity in Basketball and Classroom Mathematics," *Journal of the Learning Sciences* 17, no. 2 (2008): 143–79.

7. Eva T. H. Brann, *The World of the Imagination: Sum and Substance* (Lanham, MD: Rowman & Littlefield, 1993).

8. Charles Taylor, "Modern Social Imaginaries," *Public Culture* 14, no. 1 (2002): 91–124.

9. Robert Pace, "College Basketball: Dick Vitale's top 25 Quotes and Sayings," *Bleacher Report*, February 21, 2012, http://bleacherreport.com/articles/1071763-college-basketball-dick-vitales-top-25-quotes-and-sayings/page/2.

10. Jeremy Stahl, "Obama Takes Long View of History, Offers Hope That Trump Will Respect Democracy," *Slate*, November 9, 2016, http://www.slate.com/blogs/the_slatest/2016/11/09/obama_takes_long_view_of_history_offers_hope_that_trump_will_respect_democracy.html.

11. Eduardo Bonilla-Silva, *Racism without Racists: Color-Blind Racism and the Persistence of Racial Inequality in America*, fifth edition (Lanham, MD: Rowman & Littlefield, 2018).

12. Lois Weis, "Masculinity, Whiteness, and the New Economy: An Exploration of Privilege and Loss," *Men and Masculinities* 8, no. 3 (2006): 262–72.

13. In her insightful text *Dividing Classes: How the Middle Class Negotiates and Rationalizes School Advantage* (New York: RoutledgeFalmer, 2003), Ellen Brantlinger offers rich evidence to support this claim. Educators curious to understand more about race and privilege in contemporary schools are also encouraged to read Beverly Daniel Tatum, *"Why Are All the Black Kids Sitting Together in the Cafeteria?": And Other Conversations about Race* (New York: Basic Books, 2003).

14. Shankar Vedantam, *The Hidden Brain: How Our Unconscious Minds Elect Presidents, Control Markets, Wage Wars, and Save Our Lives* (New York: Random House, 2010), 110.

15. Two standout examples are Eric J. DeMeulenaere and Colette N. Cann, *Reflections from the Field: How Coaching Made Us Better Teachers* (Charlotte, NC: Information Age Publishing, 2013); and Jeffrey Michael Reyes Duncan-Andrade, *What a Coach Can Teach a Teacher: Lessons Urban Schools Can Learn from a Successful Sports Program* (New York: Peter Lang, 2010).

16. Mark Edmundson, "Do Sports Build Character?," in *Why Teach? In Defense of a Real Education*, edited by Mark Edmundson (New York: Bloomsbury, 2013), 74.

17. C. Richard King, David J. Leonard, and Kyle W. Kusz, "White Power and Sport: An Introduction," *Journal of Sport and Social Issues* 31, no. 1 (2007): 3–10.

18. Laura Azzarito and David Kirk, eds., *Pedagogies, Physical Culture, and Visual Methods* (New York: Routledge, 2013).

19. Laura Azzarito and Joanne Hill, "Girls Looking for a 'Second Home': Bodies, Difference and Places of Inclusion," *Physical Education and Sport Pedagogy* 18, no. 4 (2013): 351–75. Also see Symeon Dagkas and Lisa Hunter, "'Racialised' Pedagogic Practices Influencing Young Muslims' Physical Culture," *Physical Education and Sport Pedagogy* 20, no. 5 (2015): 547–58.

20. Mary Drummond and Shane Pill, "The Role of Physical Education in Promoting Sport Participation in School and Beyond," in *Youth Sport in Australia*, edited by Steve Georgakis and Kate Russell (Sydney: Sydney University Press, 2011).

21. Shane Pill, "Sport Literacy: Providing PE Teachers a 'Principled Position' for Sport Teaching in PE and a Process Through Which to Frame That Teaching According to Situated Contextual Needs," *Global Journal of Health and Physical Education Pedagogy* 3, no. 1 (2014): 54–75.

22. See note 16 above for reference, 71.

Part I

Sports and Classroom Success

INTRODUCTION

Where might sports factor into educators' understanding of their work and role? Common wisdom suggests that experience yields a wellspring of knowledge. Among practitioners, firsthand experience in front of the classroom or in the administrator's chair is considered especially valuable. Educators presumably come to know what they know by trying things out, reflecting upon what happened, and then making adjustments before trying again.

But educators do not enter into their roles completely ignorant of schooling.[1] Furthermore, what happens on the ballfield, track, or court can prove quite influential on educators and students. This begs the question of how the wellspring of practitioner knowledge is (or might be) infused with athletic knowledge. Part I thus examines the experiences of coaches and athletes to glean practical insights for K–12 teaching and leadership.

In the first chapter, Megan M. Buning and K. Jamil Northcutt contend that coaches and teachers can learn from each other if they cross the "chalk line" to engage one another as educators. To make their case, they draw parallels between the strategies of successful coaches and several prominent theories of practice within the field of education, including Vygotskian learning theory, differentiation, and team-based learning. Having themselves bridged athletic careers with careers in higher education and administration, Buning and Northcutt offer helpful intellectual scaffolds to others building similar bridges.

The author of the second chapter, Halley Gruber, also crossed over from athletics to education. A former collegiate basketball player turned fourth grade teacher, she finds the persistent and positive mindset developed on the court to be invaluable for teaching in her Title I school. Gruber recounts classroom anecdotes to exemplify how "missed shots" can yield growth moments for teachers. She credits her sports experience for setting her up to succeed with students, though she views the lessons of that experience as accessible to all educators.

The numerous lessons that sports can offer teachers are elaborated further by Heather Rogers Haverback in the third chapter. Haverback points out that John Wooden, the famous UCLA basketball coach, started out as a high school teacher and earned a master's degree in education. Wooden's well-known *Pyramid of Success* thus reflects his long-standing concern for the development of young people. His pyramid is comprised of fifteen building blocks for success; Haverback defines the blocks (industriousness, cooperation, enthusiasm, and so forth) and illustrates each through the exemplary behavior of LeBron James, the star basketball player. She also notes how each block supports good teaching.

Finally, in the fourth chapter, Alan Brown revisits the "chalk line" dividing teaching and coaching to examine the challenges of inhabiting both roles. Brown tells the story of Christopher, a real first-year high school English teacher and football coach working in a large public high school. Christopher enjoyed teaching and coaching but encountered what Brown calls *inter-role conflict* as each role made demands on his time, energy, and identity. Brown teases out specific ideas from the story for how school leaders can support teachers with managing multiple roles.

NOTE

1. A point made by Dan C. Lortie with his famous observation in *Schoolteacher: A Sociological Study* (Chicago: Chicago University Press, 1977) that thousands of student hours amount to an impressionable *apprenticeship of observation* of teaching.

ONE

Developing a Classroom Playbook

From the Locker Room to the Classroom

Megan M. Buning and K. Jamil Northcutt

One of the most common phrases in athletics is "There is no I in team." However, in some moments this lesson is forgotten and an "I" is inserted. Consider, for example, the brief anecdote of a high school softball pitcher learning to field ground balls with her high school team. Being a competitor and perfectionist, she tried fielding every ball hit near her even if out of range. She never once considered whether she was successful in throwing the runner out at first base. Eventually, she was so out of breath she had to stop.

The coach used this as a teachable moment by pointing out that the team might have a better chance of getting the runner out if this ambitious player let the fielders behind her get some of those ground balls. She had to learn that they were a better team when every player performed her role and was allowed to contribute to the team's success. Such moments reveal the many parallels between the kind of learning and teaching that happens on the field and what unfolds in the typical classroom as teachers coordinate the learning of a diverse "team" of students.

Sports and schooling have a complicated but intertwining history.[1] In the United States, as the concept of organized teams grew toward the end of the nineteenth century, the nation saw a rapid growth in public and private teams, including secondary school teams and the inclusion of female athletes.[2] Eventually, the United States became recognized more for its athletic prowess than academic strength. This might explain why sports culture often is blamed for the nation's educational decline. Some have even suggested that schools should remove sports teams altogether.[3] Yet a plethora of research shows the benefits of sport participation on a variety of student outcomes, including improved academic performance, enhanced cognitive skills and attitudes, and a lower dropout rate.[4]

Critics also are missing key similarities between the leadership work of teaching and coaching. The strongest coaches arguably interweave several core theoretical elements of contemporary teaching, including Vygotskian learning theory, differentiation, social cognitive theory, social interdependence theory, and team-based learning. Coaches and educational leaders can learn from each other if they cross the "chalk" line. To facilitate this mutual learning and promote sound classroom leadership, this chapter highlights key elements of successful coaching and the relationships to several prominent theories and approaches in education.

CONSTRUCTING A GAME PLAN

The words of Bobby Knight, the controversial yet successful college basketball coach, come to mind: "The key is not the will to win. Everybody has that. It is the will to prepare to win that is important."[5] The classroom and athletic arena are similar in that it is crucial to understand what you are doing and why. In other words, you need to have a clearly stated philosophy and plan of action for achieving short- and long-term goals. The best coaches understand the importance of a personal philosophy and getting athletes to commit to the philosophy quickly.[6]

Legendary basketball coach John Wooden illustrated this with his popular Pyramid of Success[7] used by many coaches. Different from a teaching philosophy that only describes an individual's justification and approach to teaching, a personal philosophy such as Wooden's encompasses ideas, attitudes, and beliefs encompassing the coach's vision for how the team should approach both life and sports. Wooden acknowledges that two games are being played within athletics (and academics): the game focused on winning (or success in testing) and the game of developing players' soft skills (or life lessons).

Therefore, a coaching philosophy includes methods of instruction, but it is more holistic, with clear expectations for athletes' personal characteristics and actions ranging from off-field behavior (classroom) to competition behavior (assessment). First, before crafting a philosophy, it is important to gather essential information about the players.

Determining Strengths and Weaknesses

When asked about his coaching philosophy, Hall of Fame football coach Don Shula declared, "Determine your players' talents and give them every weapon to get the most from those talents."[8] When assessing athletes, quality coaches tend to follow a cycle that can be easily adjusted for students: first, they determine what the athlete knows about the topic already; then they determine how to best communicate to the athlete; next, they determine the best combination of instruction delivery methods for the athlete; finally, they determine how the athlete is motivated to perform. Depending on team size, this process can occur for each athlete individually or in small groups.

The experiences of successful coaches at any level are likely to validate Shula's advice, as coaches must know what talents their athletes possess. In sports, assessment starts early through an extensive recruiting process. Recruiting is a luxury teachers do not have, but they still need to assess student strengths just as coaches continually assess their athletes' abilities. Notable differences in how these assessments occur can be informative for educators.

Currently, much classroom assessment relies heavily on quantitative measures from tests and quizzes. By comparison, coaching assessments largely are qualitative as coaches assess primarily through observation and dialogue to determine what athletes can do and understand. Qualitative assessment seeks to understand an individual's experiences and perspectives within the context of their setting and personal circumstances. This is useful for coaches as they guide day-to-day improvement.

Quantitative (numerical) information is more useful later in the season as coaches compare athletes within and across teams (e.g., batting average, earned run average, passes completed, successful scoring attempts). As in the classroom, coaches use a combination of formal and informal assessments (some with recorded scores and some without). For example, an at-bat statistic or progress toward first down both are assessments evaluated formatively (during practice) and summatively (during competition). Quantitative and summative data assesses growth, but qualitative and formative assessment promotes growth.

Indeed, coaches know that athletes often provide a more accurate description of their performance through dialogue. In coaching pitchers, for example, the dialogue between the coach and pitcher continues throughout the pitch performance and repeatedly through an ongoing cycle until the coach has a firm understanding of the pitcher's strengths and weaknesses. This process can continue for days, weeks, or months. The entire process of the initial evaluation requires the coach to be patient, listen, and be motivated to help the athlete through constant feedback and adjustment. Once coaches determine how individual athletes respond to different modes of instruction, they can start planning practice sessions to enhance the learning for all athletes on the team.

In this way, the assessment process that most coaches use follows the logic of Vygotsky's well-known zone of proximal development (ZPD), which posits that optimal learning occurs when the learner is presented with a challenge that builds upon what he already knows and can do.[9] It accomplishes this by first acknowledging the coach as the content expert charged with guiding the athlete toward new knowledge; second, it assumes that the athlete's skill can only be enhanced or developed by acknowledging what she already knows and is capable of doing. Similarly, teachers employing ZPD must first identify, through quantitative and qualitative measures, where students are in their knowledge about a targeted topic before they can know where to start instruction.

PROVIDING TOOLS FOR IMPROVEMENT

Once strengths and weaknesses are identified, the next step is determining the best approach to improve performance for individuals. This is a central aim of differentiation that focuses on providing foundational content, processes and environment, and culminating products in ways that meet the needs of all students. Specifically, differentiated instruction is the process of "ensuring that what a student learns, how he/she learns it, and how the student demonstrates what was learned is a match for that student's readiness level, interests, and preferred mode of learning."[10]

Ultimately, differentiation means meeting the student where he is and adjusting how curriculum is delivered by tailoring instruction delivery, goals, and output for each student.[11] Although K–12 personnel only recently have been encouraged to differentiate, coaches have been involved in this practice for years through trial and error. It could be argued that teaching a physical skill is very different from teaching a cognitive skill, and there is some truth to that argument. However, coaches and many athletes understand that physical ability can only take an athlete so far. As Yogi Berra stated, "Baseball is 90 percent mental. The other half is physical."[12]

Cognitive skills in sports help athletes learn and understand more about their mental processing to enable them to develop more control over effective movements during varying psychological states of performance.[13] Researchers in the field of sport psychology and performance have linked the mental element to physical performance by providing evidence that a variety of mental skills are connected to physical performance.[14] A tool that could benefit teachers and frequently is used by coaches for differentiating support for athletes is behavior or skill modeling.

Modeling

As a practice, modeling reflects key tenets of social cognitive theory (SCT), which posits that people learn best through observing a behavior in context, with models demonstrating desired behavior.[15] Athletes learn the most through observational learning, particularly for skill movements.[16] The more similar the model is to the learner, the greater the influence the model will have on the learner's behavior. This is particularly true in athletics.

With softball pitchers, for example, it helps when the coach can throw a pitch while the athlete observes. In this low-stress situation, the athlete can process information and focus on skill movement. She can also develop a visual image of the pitch, ask questions about the feel of the pitch, and see what creates a successful pitch (the end product). It is, therefore, critical that coaches provide live demonstrations or engage athletes in less direct forms of modeling, such as through the use of video.

Video analysis, a valuable modeling tool in athletics, is used frequently. Recent advances in technology have flooded the market with software that enables coaches to video an athlete, slow down the speed of replay for easier analysis, and even provide split-screen comparisons of movement with preprogrammed elite athlete models. Such analysis combines modeling with physical movement assessment. Some coaches record competitions, practice sessions, portions of practice, or even off-field interactions (e.g., dugout, sidelines, bench) to observe behaviors of both athletes and coaches. Body language, interactions with teammates and coaches, and verbal communication are critical to athlete development. However, video modeling extends beyond simple recording of desired behavior to behavior analysis.

Technological modeling in the classroom can be just as useful when incorporated strategically and guided by theory. A number of options, including software to assist physics teachers with video modeling, assist mathematics teachers with visually representing measurement and motion, help science teachers capture fleeting events, and assist teachers in analyzing their own communication with students.[17] Video modeling also has produced promising results when used to instruct students who have autism or certain disabilities.[18]

BUILDING A COHESIVE TEAM

Teams that work well together are vital for success. Coastal Carolina University's (CCU) 2016 baseball team is a prime example of team cohesion. CCU was considered an underdog to win the 2016 College World Series (CWS). The team had suffered devastating first-round losses but battled back to win the national championship game. Its success started with head coach Gary Gilmore's leadership and his ability to assist his athletes by helping them set realistic, attainable, and promotive interaction goals. In addition, he provided the resources and emotional support for his athletes to achieve goals when necessary. Coach Gilmore successfully taught the CCU team that the actions of one affect the outcome for all.

Indeed, another key feature of a coach's game plan, or personal philosophy, is nurturing team learning. Much of what coaches such as Gilmore practice echoes social interdependence theory, which emphasizes goal setting and group interactions.[19] The way goals are structured determines the degree of interdependence and the type of interaction among group members. Interaction can be direct or indirect and can promote or obstruct goal attainment for individuals and the team. Productive interactions require group members to work together to achieve shared goals by exchanging resources, communicating with each other, managing conflict effectively, and building trust among all members.

The CCU example illustrates how team members must trust and respect each other. They must be willing to accept differences of teammates and learn how to communicate effectively. In the classroom, students have to trust that their teammates are doing their respective jobs or they will risk jeopardizing the team's performance. Four key interpersonal and group skills are necessary for groups to function and achieve group goals. Group members must 1) learn to trust each other, 2) communicate accurately and clearly, 3) support and accept each other, and 4) learn how to resolve conflict.

Some of these skills arguably emerge by just being on a sports team, but coaches who take the time to intentionally develop these skills are the ones who typically coach the most cohesive and successful teams.[20] As coaches know, teaching trust is difficult. One way to help teammates build trust and strengthen the self is to emphasize individual accountability and responsibility. Regardless of how well a group seems to function, it is human nature for individuals to struggle with the tension between individual and group interests.

Responsibility is nurtured when individuals are made aware of how their contributions (or lack thereof) directly affect the outcome and become motivated to contribute for the sake of the team. Individual accountability is vital to successful interdependence and responsibility[21] and is accomplished by assessing individual performance compared to a standard of performance. This assessment is then shared with the group. Such transparency allows other group members to hold teammates responsible for contributing to group success. On the field, for example, transparency often is accomplished by posting performance statistics.

In the classroom, this transparency may come in the form of allowing group members to submit peer evaluations and discuss results within the group. Teachers can make this fun and incorporate positive competition by staging quizzes or tests as games. Groups can even complete assessments together and present a group response rather than individual submissions, followed by immediate peer and teacher feedback.

Coaches use other tactics to help build trust, acceptance, communication, and conflict skills that can be adapted for the classroom. One of the most popular tactics is the use of team-building activities. Ideally, these activities should be incorporated consistently and frequently during the year. Coaches generally start with small-scale skill- or non-skill-related activities built into practice that may last from five to fifteen minutes. Regardless of focus, the activities force team members to work together toward a common goal. The frequency and challenge of team-building activities depends on team needs.

A notable high-intensity example was the 2004 U.S. Olympic softball team, which took team building to the extreme when they completed modified Navy SEAL training.[22] Many options for team- and trust-building activities are suitable for the classroom.[23] Team building is appropriate for developing behavioral outcomes and building trust among members, but complex teams may require team-member skills training to improve performance.[24] With all team-building exercises, it is vital to engage students in reflection on the activity upon completion to formulate appropriate recommendations for improvement.[25]

STRATEGIC GROUPING FOR LEARNING

Good coaches know the value of strategically formed groups for skills development. Group formation should be guided by a clear goal for establishing teams of individuals. Coaches typically form independent groups based on session goals and athlete needs. Again, in line with differentiated instruction, coaches frequently adapt processes and activities within practice sessions. Over the course of a single practice, smaller groups often are nested within larger groups.

For example, most football teams' practices are structured to build from one-on-one and small-group instruction to whole team practices on the field. Practice, in other words, starts in a classroom. Teams meet in lecture rooms to be reminded of philosophy and strategy to defeat a opponent. From there, they break into special team (small-group) meetings incorporating individuals from multiple offensive and defensive units for kicking plays (e.g., punts, kickoffs, returns, extra points, and field goals).

After these meetings, the team often will split into individual meetings by position groups (e.g., linebackers, running backs, quarterbacks, etc.). In these meetings, coaches offer instructions (plays and strategies) for that day. From there, the division of position groups into increasingly smaller units continues, and athletes aid one another through peer instruction.

Peer instruction is a helpful way of ensuring differentiated instruction and working within a learner's zone of proximal development. The pro-

cess involves more-experienced athletes assisting less-experienced athletes with implementing a desired play effectively (and providing peer
modeling). Strategically, the coach creates a situation where he can freely
observe and move from group to group offering guidance where needed.
Theoretically, by incorporating peer instruction, the coach is communicating to the experienced player that his expertise is valued. He gives the
player autonomy and encourages him to learn by putting his thoughts
and physical feelings about performance into words. As for the less-
experienced player, he engages with a qualified peer and reaps the benefits of more-extensive knowledge and skill.[26]

In other situations, it may be more beneficial to form groups based on
skill or knowledge level. With quarterbacks, for example, the coach may
form small groups based on physical ability and knowledge level, then
assign each group a task to practice scaled by difficulty and complexity.
One group might practice handoffs from the center while another practices throwing mechanics. Each group is in a different place with training,
yet each is provided with appropriate tasks to complete during a practice
based on targeted goals (and all experience differentiation) within time
restraints.

The small-group work builds skills that are then used during full team
practice sessions. The focus becomes functioning as a unit, and the coach
may establish stations where groups of athletes of various positions work
together to compose the larger picture of successful performance. After
stations, the team regroups as a whole unit. The typical football practice
thus illustrates how group work can be fluid, with groups intentionally
formed and variable depending on the larger practice goals.[27] Similarly,
teachers can employ strategic use of groups for individual and collective
learning.

PROMOTING COOPERATIVE LEARNING

Forming strategic groups is one thing; developing teammates' capacity to
cooperate is another. Strategies that could be labeled as "cooperative
learning" have formed by necessity within sports, and the most successful coaches are masters at making cooperative learning work. Building on
the previous section, the goal is to structure small groups strategically so
that group members must use positive interdependence to accomplish a
common goal while holding each group member both individually and
collectively accountable for the group's work.[28] What makes cooperative
learning different from collaborative learning is the intentional focus and
creation of accountability within groups.[29]

In sports, cooperative learning is linked to enhanced self-determined
motivation.[30] In the classroom, research supports the use of cooperative
learning to promote student achievement, persistence, learning transfer,

quality of relationships between group members, and more positive attitudes toward learning.[31] Seen more in higher education classrooms, the use of cooperative learning in the K–12 setting has extended to physical education classrooms, and the findings are encouraging.[32]

One particularly powerful manifestation of cooperative learning is team-based learning. The team-based learning (TBL) approach most clearly resembles what happens on successful athletic teams. Four key principles guide TBL: 1) teams should be intentionally formed, large, diverse, and permanent; 2) students must be held accountable for pre-class work and team contribution; 3) student learning should focus on complex decision making that can be reported in simple forms; and 4) teachers should provide feedback quickly and frequently.[33] Each of these features is evident in winning sports clubs, which capitalize on the complexity and diversity of the team by ensuring that individual players come prepared and are given clear instructions and immediate feedback.[34]

CULTIVATING BUY-IN

Importantly, athletes must buy in to what the coach is selling. Some of the most successful teams have left the athletes' last names off the back of their jerseys. From experience, this keeps the focus on the organization or institution, stressing that the athletes play for the name on the front, not the name on the back. Playing for the name on the front is contagious! Indeed, the idea of playing for something larger than oneself is critical for individuals to become solid teammates. Teachers can create this sense of unity among their students by stressing the importance of the classroom unit and larger school unit. However, neither students nor athletes will buy in if they feel that their leader (coach or teacher) cannot be trusted. Kevin Plank, CEO of sports apparel company Under Armour, is credited with saying that "trust is built in drops but lost in buckets."

In sports culture, it is believed that winning is the cure for all things. But winning arguably masks symptoms and does not address underlying problems, such as the toxicity of players being allowed to violate team rules that establish culture. Consider the story of a high-performing player on a team in the National Football League who risked his team's success by breaking several team rules at a critical time in the season. This player was a great talent and possessed God-given ability that others wished they had, but he frequently found himself in difficult situations.

At one point, the team was on the verge of postseason play, which meant longevity for the staff, economic mobility for the program, and hope for the community. The head coach allowed this individual to play and ignored the player's repeated dismissal of the team's core principles.

Ultimately, the decision created dissension in the locker room, and the team failed to make the postseason. That decision compromised the coach's ability to influence the team, and the players no longer bought into the core principles of the program. The coach lost the opportunity to succeed and the ability to lead.

This story illustrates how building trust is paramount for any leader to have success. Most athletes and professionals have witnessed coaches who failed at persuading the locker room to follow their lead. By comparison, a successful coach gives clear instructions, has a plan, and conveys core principles that are demonstrated and executed no matter the circumstance. No amount of strategy or coaching will improve team success if athletes do not believe in the coach's message. The same is true for teachers and students, who must "buy in" to the fundamental message of success, and that required effort will prove motivating and be rewarding. To enrich this idea, two key strategies are presented that coaches use to facilitate athlete buy-in: strengthening relationships and effective communication.

Strengthening Relationships

As esteemed college basketball coach Mike Krzyzewski suggests, "A common mistake among those working in sport is spending a disproportional amount of time on x's and o's as compared to time spent learning about people." [35] First and foremost, successful coaches care first about each individual athlete as a person. Coaches spend large amounts of time getting to know each athlete's personal characteristics and background. A positive coach-athlete relationship is critical to motivation, group cohesion, and performance. [36] Likewise, the teacher-student relationship matters, with certain teacher characteristics (e.g., empathetic, warmth, learner-centered) having a positive connection to social functioning, behavior problems, engagement, enjoyment, and achievement. [37]

College and professional coaches start the process of forming relationships with players well in advance through recruitment. As the coach works to sell a prospective player on the merits of joining his team, he begins to form a connection with the athletes and important figures in their lives. Early recruitment tactics thus help with the buy-in and retention process. Again, although educators do not have the same advantage of a lengthy recruitment process, they can lay the foundation for students to form more interpersonal relationships and increase trust levels prior to the first day. [38]

Strategies for accomplishing this include sending short handwritten notes introducing yourself and expressing excitement; interacting through a web page or social networking site for students through the summer break; hosting short meet and greets at central locations (e.g., park, pool, library); or having students complete fun, quick surveys that will provide information about likes and interests.

Effective Communication

Teamwork and collaboration are arguably one and the same. As posed rhetorically in the Bible, "Can two walk together unless they have agreed to do so?"[39] It is common wisdom that those who agree accomplish more. This certainly is true in competitive athletics. Good teams usually are described as having great communication, a clear understanding of roles, and the focus necessary to execute winning strategies. In juxtaposition, teams that do not communicate well, lack clarity about their roles and fail to execute, trend in a negative direction and are labeled bad teams. Communication is thus vital for success.

Effective communication comes in various forms. In football, for example, the offensive coordinator communicates the play to the quarterback, who then relays the message to other offensive members of the team on the field. Each member on the field serves a different function but must receive the instruction to use his unique skill to execute his part of the assignment for the play to succeed. In essence, the goal is to advance the ball down the field of play to outscore the opponent. In order to achieve success, each player must know his role and understand the roles of teammates to collaborate on execution of the play.

Much like football, those in athletics and education must work as a team to serve the interest of the student. Although each role differs in job title, the teaching function is distinctively similar. Gaining a better understanding of these teaching techniques can aid both in the execution and delivery of information to the student. In doing so, the aims of a T.E.A.M. (Together Everyone Achieves More) can be fulfilled.

Many athletes are skeptical when they first arrive at practice. Daily, coaches work hard to address three questions on the athletes' minds: What is the coach trying to accomplish? Why does the coach want me to do what is asked? How does doing what the coach wants apply to me? These questions can be answered through clear, direct communication from a knowledgeable and organized coach. Organization and clear communication of expectations and instructions are not only necessary for athlete buy-in and success, but the athletes want them.[40] The same arguably holds for how educators interact with those they lead.

Accomplished coaches are mindful of how they deliver feedback. The most successful coaches provide feedback to athletes in the form of corrective instruction followed by praise or encouragement.[41] Athletes' perception of feedback contributes to the coach-athlete relationship. Disciplinary or critical feedback leads to negative outcomes and memories for athletes, but encouraging and constructive feedback returns positive relationships.[42] The same concept applies to the classroom. Teachers can be mindful to encourage students and offer frequent feedback that will facilitate positive interactions. Communication seems like common sense, but it is not easy and requires intentionality. How athletes and students perceive the behaviors of their leaders is the secret to successful communication.

A FINAL THOUGHT

Teaching and coaching are both hard work. Successful people, whether they are coaches, teachers, or administrators, cannot be afraid of hard work and failure. Pele, arguably the world's best soccer player, provided a fitting summary of success when he stated, "Success is no accident. It is hard work, perseverance, learning, studying, sacrifice, and most of all, love of what you are doing or learning to do."[43] The coaching strategies and best practices discussed, when put into conversation with popular theories of organization, teaching, and learning, illustrate how the hard work of educators can produce desired results. Indeed, the tactics of great coaches can be used in the classroom to enhance teacher performance and student learning. Teachers are encouraged to eliminate nonessential tasks from their schedules to make time for discovering fun and effective ways to learn from good coaches. The hope is that by recognizing parallels, coaches, teachers, and educational leaders can learn from each other and enhance the student experience.

NOTES

1. For an overview, see Robert Malina, Sharon Shields, and Elizabeth Gilbert, "School Sports: Overview, Role in Students' Social and Emotional Development," *Education Encyclopedia*. Retrieved from http://education.stateuniversity.com/.

2. A brief history can be found in Jack Berryman's "The Rise of Boys' Sports in the United States, 1900 to 1970," in *Children and Youth in Sports: A Biopsychosocial Perspective*, edited by Frank Smoll and Ronald E. Smith (Dubuque, IA: Brown & Benchmark, 1996), 4–14. Also see Vern Seefeldt and Martha E. Ewing, "Youth Sports in America: An Overview" (President's Council on Physical Fitness and Sports Research Digest, 1997).

3. For an example, see Sandra Meyer, "NCAA Academic Reforms: Maintaining the Balance between Academics and Athletics," *Phi Kappa Phi Forum* 85, no. 3 (2005): 15.

4. Some of this evidence is presented in Beckett A. Broh, "Linking Extracurricular Programming to Academic Achievement: Who Benefits and Why?" *Sociology of Education* 75, no. 1 (2002): 69–95. See also U.S. Department of Health and Human Services, Centers for Disease Control and Prevention (CDC), "The Association between School-Based Physical Activity, Including Physical Education, and Academic Performance," last updated April 2010, http://www.cdc.gov/.

5. Robert Pace, "Bob Knight: The General's Top 20 Quotes as a College Basketball Coach," http://bleacherreport.com/.

6. See Karen Collins et al., "The First Step: Assessing the Coaching Philosophies of Pre-service Coaches," *ICHPER—SD Journal of Research in Health, Physical Education,*

Recreation, Sport & Dance 6, no. 2 (2011): 21–29. Also Chantal Vallée and Gordon Bloom, "Building a Successful University Program: Key and Common Elements of Expert Coaches," *Journal of Applied Sport Psychology* 17, no. 3 (2005): 179–96.

7. John Wooden and Jay Carty, *Coach Wooden's Pyramid of Success: Building Blocks for a Better Life* (Ventura, CA: Regal Books, 2005).

8. Mark Myette, "5 Steps to Make Work . . . Not Work!" *Noomii: The Professional Coach Directory*, http://www.noomii.com/.

9. Lev S. Vygotsky, "Interaction between Learning and Development," in *Mind in Society: The Development of Higher Psychological Processes*, edited by Michael Cole, Vera John-Steiner, Sylvia Scribner, and Ellen Souberman (Cambridge: Harvard University Press, 1978), 79–91.

10. Carol Tomlinson, "Sharing Responsibility for Differentiating Instruction," *Roeper Review* 26, no. 4 (2004): 188.

11. One such method can be found in John Munro, "Session G-Effective Strategies for Implementing Differentiated Instruction," *Proceedings from 2009–2015 ACER Research Conferences*, paper 14, 2012.

12. Michael Chen, "Yogi Berra's Famous Quotes: 'Baseball Is 90 Percent Mental. The Other Half Is Physical,'" *Globe and Mail*, updated September 23, 2015, https://beta.theglobeandmail.com/.

13. For an athletically applied example, read Brent S. Rushall, "Increasing the Positive Aspects of a Sporting Experience," in *Mental Skills Training for Sports: A Manual for Athletes, Coaches, and Sport Psychologists*, fourth edition (Spring Valley, CA: Sports Science Association, 2008), 2.1–2.17.

14. For a review, see Luke Behncke, "Mental Skills Training for Sports: A Brief Review," *Athletic Insight: The Online Journal of Sport Psychology* 6, no. 1 (2004): 1–19.

15. Arthur Bandura, *Social Foundations of Thought and Action: A Social Cognitive Theory* (Englewood Cliffs: Prentice-Hall, 1986).

16. Natascha Wesch, Barbi Law, and Craig Hall, "The Use of Observational Learning by Athletes," *Journal of Sport Behavior* 30, no. 2 (2007): 219–31.

17. Olcay Sert, "Integrating Digital Video Analysis Software into Language Teacher Education: Insights from Conversation Analysis," *Procedia-Social and Behavioral Sciences* 70 (2013): 231–38.

18. A review of literature is found in Kathleen McCoy and Emily Hermansen, "Video Modeling for Individuals with Autism: A Review of Model Types and Effects," *Education & Treatment of Children (ETC)* 30, no. 4 (2007): 183–213.

19. Morton Deutsch, "A Theory of Cooperation and Competition," *Human Relations* 2, no. 2 (1949): 129–52. For application of the theory, see David Johnson and Roger Johnson, "An Educational Psychology Success Story: Social Interdependence Theory and Cooperative Learning," *Educational Researcher* 38, no. 5 (2009): 365–79.

20. John Mathieu et al., "Modeling Reciprocal Team Cohesion-Performance Relationships, as Impacted by Shared Leadership and Members' Competence," *Journal of Applied Psychology* 100, no. 3 (2015): 713–34.

21. Julie Archer-Kath, David Johnson, and Roger Johnson, "Individual versus Group Feedback in Cooperative Groups," *Journal of Social Psychology* 134 (1994): 681–94.

22. For more details, visit "How USA Gold Medal Softball Team Utilized Rugged Mental Conditioning," *Collegiate Baseball Newspaper*, http://www.baseballnews.com/old/features/stories/navysealtraining.htm.

23. See, for example, *"Team-Building and Trust-Building Activities,"* National School Reform Faculty, http://www.nsrfharmony.org.

24. Scott Tannenbaum, Rebecca Beard, and Eduardo Salas, "Team Building and Its Influence on Team Effectiveness: An Examination of Conceptual and Empirical Developments," *Advances in Psychology* 82 (1992): 117–53. For a distinction, read David Baker, Rachel Day, and Eduardo Salas, "Teamwork as an Essential Component of High-Reliability Organizations," *Health Research and Educational Trust* 41, no. 4 (2006): 1576–98.

25. Giada Stefano et al., "Learning by Thinking: How Reflection Aids Performance," *Working paper 14-093*, Harvard Business School, March 25, 2014.

26. For more on this, see Pierre Ensergueix and Lucile Lafont, "Reciprocal Peer Tutoring in Physical Education Setting: Influence of Peer-Tutor Training and Gender on Motor Performance and Self-Efficacy Outcomes," *European Journal of Psychology of Education* 25, no. 2 (2010): 222–42; and Kate Jenkinson, Geraldine Naughton, and Amanda Benson, "Peer-Assisted Learning in School Physical Education, Sport and Physical Activity Programmes: A Systematic Review," *Physical Education & Sport Pedagogy* 19, no. 3 (2014): 253–77.

27. For a comprehensive excerpt, see Alan Kornspan, "Enhancing the Performance of Individual Athletes," in *Fundamentals of Sport and Exercise Psychology* (Champaign, IL: Human Kinetics, 2009), 39–54.

28. Applied examples are presented in Karl Smith et al., "Pedagogies of Engagement: Classroom-Based Practices," *Journal of Engineering Education* 94, no. 1 (2005): 87–101.

29. Julie Siciliano, "How to Incorporate Cooperative Learning Principles in the Classroom: It's More Than Just Putting Students in Teams," *Journal of Management Education* 25, no. 1 (2001): 8–20.

30. See Lindsay Kipp and Anthony Amorose, "Perceived Motivational Climate and Self-Determined Motivation in Female High School Athletes," *Journal of Sport Behavior* 31, no. 2 (2008): 108–29; and Ronald Smith, Frank Smoll, and Sean Cumming, "Effects of a Motivational Climate Intervention for Coaches on Young Athletes' Sport Performance Anxiety," *Journal of Sport & Exercise Psychology* 29, no. 1 (2007): 39–59.

31. David Johnson, Roger Johnson, and Karl Smith, *Active Learning: Cooperation in the College Classroom*, 2nd ed. (Edina, MN: Interaction Book Company, 1998); also reviewed in Michael Prince, "Does Active Learning Work: A Review of the Research," *Journal of Engineering Education* 93, no. 3 (2004): 223–46.

32. As demonstrated in Ben Dyson, "The Implementation of Cooperative Learning in an Elementary Physical Education Program," *Journal of Teaching in Physical Education* 22, no. 1 (2002): 69–85; and Ben Dyson and Allison Rubin, "How to Implement Cooperative Learning in Your Elementary Education Program," *Journal of Physical Education, Recreation, and Dance* 74, no. 1 (2003): 48–55.

33. Larry Michaelsen and Michael Sweet, "The Essential Elements of Team-Based Learning," *New Directions for Teaching & Learning* no. 116 (2008): 7–27.

34. Although evaluation of TBL is relatively new, research is showing positive outcomes using the TBL approach. See Christopher Huggins and Janet Stamatel, "An Exploratory Study Comparing the Effectiveness of Lecturing versus Team-Based Learning," *Teaching Sociology* 43, no. 3 (2015): 227–35.

35. Mike Kline, "Mike Krzyzewski's 20 Best Quotes from His Time as Duke's Coach," *Duke Basketball*, updated March 1, 2011, http://bleacherreport.com/.

36. See Sophia Jowett and Duncan Cramer, "The Prediction of Young Athletes' Physical Self from Perceptions of Relationships with Parents and Coaches," *Psychology of Sport & Exercise* 11, no. 2 (2010): 140–47; and Nikos Ntoumanis Smith and Joan Duda, "An Investigation of Coach Behaviors, Goal Motives, and Implementation Intentions as Predictors of Well-Being in Sport," *Journal of Applied Sport Psychology* 22, no. 1 (2010): 17–33.

37. Debora Roorda et al., "The Influence of Affective Teacher-Student Relationships on Students' School Engagement and Achievement: A Meta-Analytic Approach," *Review of Educational Research* 81, no. 4 (2011): 493.

38. For more, read Nicole Dobransky and Ann Frymier, "Developing Teacher-Student Relationships through out [sic] of Class Communication," *Communication Quarterly* 52, no. 3 (2004): 211–23.

39. Amos 3:3, King James version.

40. Megan Buning and Melissa Thompson, "Coaching Behaviors and Athlete Motivation: Female Softball Athletes' Perspectives," *Sport Science Review* 24, nos. 5/6 (2015): 345–70.

41. See Andrea Becker and Gloria Solomon, "It's Not What They Do, It's How They Do It: Athlete Experiences of Great Coaching," *International Journal of Sports Science & Coaching* 4, no. 1 (2009): 93–119, as well as Andrea Becker and Craig Wrisberg, "Effective Coaching in Action: Observations of Legendary Collegiate Basketball Coach Pat Summitt," *Sport Psychologist* 22, no. 2 (2008): 197–211.

42. Examples of poor behaviors are documented in Brian Gearity, "Poor Teaching by the Coach: A Phenomenological Description from Athletes' Experience of Poor Coaching," *Physical Education & Sport Pedagogy* 17, no. 1 (2011): 79–96.

43. See Soccerlens's blog post "The Story for Pelé, in Art," *Sportslens*, updated December 12, 2011, http://sportslens.com/artofpele/86387/.

TWO

The Point of Missed Shots

Pursuing Greatness in the Urban Classroom

Halley Gruber

It is a typical day of teaching. Once again, twenty-five fourth graders are finding it a challenge to proceed quietly to the lunchroom. Per school rules, they need to walk, not run; whisper, not scream; to keep their hands to themselves and to remain "calm" in any sense of the word. At a different time and in a different place, running, screaming, and being silly are totally appropriate; however, having the ability to regulate one's behavior in a public setting is an important life skill.

A few options are available to address these actions: the herd of students screaming excitedly, bouncing soccer balls, and thundering up three flights of stairs can be ignored; the teacher could yell at them (inevitably with them); or a management strategy could be put into practice. In this situation, the last option prevails, and as a wise coach might do, the teacher asks the "team" to sit down and create a game plan. A coach might say something like:

"What do we need to work on?"

"What do we need to do to execute this play?"

"We can do this; we got it!"

Similarly, the teacher prompts the students to discuss why they need to be quiet and walk in the building; with their teacher's guidance, they diagram all three flights of stairs and troubleshoot the areas that present the most issues (e.g., teacher blind spots, fifth graders, the fire extinguish-er), and, finally, come up with ways to overcome the "recess-to-lunch transition challenge." Each student copies down the "recess-to-lunch" play into her own *playbook* (a black-and-white composition journal) and agrees to practice this a few times to achieve mastery.

Everyone has bought in, the plan is clear, and the team is a united front, so practice commences. Working together, the fourth grade class marches up and down the stairs. Occasionally, they pause to assess and regroup, consult their playbooks, and talk up teammates who are lagging to remind them that they are capable of "stairwell greatness." Patience is required as the team conducts its third run of this drill as some students still struggle to keep their voices in check or their hands to themselves. Such setbacks are not a deal breaker; the team just needs more practice. "This is okay," the teacher reminds herself. "After all, these are nine-year-olds."

Flash back eleven years to the basketball gym at the University of Hawaii, Hilo, where twelve women stood exhausted and dripped sweat on the baseline. Was it the humidity, or the fact that the team had been running the same fast-break drill for forty-five minutes? The coach was not necessarily mad but frustrated; how were the players not getting it after watching film, drawing, discussing, and practicing the play repeat-edly? The point guards never missed a beat, but the forwards and post could not seem to get the rhythm—so the team practiced.

Fast-forward to the basketball team's last tournament game in Califor-nia where they faced a statistically stronger opponent. The University of Hawaii's standings in the league and tournament would lead anyone to believe that they had no chance of winning. Yet, if one walked into the team locker room before the team was called to the floor, they would notice a different energy: a sense of assurance and excitement that the team would win. The stats, the chatter . . . nothing mattered; no one else knew what the players felt when the team captain led the pregame cheer. Victory seemed a certainty!

The team lost. The game sometimes was close, but in the end they were soundly defeated. They had moments of greatness—some players stood out and kept up—but the team still lost. In the locker room the players were crestfallen, disappointed, and frustrated, but no one quit that night or decided basketball wasn't her sport. Although it went un-said, it was understood that every player believed that the University of Hawaii should have won the game and that continued practice eventual-ly would result in fewer missed shots and success on the court.

PURSUING A GROWTH MINDSET

These two seemingly disparate scenarios—fourth-grade stairway pandemonium and the agony of a basketball loss—exemplify how the lessons of athletic experience can inform one's growth into a successful educator. The path to such growth is effectively summarized by Carol S. Dweck in her claim, "[w]hen people believe their basic qualities can be developed, failures may still hurt, but failures don't define them. And if abilities can be expanded—if change and growth are possible—then there are still many paths to success."[1] As it applies to athletes, she goes on to dispel the myth of the "natural," claiming that "[p]eople with the growth mindset in sports . . . [take] charge of processes that bring success—and that maintain it."[2]

According to Dweck, the possibility of a *growth mindset* assumes that none of us are born with set characteristics and talents necessary for success; rather, these qualities can be created, grown, or developed through concentrated effort. This is in contrast to the *fixed mindset*, or the belief that people are born smart or talented, dumb or clumsy, and will remain so regardless of a desire or concerted effort to change.

New teachers, like developing athletes, must sustain a sense of purpose and a growth mind-set for success. Often, it would seem that the individual who gravitates to athletics or teaching feels an inherent optimism that drives her work ethic and leads her to succeed. Athletes and teachers who believe they are successful arguably develop a personal identity that allows them to be winners—maybe not all of the time, but they strive to play the game and win by making the most of their losses. Among such individuals, a sense of dedication and urgency drives them in the face of challenge or a losing season; they have an almost egotistical belief that regardless of the statistics, they know they can do it. They are excited at yet another chance to get it right, to be the winner, to grow and get better.

Each person arguably is born with potential and, perhaps, a few innate advantages. For basketball players, height can be a gift, though more is needed to make one into a strong opponent and teammate. Teachers similarly may bring gifts to the classroom, such as a capacity to build relationships, but they require a growth mindset and a reflective capacity for such gifts to flourish. This self-reflection and a belief that individuals are not predestined to be who they are today, or who they were yesterday, can inspire one to work toward who one wants to become and avoid dwelling on past failures. Teachers can improve every day. They also have the opportunity to help students develop a growth mindset, thus allowing them at least some control of their future despite their circumstances.

DEFYING LOW EXPECTATIONS

Sports statistics often will suggest that one is outmatched by her opponent. Conceived properly, such signs of impending challenge can serve as a motivator—the stats can drive rather than define the athlete. Besides, stats change with every game. Years of committed practice can give the confidence that high expectations can be achieved despite missed shots. For teachers, part of the challenge is sustaining a belief that all students will be successful regardless of historically defined challenges—the expectation of low scores, poor behaviors, and the very real racial and socioeconomic barriers they face.

But students cannot do it alone. Many students in underperforming schools are confronted with the daunting expectation that they overcome two or three years of academic deficit in a matter of months. Some fourth graders must strive to reach a minimal third-grade proficiency level, which is a crucial accomplishment and predictor of future academic success.[3]

As menial as it may seem to have students walking up the stairs exhibiting self-control, it is intended to promote a growth mindset. Each student will encounter obstacles much more intimidating than mean fifth graders in the hall. In a school where nearly all students receive free or reduced lunch, it is vital to recognize and heed the research that shows that 22 percent of children living in poverty fail to graduate high school, a number that increases by 10 percent for students who have spent most of their short lives in poverty.[4]

To believe genuinely that students can beat the odds, a teacher must call upon the kind of optimistic growth mindset that carries athletes physically and emotionally through losing seasons, demanding coaches, and two-a-day practices. If one refuses to believe that students are defined by achievement statistics, then one must strive to change these numbers with every lesson. Great teachers, like great basketball players, believe in upsets.

Significantly, buzzer beaters and upsets do not just happen; they are the products of hard work, dedication, practice, and a commitment to success in spite of challenges. The connection between athletes and teachers also can be seen in their commitment to stay optimistic when faced with a cyclical challenge as each new season brings its trials and tribulations. Some challenges are familiar, others are novel. Players on the basketball court know what to expect: two halves, ten players, one ball, one set of rules, and one objective. Teachers similarly know what to expect heading into each school year: a class of students, lesson plans, state standards, testing, and assessments. Yet, any athlete or teacher will point out that no two games, seasons, classes, or years are alike. Even though the classroom or gym remains the same, and the plays and curriculum look familiar, different results are inevitable.

High-level competitive sports and teaching in challenging, hard-to-serve schools can be thankless and offer little predictability, certainty, or success. Players and teachers who have a fixed mindset and a reliance on statistics and historical patterns often will feel defeated before the year has begun. To achieve success at a high level and survive in more challenging schools and institutions, teachers must have a conviction of accomplishment, be passionate about the job, ignore the potential to fail, and possess a work ethic that matches their passion. As the following story of Jeremiah illustrates, blind determination and a growth mindset can lead competitive athletes and passionate teachers to come back, lace up, and commit to another season regardless of last year's stats.

SUSTAINING COMMITMENT

Experience teaches that effort and commitment can be derailed by unforeseen and possibly irreversible factors. These factors may impact both the performance of and the payback for a teacher or athlete. Following a setback such as an injury, an athlete may not have the opportunity to return to the playing field; fortunately, most teachers do. Serving as a teacher of record for the first time can be extremely difficult. The students test the new teacher in unpredictable ways, and some of their life stories can evoke tears.

Even in the second year, it can be difficult for teachers to build positive momentum. Doubts can creep in after a number of disheartening lessons, phone calls home, and lunch-to-recess transitions. But, then, one student can make a huge difference. The student of this story, a nine-year-old boy named Jeremiah (pseudonym), was an unusual challenge who taught his teacher a valuable lesson in never giving up on one's students. A tall, large, and outspoken boy of color, he had a history of "defiant behavior" and required a variety of behavioral interventions and a safety plan. Jeremiah brimmed with academic potential, though he was rarely interested in the curriculum. Working with him brought to mind those basketball games that left one exhausted but feeling like the most incredible player in the gym, the games that erase all of the bad days and rekindle one's love of the sport.

Jeremiah offered many tests for a new teacher: He frequently refused to come in from recess, he refused to sit in his chair, and he engaged in innumerable outbursts. Giving up was tempting. But instead, a game plan was developed that centered on building a stronger relationship between the teacher and Jeremiah. This entailed attending his football games, getting to know his family, staying with him after school, and letting him come into the classroom early. The mission was to understand him better so he could be empowered and supported toward realizing his enormous potential. A lot of other plans were drafted for him and the teacher. Early on it became clear that all strategies would need frequent reevaluation, and all moments of success needed to be acknowledged and celebrated.

Progress was made that first year; then, life intervened. During the following summer Jeremiah's family moved out of the school district, and he left the building for good. It was an emotional moment, realizing that this valued relationship would be severed. Jeremiah's presence in the halls and classroom would be missed, as would the pleasure of seeing the mounting evidence of his growth and success.

Perhaps the feeling of loss was mutual. The young man had offered helpful reminders of what commitment can achieve. As the new school year began and the pressures of teaching mounted, an email arrived from Jeremiah. He shared his first essay and presentation from his new literacy class accompanied by a note that read, "Hope you are having a good year Ms. Moseley, I thought you would want to read this. Miss you." Just like that, doubts diminished, and hope emerged for the best season yet.

Moments such as this can inspire teachers who face adverse experiences in the classroom to return, but it takes more—an emotional connection to students and the "game" of teaching. Educators face a Sisyphean task, rolling boulders up mountains in ten-month cycles, each August arriving back at the base again. At the start of each year teachers must call upon an internal drive similar to what competitive athletes possess when they muster the strength and courage to return to practice and face the possibility of loss.

Indeed, regardless of past failures and daily setbacks, teachers and athletes alike must hold on to moments of significance that reaffirm this belief: *this is where I belong and where I feel best about myself.* Such moments serve as reminders of one's unique abilities for making an undeniable impact on a game or student. Jeremiah's email confirmed that his teacher had made a difference for him despite the early stumbling blocks.

A PHILOSOPHY FOR SUCCESS

The emotional drive to make a student's time in one's classroom a positive, even life-changing, experience can become all-consuming. Teachers who are former athletes are uniquely positioned to make an impact. Such teachers display a capacity for strategic planning, demonstrate relentless effort, and are hardwired to adopt a team-oriented approach to their work. They thrive on the pursuit of success and acknowledge that, even though the odds may be stacked against them, they won't quit. Regardless of the challenges, these teachers survive by viewing the season as young—anyone's game—and have the mindset that they have time to succeed and prevail. The feeling is heightened by an inner drive to achieve and the nagging sense that they can and will succeed.

Athletes all over the world dedicate their lives to their sport, spend hours a day practicing and fine-tuning their skills. At some point or another, and more often than not, all of them experience failure, loss, defeat, physical and mental strain, and even injury. In short, they "miss shots." How they transform such experiences into wisdom and growth separates those who ultimately succeed from those who do not. Great athletes know that more can be learned from the worst games and missed shots than from victories and easy buckets.

Like athletes, teachers should not only celebrate their wins, but also welcome the lessons found in missed shots. Teachers can always choose to improve. They cannot pick their class or coworkers, and they cannot protect students from all of the challenges of the world. But just as a bad game last week demands a great game next week, a poorly executed lesson means that tomorrow's lesson has to be twice as good. All teachers, especially those serving in the most disadvantaged schools, should feel an urgency to improve and to experience the immense satisfaction of leaving the classroom each day knowing that they left it all on the court.

NOTES

1. Carol S. Dweck, *Mindset: The New Psychology of Success* (New York: Random House, 2006), 39.

2. Dweck, *Mindset*, 101.

3. Donald J. Hernandez, *Double Jeopardy: How Third-Grade Reading Skills and Poverty Influence High School Graduation* (Baltimore: Annie E. Casey Foundation, 2011).

4. Hernandez, *Double Jeopardy*, 8.

THREE

Climbing the Pyramid of Success in a High-Stakes Environment

Heather Rogers Haverback

Success is peace of mind which is a direct result of self-satisfaction in knowing you made the effort to become the best you are capable of becoming.
—John Wooden[1]

Appropriately framed, the game of basketball is a strong example of leadership and cooperation. Much like schools, where one teacher cannot do it all, basketball also requires many people to work together for the attainment of collective success. Two basketball icons, John Wooden and LeBron James, are exemplars of this vision of success. It is noteworthy that John Wooden, deemed by many to be the greatest college basketball coach of all time,[2] did not focus on "winning," but rather focused on success. The distinction is a cornerstone of his philosophy, summarized in his well-known Pyramid of Success.

LeBron James led the Cleveland Cavaliers to the 2016 NBA championship, an achievement of great import for a suffering city whose last championship was 1964, though arguably it was LeBron's focus on becoming a successful leader rather than on winning that produced the result. In this chapter, John Wooden's Pyramid of Success is presented, with LeBron offered as a model and inspiration for how teachers might benefit from the Pyramid's framework.

WINNING VERSUS SUCCEEDING

One could argue that many aspects of today's society have been set up to focus on "winning" rather than on success. Here the term *win* refers to the experience of having a victory in a competition. This arguably can be done whether or not one reaches one's full potential. For instance, if a sixteen-year-old were to compete against a five-year-old in a game and win, she could do so without successfully playing her best. Wooden's definition of *success*, by comparison, is found in the satisfaction of putting forth one's best effort. Crucially, success differs from winning in its focus on accomplishing one's goals, which may not necessarily include winning, but rather playing or competing well.

In contemporary K–12 public education, standardized testing arguably has perpetuated a need to compete and thus to win. Federal education policies in particular have created a competitive, high-stakes environment within education. During this era of accountability, all stakeholders in education (teachers, parents, administrators, etc.) are accountable for student achievement and effort.[3] Much of this accountability, spurred by the 2001 No Child Left Behind Act, is high stakes due to the linking of test scores to funding.[4]

More recently, while working on the reauthorization of the Elementary and Secondary Education Act, the Obama administration offered funding based on the program Race to the Top. The program offered competitive education grants to school systems willing to make improvements. Though ostensibly about promoting innovation for collective success, the effort's competitive design framed reform efforts as "winning," or beating one's opponents for limited funding.

Similarly, in an effort to establish learning goals for all students, the Common Core State Standards were created through the National Governors Association Center for Best Practices and the Council of Chief State School Officers. These standards were created with teachers' input and are meant to prepare students for college and career readiness.[5] Unfortunately, in conjunction with the testing regime, this policy focuses schools' attention on "winning" by meeting score requirements to procure funds from a limited pot. In some cases, this has led to a "teaching to the test" mentality that does not focus on the whole child. Likewise, schooling becomes a zero-sum game for parents, as they seek to put their children in the "better" schools, thereby negatively impacting the "worse" schools (i.e., white flight).

Despite these policies, test scores have not improved over the past two decades.[6] One possible reason for this stagnation is that the accountability climate has left many teachers and administrators feeling the need to win instead of pursuing success through patient, student-driven efforts at true mastery of content material. One could argue that through such pursuit, students can attain a deep understanding of the material, be able to demonstrate that understanding in various situations (not only answer a question on a test), build upon that knowledge, and become intrinsically motivated to learn.

With the continuously swinging pendulum of public education, all teachers need to take on the greater challenge of being leaders who are focused on the success of all students. As shown, creating an atmosphere that focuses on the growth of the whole student is analogous to the Cleveland Cavaliers' efforts to hone in on the strengths of the whole team. Indeed, the 2016 Cavaliers' success was created by the hard work, skill building, and collaborations within the team, enabled in no small part by the team's superstar, LeBron James.

JUST A KID FROM AKRON

Like the teacher who leads in the classroom and community, many athletes act as leaders. When the economy hit on hard times in the northeast Ohio region, sports kept the spirit of Cleveland alive. During harsh winters and a failing economy, many Clevelanders continue to live for professional sports. Although rifts exist in education and class, sports bond the rust-belt city. Born and raised in Akron, Ohio, LeBron James was the son of a teenage mother who grew up with an innate understanding of this bond. Despite the societal odds working against him and those in his situation, he used his athletic talent and worked on his on- and off-court skills to better himself and, later, his community.

LeBron, as his fans call him, is the epitome of the "rags-to-riches" story, though he has admirably used his success to help others. While he played for his high school team, St. Vincent-St. Mary, fans would go to watch him lead his team. Cavaliers' fans lived with great hope that he would be drafted by their downtrodden team. In storybook fashion, he was drafted by the Cleveland Cavaliers as the overall number one pick in 2003, and eventually he took the Cavs to the NBA finals in 2007.

In 2008, LeBron announced via a special televised event that he would move to the Miami Heat. LeBron was focused on winning an NBA championship, which was not received positively by many fans.[7] This move did, in fact, lead to his winning his first championship; however, it seemed that he did not feel successful in the way Wooden frames it and he returned home in 2014 to take on the challenge of succeeding in Cleveland.

While in Miami, he came to understand what it takes to deliver wins, so he decided to share that knowledge by mentoring the players on the Cleveland Cavaliers. After losing in the finals with a depleted team in 2015, he continued to work hard and became a champion in 2016. To the people of Cleveland, though, the Cavs were just as much a success in

2015 as in 2016 because of the leadership LeBron showed in losing and in winning. In other words, he was a success.

Today's classrooms desperately need teachers who are focused on the success of their students. Much like the city of Cleveland, the most under-served schools are the most in need of such leaders. Research repeatedly shows how poverty and parental education are linked with student achievement.[8] Nearly one in five teachers quit the profession within the first five years, with the lowest-salaried teachers exiting most frequently.[9] Too often, quality educators leave inner-city schools serving primarily students of color for the relative comforts of suburban schools. Just as LeBron fulfilled his commitment, teachers who choose to work in under-served schools exhibit their commitment to those most neglected by the education system.

The focus in this chapter is on LeBron James because he embodies the spirit of Wooden's Pyramid of Success by showing strong leadership skills both on and off the court. Similar to teachers in schools who are working to meet the numerous needs of their students, LeBron keeps his eye on the ball while remembering what is important in life. Not only did he bring Cleveland the first championship in decades, he also pledged to help others within education by sending one thousand deserving students to Akron University through his I Promise program.

In an era of test-based accountability, the teaching game has changed. However, most educators probably would agree that succeeding in the classroom is a far greater achievement than passing a test. Success is working within the daily grind of the school year to make a difference in the lives of students. Although LeBron is aiming for championships, he embraces the challenge of seeking greater success within himself. Teachers can benefit from doing the same when teaching their students.

THE PYRAMID OF SUCCESS

John Wooden is deemed by many to be the greatest college basketball coach of all time. Having started as a teacher and then enlisting in the navy, he continuously gave back to society; moreover, he was a civil-rights activist. In 1947, the team he was coaching won their division. After the win, Coach Wooden refused to play in the championship be-cause African Americans were not allowed to play. In fact, he refused to play until his entire team could play together, which they did in 1948.[10]

Later in his career, Coach Wooden led the UCLA Bruins to ten cham-pionships over a twelve-season span, and he embodies what it means to be a champion, role model, and leader. He stated that one can lose when he wins and win when he loses. He believed in doing one's best in what-ever it is one is doing. Thus, if one accomplishes doing one's best, one has succeeded, even if one does not win. His leadership skills did translate to winning at a remarkable rate as both a player and as a coach, but it was his concise and modest messages to his players on how to be successful in life that contributed to a leadership philosophy that is revered to this day.

Coach Wooden formalized his philosophy into a Pyramid of Success based on his experiences as a teacher and coach. Much of it reflected his belief in the central importance of character, or who you really are and not necessarily who others think you are. Inspired by his father, Mother Teresa, and Abe Lincoln, Wooden created his scheme over two decades. The Pyramid is constructed from fifteen building blocks with which Wooden thought success was created: industriousness, friendship, loyalty, cooperation, enthusiasm, self-control, alertness, initiative, intentness, condition, skill, team spirit, poise, confidence, and competitive greatness.

Wooden argued that these building blocks are applicable to all areas of life. His Pyramid of Success has been admired widely by corporations searching to develop leadership within their ranks, scholars examining the psychological dimensions, and coaches looking to improve their educational capacities.[11] In what follows, Wooden's maxims, the Pyramid's building blocks, and LeBron James's example are offered as guides for educators seeking personal growth toward a more holistic way of achieving success in the classroom.

Industriousness

> In plain and simple English this means hard work. Very hard work.
> There is no substitute for very hard work when it comes to success.[12]

Hard work is at the forefront of what happens in the classroom and on the court. LeBron shows his industriousness by continually learning from mentors and, in turn, teaching novice players. This is exactly what he has done in returning to Cleveland following his stint in Miami, where he was mentored by Pat Riley and his friend and 2006 NBA champion, Dwyane Wade. LeBron is often called a "coach on the floor," as he is constantly giving back to his teammates by imparting knowledge and taking pride in giving an assist on a basket as opposed to dunking the ball himself; he understands the value of getting his teammates "into the game."

This industriousness is paramount to LeBron, as he wants to focus on making each possession a productive one regardless of who scores. The classroom equivalent can be seen on any given day in schools around the country when teachers apply the same level of hard work to create a learning environment that meets individual learners' needs. Moreover, teachers are lifelong learners who learn from mentors and teach mentees; knowledge transfer is not just from teacher to student, but sometimes from superstar to burgeoning player.

Friendship

> The two qualities of Friendship that are so important are respect and camaraderie. To me these are the most noteworthy characteristics of true Friendship as it pertains to leadership. Think how much you'll give when asked to do so by someone you respect and with whom you share camaraderie. You will give plenty, all you've got.[13]

Friendship means a great deal to LeBron, and he may have learned the true meaning and value of these terms after leaving Cleveland. It could be argued that he joined the Miami Heat due to his friendship with Dwyane Wade, but also, while growing up in Akron, LeBron had a close network of friends. In a biographical portrait of the player, Rich Thomaselli notes how LeBron continues to have a positive relationship with these childhood friends.[14] In fact, he and three of his friends from Akron created LRMR Marketing, a sports-marketing firm.

Friendships and caring relationships are also needed between teachers and students in the classroom. Past research has shown that when teachers are able to create a positive relationship with individual students in their class, the student will see the school as a supportive space for rich engagement built upon relationships defined by closeness, warmth, and positivity.[15]

Loyalty

> Loyalty from the top inspires Loyalty from below. It is a most precious and powerful commodity and it starts with the leader.[16]

LeBron demonstrates loyalty, which has often come with a price. First, he is loyal to his friends. In fact, the motto of LRMR Marketing is "A Bond Formed in Grade School. A Partnership Forged from Loyalty."[17] Second, he has loyalty to the cities of Akron and Cleveland. He takes pride in playing and raising his children in northeast Ohio near where he grew up. This loyalty was questioned when he played in Miami. However disappointed, his loyal fans knew LeBron was determined to return to Cleveland. It was this loyalty that made his return so important. In turn, his friends, family, and the fans in his city are loyal to him; any animosity that arose from his initial departure arguably is gone.

Likewise, it is admirable when great teachers remain in the communities that need them most. Their loyalty is evident in the tough choices they make regarding what to teach, how much money to spend out of their own pocket, and how much of themselves to give to their students. Teachers who feel the bonds of friendship and loyalty to a historically underserved school exemplify this quality of success.

Cooperation

> Sharing ideas, information, responsibilities, creativity and tasks is a priority of good leadership and great teams. This is Cooperation.[18]

LeBron shares both his ideas and the ball with his teammates. He has a "pass first" mentality. While watching LeBron play on the court, it is easy to see how much he cares about the growth of the individual players on his team. He directs their movements and oftentimes passes the ball to them in an effort to help their growth, despite many times having an open shot himself. He does this even if it costs them the shot.

The sharing of ideas and care for students are both essential to the academic team's success; this breeds enthusiasm among teachers and students. For example, common planning time conducted in interdisciplinary teams is widely seen by middle school educators as vital to the students' education, as it is a time in which teachers who share the same students meet regularly as a group during the school day to discuss student needs, plan for classes, prepare, and evaluate.[19]

Research suggests that teachers who participate in common planning time perceive several benefits to their ability to work with others, to the open lines of communication with the team leader, and to their high expectations for student achievement.[20] Thus, great cooperation occurs between teachers from different departments, much like well-timed passes and assists on the court.

Enthusiasm

> Your heart must be in your work. Your energy and Enthusiasm stimulates those you work with.[21]

LeBron's enthusiasm is infectious. He gives all he has to his family, team, and the community. When fans were introduced to LeBron as a high school player, his enthusiasm for the game, for his friends, and for his school was clear; and it translated into many successes. His trajectory is similar to the trajectories of some teachers who find their desire to teach when they are young students.[22] This enthusiasm for teaching gets passed down from enthusiastic teachers, and enthusiasm for pedagogy ensues throughout their careers. We must continue to foster this enthusiasm in teachers, especially as the job becomes more difficult with more stringent expectations placed on classrooms to achieve high test scores.

Self-Control

> Control yourself so others won't have to do it for you.[23]

Coach Wooden knew that having self-control in any aspect of learning is of great import if one is to master a task. It is obvious that the majority of professional athletes also have great self-control, and those that do not stand out from the rest, usually in their bad behavior on and off the court. To be a professional athlete, one needs to practice, avoid temptation, and keep health at the forefront of their lifestyle. LeBron James works very hard on the court and is a family man off the court who is rarely, if ever, characterized negatively in the media.

Self-regulation is a process in which the learner activates and sustains ideas and behaviors to achieve a goal.[24] Parents and teachers can teach self-regulation by emphasizing the value of encouraging students, modeling self-regulation, and using good strategies; teachers, like LeBron is to his teammates and the fans, must self-regulate in order to be present and effective in the daily lives of their students.

Alertness and Intentness

> Be persistent. Be determined. Be tenacious. Be unrelenting.[25]

Wooden observed that when a person is at the top of his game, he is alert and will not back down. Watching him plan, LeBron's energy on the court is energizing. He takes control by eyeing the entire court and building momentum within the team. Never was this more noticeable than when the Cavs were down three games to one in their best-of-seven series with the Golden State Warriors. LeBron's alertness and intentness were on full display for the next three games, culminating in three straight victories.

In the classroom, especially those classrooms where children are frustrated easily, teachers need to be able to stay the course and lead. In fact, children within classrooms who struggle need teachers who exhibit a high degree of alertness and intentness. For example, if a child has a reading difficulty, such as dyslexia, the teacher will need to work that much harder. It may be difficult to diagnose the child and find tools to teach her what she needs to know.

But the unrelenting leader will go the extra mile to ensure that she is ready to meet all of her children's needs, even when it is difficult or seems as insurmountable as being down three games to one. Moreover, through modeling such behavior, the successful teacher demonstrates to the child the benefits of relentless determination in learning; this learning is the success that John Wooden describes.

Initiative

> Failure to act is often the biggest failure of all. Initiative is the ability to act. Simple as that. You must prepare thoroughly in all ways. If you have done that you must then summon the wherewithal to apply Initiative. Failure happens. None of us is perfect but you must train yourself not to fear failure. Fear instead inaction when it is time to act.[26]

Wooden felt that initiative is based on making decisions and thinking for oneself. One should not be afraid of failure but should learn from it. In 2010, LeBron thought independently and announced his departure from the Cleveland Cavaliers; he wanted to win a championship and felt that the Miami Heat offered him the best opportunity. This understandably elicited a negative response from Cavs fans.

In response, Cavaliers owner Dan Gilbert wrote a scathing open letter to LeBron in the *Cleveland Plain Dealer*.[27] In the letter, Gilbert wrote that the hometown hero was a coward who had betrayed the fans and city. James's no. 23 jerseys were burned in the streets. Yet in Miami he won two championships. He was a "winner," but he did not feel "successful." In 2014 both Gilbert and LeBron showed initiative again by apologizing to one another for their mistakes, and LeBron came home.[28]

In the classroom, teachers show initiative every day, acting as leaders and taking on challenges by working with students and in schools that are not always easy. Simultaneously, the twenty-first-century classroom is more diverse than ever, and teachers are challenged with meeting each student's individual needs while working to have each child succeed within the classroom. Successful teachers leave their comfort zone and find new ways to reach each student and connect their classroom as a community. When one idea fails, taking initiative to find another way is vital to success.

Condition

> You must be in physical Condition, but you must also have mental and moral Condition.[29]

Being in shape and working on your skills is essential. After losing in the NBA finals in 2014 with the Miami Heat, LeBron devoted himself to returning to Cleveland for personal reasons, but once his course was set, he dedicated his summer to getting in better shape before returning to Cleveland. He had learned that he needed to prepare himself to play quicker. For sixty-seven days he ate nothing but meat, fish, fruit, and vegetables.[30] LeBron was intent on leading by example before the season even started.

Teachers work each day to continue to hone their pedagogical practices, as well as learn new ways in which teaching can be fun and interesting. However, teaching is more than just understanding the pedagogy; teachers need to be in top mental and moral condition. They have to come to the classroom alert, ready, and prepared every morning. Successful teachers act as role models for their students. Every child remembers a favorite teacher, similar to the way many children remember their favorite ball player. Whether teacher or athlete, being a role model of commitment to one's fitness to succeed is part of the job.

Skill

> Mastery of the skills you need in your job requires learning and it is
> why leaders and those who are high achievers are lifelong learners. [31]

LeBron practices constantly—three times a day, five times a week—even
though he is one of the most successful athletes of all time. In fact, LeBron
has won MVP four times and led all players in the 2016 NBA finals in
points, rebounds, assists, blocks, and steals—something no other player
in league history had ever done before.[32] Similar to practicing a sport,
successful teachers continue to take classes, practice the teaching of lessons, and work to motivate their students on each given subject. Skill
development is so important to teachers that they are encouraged to further their education, and a reported 56 percent of teachers hold a master's
degree or higher,[33] which can lead to a growth in pedagogical practices
and experiences. Despite knowing and understanding both pedagogy
and content knowledge, successful teachers work hard to master their
skills and act as lifelong learners.

Team Spirit

> I did not want a person on our team who was reluctant to sacrifice for
> the good of the team. I prized the individual who was eager to sacrifice
> for our common good.[34]

Wooden believed that team spirit was an act of selflessness. He focused
on choosing teammates who would raise the team up, not just win. This
spirit is also found within schools across the country. Many can remember attending pep rallies in high school, the excitement of the game, the
thrill of cheering, and the hope of the pending game. One could argue
that one of the most peaceful gatherings included a highly attended
sports event, the Cleveland Cavaliers' NBA championship parade. The
basketball team motivated the entire city to act selflessly, celebrating the
team in a peaceful but excited way.

Teachers cannot control who enters their classrooms at the beginning
of each year, unlike LeBron, who has had some say in personnel decisions and even coaching decisions in his career. But teachers do have a
great say in who exits their classrooms at the end of each school year.
Successful teachers lead with such spirit and build community by celebrating students' numerous successes.

Poise and Confidence

> Success is never final, failure is never fatal. It's courage that counts. [35]

On the court and in the classroom, poise and confidence are key to having others' attention. Few have more poise and confidence on the court

than LeBron. This was shown in his stance when the Cavaliers were down in the 2016 NBA finals. No team ever had overcome such a deficit. However, when LeBron got on the court, he was extremely confident. What was happening in his mind only he knew, but his opponents and teammates saw someone who was ready and able to bring home the next three games and the championship.

The success-oriented teacher exudes poise and confidence in the classroom and can build such confidence in her students. Whether implementing a lesson or meeting with parents, coming across as confident will put parents and students at ease. Moreover, the successful teacher, like quality athletes, builds confidence by setting goals, working steadily toward those goals, and continuing to work, even when the student has difficulty.

For example, teaching elementary students new mathematical problem solving can seem overwhelming. However, if students feel that their teachers have confidence in their ability to learn, the students will work hard at achieving their goal. Many of today's classrooms present long odds, but with poise and confidence in the face of failure, success is attainable.

Competitive Greatness

> Don't whine. Don't complain. Don't make excuses. Just get out there, and whatever you're doing, do it to the best of your ability.[36]

Wooden and LeBron have shown competitive greatness within the game of basketball throughout their careers. Wooden believed that competitive greatness was doing your best every day, no matter the task or the activity. This is particularly important for a superstar such as LeBron, who took on a team not necessarily built for instant success and gave it his all for the Cavs to compete at a higher level. In this way, LeBron does much more than the average NBA player.

Indeed, what he did for Cleveland is, seemingly, the equivalent of what teachers must do in today's classrooms. When teachers enter the classroom each morning, they have to be prepared to be 100 percent available to their students. Likewise, despite teachers' feelings about standards, they need to lead their classes in learning the material. A teacher's personal needs and feelings are left at the door; the needs of the students come first. Moreover, a teacher may have thirty or more children in class, each bringing the benefits and limitations of their unique circumstances. This is when a teacher needs to be a leader, on top of his game, and ready to meet the children's needs so they might be successful.

CONCLUSION

As teachers, coaches, and education leaders reflect upon their daily work in K–12 schools, it is important for them to appreciate what success means to them and their students. Are they aiming to win the game of education? Or are they after something more meaningful, arguably more ambitious? Teachers face an uphill battle each day and each school year. Although it may seem that teachers are down three games to one in the NBA finals, success in the fullest sense of the term is possible. Coach Wooden would encourage teachers to lead their classrooms by supporting students to do their best to learn, not just to pass a test. He would also support their commitment to the school communities most in need of great leaders.

Although Cleveland fans have great expectations for their teams, admirably they have stuck by those teams each nonwinning season with loyalty and perseverance. Likewise, communities must stick by their schools and support the many LeBron-like teachers who work to exemplify Wooden's Pyramid of Success. It is these teachers who find peace of mind through the pursuit of success, no matter how small or seemingly insignificant. They know that each day in the classroom they are putting forth the effort to become the best they can be.

NOTES

1. John Wooden, *John Wooden, Coach & Teacher*, www.coachwooden.com.

2. See, for example, John Feinstein's piece in the *Washington Post*, "John Wooden: Untouchable Record, Incomparable Man," June 5, 2010.

3. Allan C. Ornstein, Daniel U. Levine, Gerry Gutek, and David E. Vocke, *Foundations of Education* (Boston: Wadsworth Cengage Learning, 2014).

4. For more on this, see the U.S. Department of Education's *No Child Left Behind: A Desktop Reference* (Washington, DC: ED Publishers, 2002).

5. *Common Core State Standards Initiative* (Washington, DC: National Governors Association Center for Best Practices and the Council of Chief State School Officers, 2010).

6. U.S. Department of Education, *The Nation's Report Card: A First Look: 2013 Mathematics and Reading* (Washington, DC: Institute of Education Sciences, 2014).

7. A sentiment captured in Greg Maiola's article for *Bleacher Report* titled "LeBron James: Miami Heat Superstar Is the Most Hated Man in All of Sports," February 27, 2012, http://bleacherreport.com/articles/1082804-LeBron-james-is-the-most-hated-man-in-all-of-sports.

8. See note 6 for reference.

9. Lucinda Gray and Soheyla Taie, *Public School Teacher Attrition and Mobility in the First Five Years: Results from the First through Fifth Waves of the 2007–08 Beginning Teacher Longitudinal Study (NCES 2015-337)* (Washington, DC: National Center for Education Statistics, 2015).

10. Biographical information accessed online, see note 1. Additional information provided by John Wooden and Steve Jamison, *Wooden: A Lifetime of Observations and Reflections On and Off the Court* (Chicago: Contemporary Books, 1997).

11. An example of how the pyramid has been studied is Deanna Perez, Stefanee Van Horn, and Mark P. Otten, "Coach John Wooden's Pyramid of Success: A Comparison to the Sport Psychology Literature," *International Journal of Sports Science and Coaching* 9, no. 1 (2014): 85–101. Those interested in learning more about Wooden's philosophy are encouraged to read *Wooden on Leadership: How to Create a Winning Organization* (New York: McGraw-Hill, 2005).

12. Quote by John Wooden accessed at Wooden's official website, "Pyramid of Success," http://www.coachwooden.com/pyramid-of-success.

13. See note 12 for reference.

14. Rich Thomaselli, "All the King's Men: The LeBron James Version of 'Entourage,'" *Advertising Age*, July 17, 2006, www.adage.com/article/news/king-s-men-LeBron-james-version-entourage/110516/.

15. Bridget K. Hamre and Robert C. Pianta, "Early Teacher-Child Relationships and the Trajectory of Children's School Outcomes through Eighth Grade," *Child Development* 72, no. 2 (2001), 625–38.

16. See note 12 for reference.

17. LRMR, "LeBron James, the Businessman," www.LeBronjames.com/post/category/thebusinessman.

18. See note 12 for reference.

19. Richard Kellough and Noreen Kellough, *Teaching Young Adolescents: Methods and Resources for Middle Grades Teaching* (Upper Saddle River, NJ: Pearson Merrill Prentice Hall, 2008).

20. Heather Rogers Haverback and Molly Mee, "Middle School Teachers' Perceptions of the Benefits and Barriers of Common Planning Time," *Journal of Curriculum and Instruction* 7, no. 2 (2013): 6–19.

21. See note 12 for reference.

22. Molly Mee, Heather Rogers Haverback, and Jeff Passe, "For the Love of the Middle: A Glimpse into Why One Group of Preservice Teachers Chose Middle Grades Education," *Middle Grades Research Journal* 7, no. 4 (2012): 1–14.

23. See note 12 for reference.

24. Dale H. Schunk, "Goal Setting and Self-Efficacy During Self-Regulated Learning," *Educational Psychologist* 25 (1990): 71–86.

25. See note 12 for reference.

26. See note 12 for reference.

27. Dan Gilbert, "Dan Gilbert's Open Letter to Fans: James' Decision a 'Cowardly Betrayal' and Owner Promises a Title Before Heat," July 9, 2010, www.cleveland.com/cavs/index.ssf/2010/07/gilberts_letter_to_fans_james.html.

28. Mitch Albom, "Dan Gilbert Tells How He and LeBron James Mended Fences," *USA Today Sports*, July 13, 2014, www.usatoday.com/story/sports/nba/cavaliers/2014/07/13/dan-gilbert-LeBron-james-buried-the-hatchet/12596623/.

29. See note 12 for reference.

30. The Postgame Staff, "LeBron James Shares the Four Different Foods He Ate During His Summer Diet," September 29, 2014, www.thepostgame.com/blog/training-table/201409/LeBron-james-shares-four-foods-he-ate-his-summer-diet.

31. See note 12 for reference.

32. Fox Sports, "This Unbelievable Stat Illustrates Just How Great LeBron James Was in the Finals," June 19, 2016, www.foxsports.com/nba/story/LeBron-james-cleveland-cavaliers-nba-finals-game-7-061916.

33. U.S. Department of Education, *Digest of Education Statistics, 2014 (NCES 2016-006),* 2016.

34. See note 12 for reference.

35. See note 12 for reference.

36. See note 12 for reference.

FOUR

Examining the Professional Identities of Academic Teachers and Athletic Coaches

A Case Study of a First-Year Teacher-Coach

Alan Brown

The socialization of beginning teachers is a process complicated by the multiple social positions many educators face in American schools. With every educational role comes a set of expectations that reflects the norms required of the person who fills that role.[1] The negotiation between an educator and his educational responsibilities has been made more challenging when teachers take on additional roles, including the role of athletic coach, in the school setting.[2]

Part of the reality shock that many beginning academic teachers who are also athletic coaches—referred to hereafter as teacher-coaches—face is the result of role overload, the struggle to keep up with the demands of role expectations, as well as inter-role conflict, when the expectations of multiple roles seem incompatible with one another.[3] Both role overload and inter-role conflict can lead to role stress, a condition in which conflicting roles can cause anxiety or apprehension,[4] which could lead teaching or coaching to become a career contingency.[5]

Researchers have brought to light the challenges of balancing academic and athletic roles. Diane Drake and Edward Hebert, for example, conducted case studies of two teacher-coaches, both of whom struggled to balance multiple roles after several years of experience based on stresses related to inter- and intra-role conflict, the school context, and family life.[6] Alan Brown described the socialization of a first-year educator who expressed feelings of isolation as the only ninth-grade world history teacher and the only women's athletic coach in her rural high school.[7] As a first-year teacher-coach, she was faced with a challenging load that included teaching three sections of world history; coaching volleyball, basketball, and softball; engaging in other professional obligations (e.g., paperwork, meetings); and balancing family responsibilities and social activities. Meanwhile, other researchers have discussed the importance of examining how teacher-coaches can "reduce tensions and maximize complementarity across the responsibilities"[8] that include academic teaching and athletic coaching.

With these stories in mind, the purpose of this chapter is to allow K–12 teachers and leaders to explore the experiences of a novice teacher-coach—Christopher (pseudonym), a twenty-five-year-old white male in his first year as a high school English teacher and football coach—and investigate the demands of balancing academic and athletic positions in secondary schools. Christopher's experiences will be viewed through the framework of occupational socialization[9] and, specifically, the latter two stages of professional and organizational socialization, which encompass Christopher's professional preparation for and induction into the full-time positions of academic teaching and athletic coaching.

This chapter will focus on Christopher's first semester teaching and coaching in a large public high school in the southeastern United States after graduating from a university teacher education program. His story is part of a multiple-case study involving first-year, core content area teacher-coaches in secondary schools. The researcher conducted three separate case studies that involved weekly observations of teacher-coaches, multiple interviews with primary (i.e., teacher-coaches) and secondary (e.g., department chairs, mentors, athletic directors, principals) participants, and artifact analysis used to enhance, support, or challenge previous data.

Findings were synthesized using a system of theoretical sampling, a data collection method whereby concepts develop in response to their properties, variations, and relationships.[10] This inductive process[11] was based on constant comparative analysis consisting of open, axial, and selective coding,[12] which in Christopher's case produced themes that encompassed his teaching and coaching induction, workload, expectations, and experiences with implications related to role overload, inter-role conflict, role stress, and prioritizing academics and athletics.

Although case studies are not intended to be generalizable, Christopher's experience, however unique it may seem, will provide a lens through which teachers, coaches, and school leaders can better understand the social positions of academic teaching and athletic coaching as well as the identity formation processes of beginning teacher-coaches, including how professional qualities developed through the roles of teaching and coaching can positively *and* negatively impact their overall performance.

PROFESSIONAL SOCIALIZATION

Professional socialization is the stage of occupational socialization that consists of career preparation. For K–12 teachers, this preparation often includes either university preservice teacher education or some form of nontraditional alternative certification. Christopher entered a university teacher education program partially interested in teaching history but primarily wanting to coach athletics. He vividly recalled the moment when teaching became his main priority:

> My sophomore year in college, I was helping tutor a guy who was on the football team . . . and realized how behind he was. I decided I wanted to teach more than I wanted to coach, [and I] kind of gave up on the coaching thing. I switched over to English not too long after that . . . just because I realized how hard a time a lot of people have with communicating their ideas.

Soon after this experience, Christopher put his interest in coaching on hold and began to pursue a bachelor's degree in secondary English education (grades six to twelve) without giving much thought to connecting his lifelong interest in sports to his intended major.

Christopher applied for countless teaching jobs near his university during the spring and summer months before finally being hired. During that time, he received a total of three calls and only a single job offer, a position teaching English II and English III at a local high school. The caveat to the position was that it would require a few extra responsibilities: that is, assistant football coach, assistant varsity boys' and girls' soccer coach, and junior varsity boys' soccer coach. Christopher was not concerned about coaching soccer based on his extensive background with the sport, but football was a different matter. He had never played the game as a youth.

Christopher admitted his focus was on finding a teaching position out of college. However, with an abundance of English candidates in the system, he grew to understand that a willingness to coach athletics might help him land a job. As it turns out, coaching athletics was a necessary credential. When asked about the hiring process, his principal acknowledged seeing a total of 250 applicants in the system for two English positions, so he did not have to look far to find qualified candidates. He said Christopher stood out for two reasons: (1) his potential as an academic teacher and (2) his willingness to coach football and soccer. His principal went on to say:

> With a [large] football team and five coaches on campus, we went into
> the interviews with Christopher knowing that not only was [coaching]
> a priority, but it was pretty much non-negotiable that we had to hire
> athletic coaches.

When he found out that Christopher had experience with soccer, the
principal was relieved because there had not been a single soccer coach
teaching on campus the previous year, a situation he felt was "un-
healthy" for the school. Although Christopher initially was skeptical
about coaching two sports as a first-year teacher, a close friend justified
his time commitment by telling him that mentoring through athletics
might be valuable in building relationships with many of his students.
Soon after, Christopher accepted the position and entered his first year of
teaching and coaching with an open mind and a desire to become successful in both roles.

ORGANIZATIONAL SOCIALIZATION

Organizational socialization is the final stage of occupational socialization and consists of the induction phase as a person enters the chosen
profession. For Christopher, his organizational socialization consisted
primarily of his introduction to the roles of academic teaching and athletic coaching.

Teaching and Coaching Induction

Christopher's introduction to his new school first occurred in the context of football during summer workouts as he was asked to serve as the
strength and conditioning coach based on previous employment as a
personal trainer. Summer workouts began around 6 a.m. daily and ran
until just before noon. When asked about his preparation for the coaching
role, Christopher recollected how naive he was about what it meant to be
a coach. "I didn't know what to expect. . . . I remember going to a coaching conference and calling [the head football coach] and asking, 'What do
I wear, man?' I just didn't even have a clue about the culture."

Christopher's athletic director acknowledged that learning the concepts and principles of the school's coaching philosophy was a difficult
process for Christopher, or as the team's defensive coordinator called it,
"a trial by fire." Indeed, coaching served as Christopher's most profound
learning curve as he started the season scared to make a mistake while
leading basic drills but then slowly progressed to the point of taking on
more significant responsibilities (i.e., teaching football skills and techniques).

In hindsight, Christopher appreciated participating in the summer
workouts because they served as a prologue to his teaching experience

and an introduction to many of the students, teachers, coaches, and administrators in the school. However, coaching quickly became a source of fatigue as the grueling schedule took its toll. Even in the summer, Christopher remembered how coaching impacted his attempts at lesson planning. "[When] you're up here [at the school] that much, and you're doing physical stuff outside in the 110 degree heat, the last thing you want to do is to go home to shower and come back to [write] lesson plans."

Teaching and Coaching Workload

In the fall, Christopher's normal workday began around 7:30 a.m. and ended well after 5 p.m. The school day ended at 3:20 p.m., in which time Christopher generally had taught three classes, planned for the upcoming school day, graded essays, and completed other school responsibilities (e.g., hall duty, lunch duty). He would then make his way to the teacher's lounge to change clothes before arriving at the practice field at approximately 3:40 p.m., where he worked mostly with junior varsity offensive players, including receivers, backs, and tight ends.

Because players participated in weight training and conditioning drills during a fourth period physical education class at the same time as his fourth period English class, Christopher missed out on that part of the daily workout and usually left the school around 6 p.m. on most afternoons. During the two to three game days a week, he found himself at the football field later into the evening, 8 p.m. at the earliest for middle school games and 11:30 p.m. at the latest for varsity games. Once at home, Christopher was a night owl who often suffered from insomnia, and he admitted that the stress of coaching did not help his sleep pattern.

During the season, Christopher also spent his Saturday afternoons and/or Sunday mornings watching film from the previous game to break down defensive fronts and blitzes before the coaches' meeting on Sunday afternoons. During these Sunday meetings, the coaching staff would watch game film, preview upcoming games, probe schematic changes, and discuss any necessary personnel adjustments before meeting with the team. For Christopher, weekend meetings and practices made for long school weeks during the football season.

Teaching and Coaching Expectations and Experiences

When asked about the primary focus of novice teacher-coaches, Christopher's principal said it was "extremely important that they be able to manage their classes, establish a rapport with students, [and] effectively instruct . . . students [in their content area]." This proved difficult as Christopher struggled to handle discipline issues while simultaneously attempting to increase the academic rigor of his English classes, in part due to his lack of experience but also due to a lack of resources. As a result, he used curricular supports from a number of sources, including other teachers, the internet, the library, and class textbooks. "It's a beggar's market," he acknowledged. He quickly learned the importance of flexibility because "you never know what's going to be thrown at you in a school," or, as his department chair put it, "You find out some days you're not in control . . . as much as you would like to be."

Christopher's expectations of himself were much higher in teaching than they were in coaching. This notion was supported by his principal who acknowledged, "I'm very understanding of maybe some shortcomings in athletics if I see that the effort is there . . . [but] we have to have a teacher doing an outstanding job in the classroom." Christopher prided himself in teaching students to learn to think deeply and meaningfully about the English language arts curriculum. On one writing assignment early in the semester, he told students he would not grade them on grammar or organization; "I just want to see your thoughts," he said. His goal was to make his classroom more learner-centered by involving students in deep thinking and whole-class discussions.

When asked about his teaching style, Christopher explained that he used a discussion/lecture format. "[There are] very few PowerPoints. I get up. I show you something. I tell you something. I write it on the board. We talk about it." Later in the semester, though, he began to understand that he had indeed focused too much on lecture and not enough on discussion, or activity, in part because his own voice as the teacher tended to overwhelm the conversation.

The disadvantage of Christopher's approach to teaching was that he struggled to keep students engaged early in the semester despite his most sincere efforts. This was especially true in his standard-level classes, where students were just as likely to fall asleep as they were to pay attention or misbehave. A perceived lack of student motivation led to many frustrations, such as on the following occasion when the principal dropped by for an unannounced observation:

> Some kids didn't bring their books, and half of them didn't read. So I said, forget about it. I'm not discussing it. I'm not going to go over something to give you guys a day off where I get to tell you what all happened [in] the first four chapters. You guys will have to do this [assignment]. So I made them get in small groups to read.

It turns out that motivation was also a concern in his advanced classes. In Honors English 11, for instance, he quickly realized that students had other commitments and priorities, namely AP courses that students felt were more important for college, meaning his English class would take a backseat at times.

Early in the semester, Christopher became afraid that too many of his students were failing, and he worried how this trend might look to the administration. He struggled with his desire to provide a rigorous course of study while avoiding "dumbing down" the curriculum to ensure that students passed the state graduation exam. In general, Christopher preferred to get as much of his grading done during the school day as possible—primarily during his planning period—because he felt the quality and timeliness of his responses were often better than if he took home work in the evening.

In one interview, Christopher mentioned, "I have a stack of papers and tests in [the homework bins] that have been sitting there for a couple days. You know, the papers don't have to be given back until I'm ready for them to go back. . . . There's no sense in handing back a paper until you're ready for them to write another paper." However, his own lack of motivation toward grading stood in stark contrast to his regular engagement in breaking down defensive fronts and blitzes after football games because he felt a greater sense of urgency due to the expectations set forth by the coaching staff.

Ultimately, although the bulk of Christopher's time beyond teaching and coaching was spent planning his classes and assessing student work, the expectations placed on him by the football program often were more intense:

> I do feel more pressure from football. With teaching and stuff, if I don't get my papers done, the only people I have to tell are the students and myself. And with the students, I can say, well, I didn't get it done because honestly we need to focus on this [content], and I can shift the focus. I'm more in control. Football, though, if I don't get that video broken down by 2:00 on Sunday, the head coach is hurting; the offensive coordinator is hurting; the offense is hurting.

Aside from breaking down game tapes, the bulk of Christopher's responsibility was managing players—like classroom management in the academic setting—and throwing passes to receivers during practice drills. His primary responsibility during football games was to record the offensive plays called by the head coach, who also served as the offensive coordinator.

As the season moved forward, and Christopher became more comfortable with the system, he began to do more teaching on the practice field and on the sidelines during games. However, one of his frustrations involved his players' lack of seriousness on the field.

> I was sort of surprised how much of a social scene it was. . . . [When I played sports and] the whistle blew, there was no more talking. It was we've got a job to do because fun in soccer and basketball wasn't joking around with your friends. Fun was getting out there and making a play, getting out there and winning the game.

As a result, Christopher expected his players to give all of their energy to the team, just as he expected his English students to be actively engaged in class. During times when those expectations were not met, whether in the academic *or* athletic settings, Christopher sometimes struggled to maintain control of his emotions.

IMPLICATIONS

Role overload and inter-role conflict. Christopher's classroom demeanor was relatively relaxed early in the semester due to his conversational nature and his interest in promoting classroom discussion. As a result, at times his students were unsure whether he was being serious or playful.

As the football season progressed, Christopher's speech patterns changed noticeably. Specifically, parts of Christopher's coaching lexicon made their way into the classroom. For example, Christopher began using the word "son" to describe his football players early in the season. Although this term often was emphasized by the older and more experienced coaches, Christopher picked it up quickly and was routinely heard using phrases such as "I'm trying to teach you something, son," both on the football field and in the English classroom. Although a fatherly tone may have a different connotation for older coaches or even older noncoaching teachers, Christopher began to understand that coaching football was hurting his ability to communicate with students due to the hostile intensity that accompanied his interactions on the football field.

The very nature of Christopher's socialization into teaching via coaching created a mentality that did not always represent his generally positive outlook or his desire to help students communicate effectively. Separating the roles of teaching and coaching was challenging for Christopher because the athletic relationship with the football players he taught was built prior to the academic relationship in the classroom.

As fatigue set in early in the semester, Christopher's authoritative nature combined with his use of sarcasm to make him feel almost confrontational with students who misbehaved or were not focused. Instinctively, the coaching mentality in which some coaches try to maintain a dominant position at all costs, and one in which the first reaction generally was "drop and give me ten [pushups]," took over for Christopher in these circumstances. For the football players in his classes, he could simply warn them of "gassers." However, this approach rarely worked with nonathletes, which became problematic for a novice teacher with so few classroom management tools under his belt.

Christopher called the combination of teaching and coaching an "emotional roller coaster" that at times left him seeking "a good balance between intensity and anger":

> You can go from having a great day in school where you're feeling great about yourself and go to coaching and the kids are down. They don't feel like being there, and that pulls you down. . . . Then you go home and come back the next day, and you're in a bad mood. The kids

are still in a great mood because they had a great day yesterday. . . . It's just all up and down, up and down.

As the end of the football season coincided with fall break, Christopher was given a much-needed rest that allowed him to return to the classroom refreshed and with a more positive outlook. Although classroom management was always a struggle, his intentional increase in the use of constructive feedback provided Christopher with more meaningful opportunities to engage his students in dialogue. Whether in teaching or coaching, Christopher came to believe that different students needed different forms of encouragement to live up to their potential. For some students and athletes, the situation necessitated raising his voice, whereas for other students it meant pulling that individual aside for a quiet chat.

As the football season ended, Christopher acknowledged being more patient and less frustrated with minor behavioral issues, both of which drastically improved his classroom management and overall rapport with students. Nevertheless, the line between positive and negative teaching behaviors was a fine one. Although a calmer demeanor in the classroom benefited Christopher, his principal, a long-time athletic coach, suggested that sometimes academic teachers need to be more demonstrative in their approach to classroom management:

> I think teachers could get fired up, jump up and down like coaches. Show some enthusiasm. Those athletes better not straggle up on a football field late for practice, or the basketball court. Teachers should demand the same thing with them coming in class. No excuses in athletics.

Nonetheless, Christopher's attitude evolved during the fall semester, and he admitted that football showed him "a lot of what I don't want to be like [as a classroom teacher]. . . . I definitely like myself a lot more when I'm not coaching football."

Role stress. On occasion the implementation of learner-centered teaching strategies takes a backseat to PowerPoints and worksheets due to the massive responsibility and subsequent fatigue of teaching and coaching during the athletic season. Christopher acknowledged this point in a telling interview late in the semester that outlined not only how the roles of teaching and coaching can conflict, but also how the stresses of these multiple roles can affect the decision-making processes of novice educators.

> Sometimes coaching can get in the way. And to be honest, sometimes teaching can get in the way. It becomes a problem sometimes because when it comes down to me being so tired that I can't get in here and do this [lesson planning], or I'm tired so I'll grade my papers tomorrow; kids need those grades back and that's hurting them. Or maybe my lesson would have gone better if I had made that worksheet or that

> PowerPoint. Well, other stuff got in the way. I have another job to do,
> and I also teach class, but I have to do it a different way because in
> order for me to teach class, I've got to have this coaching job. In order
> for me to have this coaching job, I have to be here [teaching].

Christopher's struggle with role stress occurred primarily during the athletic season, and thus it seemed appropriate to wonder how things might
have turned out differently had Christopher focused solely on teaching
during the fall semester before coaching a winter or spring sport.

Prior to the fall semester, coaching took up much of Christopher's
time thanks to summer football workouts. "I did feel like I was coming
here to do the teaching, but definitely coaching took up more time," said
Christopher. As the semester began, his sense of balance seemed to improve when he learned how to leave teaching and coaching behind each
day:

> I was stretched the first couple of weeks with everything and running
> myself ragged with football and teaching. I was taking papers home
> and grading them all the time. . . . I grade at school [now] because if I
> take it home, I'll have a meltdown.

Much of that grading began to happen at school because Christopher
took greater advantage of his planning period, a shift that he credited to
the stress of football and wondered if he would have learned to use his
time as efficiently without coaching. He also had extra time for himself in
the evenings for personal activities such as working out, playing basketball, and visiting his girlfriend or family, which not only helped him
avoid being "on edge" at school the next day, but also improved his
ability to sleep at night.

Prioritizing academics and athletics. Despite the stresses Christopher
faced in coaching, he never treated coaching itself as a career contingency. In fact, he took great pride in improving as a football coach as his
student-athletes improved as players. However, Christopher believed his
interest in football may have had more to do with his social interactions
with players and fellow coaches than with the role of coaching itself.

On one occasion, after a long touchdown run early in the season,
Christopher was so energized that he left the coaching box to celebrate as
the players ran off the field. The incident, a surefire penalty if observed
by referees, was caught on tape and showed Christopher chest·bumping
his running back on the twenty-yard line. In the coaches' meeting two
days later, several of the coaches teased him about the situation while the
head coach smirked before firmly suggesting that Christopher should be
happy a penalty was not assessed against the team. In that moment,
Christopher's emotions clearly got the better of him due to his excitement
for his players.

Christopher mentions learning a lot about motivating players on the
football field as a result of his interactions with students in the classroom,

including providing individualized instruction and continuous feedback. Despite the potentially negative impact of his coaching mentality on classroom discourse with students, Christopher still held the belief that coaching can be beneficial in terms of classroom management. He suggested this benefit is observable in students who believe, "Oh, he's a coach, [so] he means business rather than oh, he's a teacher, and he's just really angry."

Yet, Christopher also fought against the perception of teacher-coaches as nonacademics by pitting himself as a teacher of literature who pushed critical thinking, active discussion, and intensive writing as opposed to teacher-coaches whose pedagogical techniques consisted of more passive forms of engagement such as PowerPoints and worksheets. Early in the semester, his department chair recalled a conversation he had with Christopher about prioritizing academics and athletics:

> [Christopher] was forthright and upfront about it from the beginning. "I know this is the perception of coaches, and I am not that way. Academics are my focus, and I want everyone to know that." He just said that to everyone. "I'm not going to be one of those coaches [who puts athletics over academics]."

THE PROFESSIONAL IDENTITY OF A TEACHER-COACH

From the time Christopher was hired, he made a point to stress that he was a teacher first and foremost, despite the pressures and time commitment of the coaching role. Members of the English department worried that athletics might overwhelm him during the football season, but "his focus is definitely on teaching, not the coaching, and he's excited about [teaching], and he likes it," said his department chair. Even on the football field, Christopher was more than willing to discuss teaching when the opportunity arose. On one occasion, during the middle of practice, he began talking quietly but excitedly about his most recent class session in which he had taught his favorite poem, "The Love Song of J. Alfred Prufrock," by T. S. Eliot. He then proceeded to explain some of the more interesting connections students made all while barking out instructions to his players during a football drill.

Part of Christopher's professional identity is the result of how he preferred to be addressed by others in the school. Although many teacher-coaches introduced themselves as "Coach," rarely did Christopher. During one grammar lesson on subject/verb agreement, he used his name as the subject of multiple sentences, always referring to himself as Mr. [last name]. When asked, Christopher said, "Not many students call me Coach. I don't mind if they do, but I don't introduce myself as Coach [last name]."

Accepting the label of "coach" was not something that came without serious consideration for Christopher. Although he realized that many students built a strong rapport with coaches, his preference was always to be "taken seriously as a teacher" in the academic setting. As a result, his classroom walls were filled with posters of respected authors and poets (e.g., Dickinson, Hemingway, London, Poe, Twain, Whitman), not sports figures.

When asked about being a teacher-coach, Christopher replied, "I'd honestly like it to be teacher-coach instead of coach-teacher." Regarding his future plans, Christopher admitted not knowing what was in store for him except that he hoped it involved teaching. "He's one that will probably be recommended for moving up into higher level—even AP—classes because he's that type of teacher," remarked his department chair. He's a "world-changer," said his defensive coordinator, "real teacher of the year material."

In the end, Christopher's professional identity was perhaps most successfully confirmed by listening to what his fellow football coaches had to say about him. The most telling of these conversations came from a small group of coaches sitting around after practice late in the season. Long after players had left for the day, a coach inquired as to Christopher's whereabouts, to which another coach replied, "[He is] probably writing lesson plans or grading essays." The group of coaches laughed, all nodding in agreement, before moving on to the next topic of conversation.

CONCLUSION

An argument can be made that sports are overemphasized in the social culture of K–12 schools [13] and that academic teachers should focus solely on their students' learning and not extracurricular pursuits. However, as long as classroom teachers are allowed, and encouraged, to coach athletics, important lessons can be learned from their experiences. In observing teacher-coaches such as Christopher, educational stakeholders can learn how much time and energy they devote to their students and players. Based on these observations, educational leaders also may learn a lot about effective teaching and coaching.

Athletic coaches, in particular, may be able to learn a lot from effective teachers, specifically those who have a willingness and ability to recognize diverse learning styles, connect learning styles to methods of instruction, offer a balance of positive feedback and constructive criticism, model effective practices and techniques, empower students' voices, engage students in structured small-group activities, teach detailed communication techniques; use higher-order and reflective thinking, encourage players to think critically about their own experiences through written reflection, and create various forms of assessment to measure players' learning and developmental growth.

On the flip side, teachers can learn a lot from coaches. Other scholars have led the way on this work.[14] To their recommendations, it is worth noting that successful athletic coaches often are good at keeping the activities moving at a brisk pace, establishing and practicing routines, providing structure that allows students to teach one another, beginning promptly and playing until the whistle blows (or the bell rings), making accountability meaningful and tangible, taking advantage of video reflection tools that can affect pedagogy positively, and assessing learning at every turn.

In reflecting on Christopher's experiences, he still has a lot to learn about teaching English, coaching football, and navigating the social culture of an academic institution after his first year as a teacher-coach. At times he experienced role overload and inter-role conflict, which undoubtedly led to role stress. Through it all, Christopher impressed with his ability to reflect on his successes as well as his shortcomings. Even when he struggled to balance not only the roles of teaching and coaching, but also his professional responsibilities and personal interests, he recognized how his experiences in the classroom and on the athletic field had the potential to complement one another.

In an interview a year after the study's completion, Christopher acknowledged being more competent and prepared for teaching and coaching in year two. By then he emphasized collaborations and interactions with colleagues *and* parents, professional development in education *and* sport, and participation in and/or attendance at school activities to support *all* students, not just student-athletes. He was using more small-group work in lieu of whole-class discussion to empower and engage students, which he believed would help them find their own voices and allow him to serve as more of a facilitator during classroom conversations.

Christopher also recognized that his greatest success in athletics was "learning how to be [himself] while coaching" while also teaching his sport in a way that met the developmental needs of his learners. About the coaching mentality, he said, "Some kids respond to other coaches who are more intense. . . . I like people to hear me when I'm happy and not when I'm upset about something." He says that same sentiment still applies to his classroom, and his rapport with students has improved as a result.

Based on the findings from Christopher's case study, many questions remain about how to best support novice teacher-coaches: What role(s) should athletic coaching play in the hiring processes of academic teachers? How can teacher-coaches achieve an appropriate balance in the dual roles of academic teaching and athletic coaching? In what ways may the social positions of academic teaching and athletic coaching conflict with and/or complement one another? What are the challenges for beginning teachers who take on the role of athletic coaching prior to the role of classroom teaching?

The follow-up interview with Christopher ended with him reflecting on his experience and providing advice applicable not only for beginning teacher-coaches, but also for school leaders and mentors who work with first-year teachers and coaches. In his own words, Christopher offered the most important lesson he learned about his social position within the dual roles of teaching and coaching, one that serves as a fitting conclusion to this chapter:

> If I could go back, I would tell myself, don't forget why you're here, and the main reason you're here is to teach. That's what got me a job. I didn't get a job because they want me to coach football. They needed an English teacher. They can get a football coach anywhere. They don't need me for soccer. The can get one anywhere. Of course, they like me coaching, [but] at the end of the day, they pay me a lot more for teaching than coaching. At the end of the day, too, you teach a lot more kids than you coach, and you spend so much more time with the kids in the classroom than you do on the [athletic] field, so don't let the [athletic] field distract you from what you're really [to accomplish].

NOTES

1. George H. Sage, "The Social World of High School Athletic Coaches: Multiple Role Demands and Their Consequences," *Sociology of Sport Journal* 4, no. 3 (1987): 217.

2. Alan Brown, "Gender Integration of a Core Content Area Teacher/Athletic Coach in the Rural Southeastern United States," *Sport, Education and Society* 17, no. 5 (2012): 629.

3. Diane Drake and Edward P. Hebert, "Perceptions of Occupational Stress and Strategies for Avoiding Burnout: Case Studies of Two Female Teacher-Coaches," *Physical Educator* 59, no. 4 (2002): 171.

4. See note 1 for reference, 217.

5. Hal A. Lawson, "Toward a Model of Teacher Socialization in Physical Education: The Subjective Warrant, Recruitment, and Teacher Education," *Journal of Teaching in Physical Education* 2, no. 3 (1983): 7.

6. See note 3 for reference, 172.

7. See note 2 for reference, 627–46.

8. Angela O'Connor and Doune MacDonald, "Up Close and Personal on Physical Education Teachers' Identity: Is Conflict an Issue?," *Sport, Education and Society* 7, no. 1 (2002): 49.

9. Matthew D. Curtner-Smith, Peter A. Hastie, and Gary D. Kinchin, "Influence of Occupational Socialization on Beginning Teachers' Interpretation and Delivery of Sport Education," *Sport, Education and Society* 13, no. 1 (2008): 99–101.

10. Juliet Corbin and Anselm Strauss, *Basics of Qualitative Research*, 3rd ed. (Los Angeles: Sage, 2008).

11. Sharan B. Merriam, *Qualitative Research: A Guide to Design and Implementation* (San Francisco: Jossey-Bass, 2009).

12. See note 10 for reference.

13. Amanda Ripley, "The Case against High-School Sports," *Atlantic* (October 2013): 47–53. See also Steven Conn, "In College Classrooms, the Problem Is High School Athletics," *Education Digest* 78, no. 4 (2012): 21–24.

14. Jeffrey Duncan-Andrade, *What a Coach Can Teach a Teacher: Lessons Urban Schools Can Learn from a Successful Sports Program* (New York: Peter Lang, 2010). See also Ronald Gallimore and Roland Tharp, "What a Coach Can Teach a Teacher, 1975–2004: Reflections and Reanalysis of John Wooden's Teaching Practices," *Sport Psychologist* 18, no. 2 (2004): 119–37.

Part II

Sports and Identity

Sports and Identity

INTRODUCTION

What does it mean to be a student and an athlete? Questions of identity swirl within the typical school community as diverse individuals interact to assemble colorful portraits of who they are and want to be. Part I explored the ways in which educators can and do use the cultural hues of sports participation to envision their work. Alan Brown left off with a discussion of the dual identities of teachers also serving as coaches. Students deeply committed to playing sports are likely to feel the same way, with the person inscribed on the jersey seeming different from the person of the same name written atop the exam or book report.

Whether one believes that identities are rigid and forged internally or that they are fluid and form socially,[1] the consensus is that identity matters. Being an active participant in students' identity construction is arguably a crucial part of teaching, coaching, and leading. Part II looks at dimensions of identity and athletic participation from several angles. Each author explores identity through a different theoretical lens, with explorations grounded in compelling stories and personal experiences.

In the fifth chapter, Robert D. Greim starts things off with a recommendation to notice the various signals that coaches and athletic directors send student-athletes about their developing identities. He argues that concern for the whole student can get lost among the multitude of competing priorities in the K–12 environment. Student-athletes, in particular, are at risk of harm from homophobia, racial intimidation, and damaging views of immigration status, among other things. Greim provides tools for assisting young athletes in the development of healthy identities.

As with Greim, De'Andre L. Shepard seeks effective ways of supporting student-athletes on and off the court. He begins the sixth chapter by observing how the gymnasium door demarcates two sides of the school:

an academic side and an athletic side. Drawing upon theories of identity development put forth by Erik Erikson and Henri Tajfel, Shepard characterizes the formation of an athletic identity before highlighting aspects of the subculture on the athletic side, including team membership, relationship building, and social status. He then offers a teacher-developed high school leadership initiative as an example of how educators might enable student-athletes to bridge the two sides of the school building and their twin identities.

In the seventh chapter, Antonio E. Naula-Rodríguez goes outside the school to study youth sports in a neighborhood recreation center for insights of possible value inside the school. Naula-Rodríguez unpacks the social and linguistic dynamics of the center's female athletes of color while observing teams in the youth volleyball and basketball leagues. He notes the presence of cultural signifiers and ways in which players mark their identity as athletes. The coaches, he also suggests, may be reinforcing racialized expectations of their athletes of color.

Race is a central concern for Michael Domínguez in the eighth and final chapter of Part II. He contends that athletic participation is often treated by the dominant white culture as an indulgence, thus diminishing its profound importance to the identities of youth of color. Throughout the chapter, Domínguez intersperses his analysis with the unfolding story of his relationship to Noah, a late-arrival immigrant, young black man, and excellent athlete. The tragedy of Noah's experience underscores how the assets of racialized youth often go unrecognized in schools.

NOTE

1. For a rich theoretical discussion of these opposing views of identity, see Martin J. Packer and Jessie Goicoechea, "Sociocultural and Constructivist Theories of Learning," *Educational Psychologist 35*, no. 4 (2000): 227–41.

FIVE

Toward an Expansive View of Student-Athletes beyond the Court

Robert D. Greim

Walk into the office of any coach or athletics administrator and ask yourself which books, posters, photographs, and inspirational plaques are on display, and which are absent. Keep in mind three considerations when asking these questions:

1. Does the employee recognize and incorporate into her daily routine the cultural icons, historical figures, and concerns related to the student's heritage and identity?
2. Has the employee taken into consideration life factors impacting the holistic development of the student beyond wins, losses, and workouts?
3. Does the employee encourage students to participate in activities outside the scope of athletics?

Although a brief glimpse into a single office within an institution might not reveal the entirety of the climate for the team or the department, it can be illustrative of that employee's worldview, concerns, and priorities.

Many outstanding coaches possess a wealth of knowledge related to their sport, motivation, leadership, work ethic, and the like. Factors such as the age of athletes, level of competition, and team or institutional mission can lead a coach's primary charge to range from teaching sport-specific skills, to winning championships, to creating a revenue stream;[1] however, for coaches in K–12 education, a concern for the growth and well-being of the whole student should be placed above all else. As such, it is important that coaches possess an understanding of student development and an appreciation for the lived experiences of their student-athletes outside the athletics environment.

The purpose of this chapter is to inspire educators and provide them tools to begin conversations between coaches, faculty, and administration at their institution or district to further enhance the educational experience of student-athletes.

STUDENT-ATHLETE STRESSORS

Because student-athletes spend a majority of their time practicing, conditioning, rehabilitating injuries, traveling for competition, and studying game film with teammates, a great deal of their identity is attached to their athletic endeavors.[2] Accordingly, it is natural for coaches and athletics administrators to concentrate their concern for student-athlete well-being along these athletically related lines.

However, in addition to these athletic stressors, student-athletes are experiencing the same developmental challenges as their nonathletic peers, including the evolution of their social, emotional, and sexual identities.[3] Student-athletes who identify as lesbian, gay, bisexual, or transgender can face additional stressors of identity suppression and internalized homophobia, which can result in psychological distress.[4] Student-athletes of color can experience additional stressors including intimidation, fear for personal safety, and discrimination.[5] Immigrant students can face severe disadvantages, conflicting identities, and discrimination as well.[6]

At one urban school in the Midwest, a low-income African American student-athlete transferred in to begin her junior year after her parents had experienced a very contentious separation in a neighboring state. The mother, with whom the student lived, was addicted to drugs. The father, during this time, was sentenced to prison. The student, who identified as lesbian but had not come out to her family, used her participation in basketball as an outlet for her stressors and hoped to earn a college scholarship as a means to improve her life.

Unfortunately, the young woman's basketball coach, unaware of her identity issues and indifferent to her lived experiences, unwittingly created a hostile environment for the student off the court. The coach held team events and only invited members to bring their *boyfriends*, not *partners*. The coach did not permit students to wear their hair in cornrows and made them wear dresses for team pictures. The coach, who was white, was from and continued to live in an upper-middle-class suburban gated community, reinforcing the disconnect perceived by members of her team. By the end of that school year, the student quit the team and transferred to another school.

Athletic departments can help combat these stressors by familiarizing coaches and administrators with the cultures and lived experiences of their student-athletes as well as their developmental concerns, thereby providing not only an escape from these stressors through physical activity, but the safe space of knowing a role model cares about them beyond the field of play.

Coaches who are just as familiar with Mike Rose's *Why School* or David Elkind's *The Hurried Child* as they are with Mike Krzyzewski's *Leading with the Heart* will be more likely to recognize and address life factors that are adversely impacting their student-athletes. Coaches who display a poster of social justice issues alongside the schedule of home sporting contests are those more inclined to encourage student-athletes to explore their identity and broaden their social circles.

Encouraging staff members to openly acknowledge and appreciate these issues can lead student-athletes to feel as though they matter to the department as a whole person, thereby avoiding any marginalization they might otherwise have perceived and leading to greater personal growth, improved student learning, and perhaps even a more successful team.[7]

A Coach's Influence

The influence of coaches on student-athletes extends beyond the field into motivation and socialization[8] as well as health behaviors.[9] It is important, therefore, for coaches to be cognizant of this potential impact and understand the consequences of their interactions with young athletes. Although there are bound to be teachable moments for the student and other contentious moments throughout the life cycle of the coach-student bond, department leadership should include training sessions for healthy relationship maintenance as part of the staff's professional development. In a recent study, Angela Cora Garcia found the "most prevalent negative aspect of high school sports participation was a problematic experience with a coach."[10]

It is thus worth recognizing the disparate impact a coach has on the student-athlete experience. Aside from a moral obligation to provide a healthy environment, K–12 institutions also have legal duties and standards of care for students,[11] thereby reinforcing the need for intentional interpersonal and cultural awareness.

Coaches can influence another climate factor identified by Claude Steele as *stereotype threat*, which he describes as "exposure to negative images and stereotypes about one's group [which] can lead to chronic self-doubts, low self-esteem, low performance expectancies, and the like, and these states, in turn, can undermine school performance."[12] For example, a biology teacher might believe that girls are not as likely to pursue a science-related career as boys, and therefore subconsciously might include the girls less in class discussion and not highlight achievements of female scientists as much as male scientists.

Although stereotype threat might not be felt by athletes on the field of play, student-athletes might sense it in the locker room, the coach's office, the coach's classroom, or in the coaching staff's language. Regardless of the time and place, these triggers, even when presented unintentionally, can adversely impact the student's social interactions or self-worth.[13] As such, a coach or athletics administrator should take steps to ensure that their traditions and actions do not contribute to the marginalization or stereotyping of any student. This can be done by incorporating a diverse array of books, images, and role models into their surroundings, references, and vocabulary.

Other less obvious factors that could adversely impact the student-athlete include the micro-aggressions of low expectations and mispronunciations. Micro-aggressions are subtle discriminatory acts, often unintentional, that indicate hostility or discrimination toward members of a social category.[14]

First, the language a coach uses with students can validate or invalidate their expected contributions to the team and even impact their life outcomes.[15] Even though most teachers report being able to suppress any application of stereotyping they might identify,[16] students' perceptions of "such microaggressions toward [their] intellectual capabilities and behavioral expectations have grave effects on their sense of self."[17] Examples of micro-aggressions might include a coach or teammate saying or allowing others to say *that's so gay*, or referring to a team of young men as *boys*, which could have historically racial undertones.

Second, coaches should be mindful of the proper pronunciation of student names, as repeated mispronunciation suggests a lack of concern for the student's cultural heritage, thereby impacting the student's socio-emotional well-being and, in turn, his learning, motivation, and performance.[18] Educating coaches about possible biases based on stereotypical expectations might decrease negatively reinforcing behaviors and make for a healthier team climate and student experience.[19]

RECOMMENDATIONS

Although teaching proper skill and technique may be the primary job of a coach in K–12 education, the fact that very few of her students will experience playing sports professionally or even in college (see table 5.1) adds credence to the importance of expanding a coach's considerations for success beyond the court.

Table 5.1.   Table 5.1. Probablility of Competing Beyond High School, 2014. Statistics accessed at http://www.ncaa.org/about/resources/research/ probability-competing-beyond-high-school.

	Total U.S. High School Participants	% Continuing on from High School to NCAA	% Continuing on from NCAA to Professional
Men			
Basketball	486,567	7.0	1.1
Baseball	541,479	3.5	9.7
Cross-Country	250,981	5.7	—
Football	1,083,617	6.7	1.6
Golf	148,823	5.8	—
Ice Hockey	35,875	11.3	6.6
Lacrosse	108,450	12.1	—
Soccer	432,569	5.7	1.4
Swimming	137,087	7.1	—
Tennis	157,240	5.2	—
Track and Field	578,632	4.9	—
Volleyball	54,418	3.3	—
Water Polo	21,626	4.8	—
Wrestling	258,208	2.7	—
Women			
Basketball	429,504	3.9	0.9
Baseball	221,616	7.3	—
Cross-Country	60,549	9.7	—
Football	72,582	7.2	—
Golf	9,418	23.1	—
Ice Hockey	84,785	13.0	—
Lacrosse	375,681	7.2	—
Soccer	364,103	5.4	—
Swimming	166,838	7.4	—
Tennis	182,876	4.9	—
Track and Field	478,726	6.0	—
Volleyball	432,176	3.9	—
Water Polo	19,204	6.0	—

Administrators and coaches can use the following Team Profile Worksheet (see figure 5.1) to assess their cultural awareness and identify strategic initiatives in concert with their colleagues (e.g., counselors, teachers) for the benefit of students. Coaching staff should complete the top box during the first all-team meeting and the second box together with the school's registrar by the end of the first week of practice. Counselors should then complete the third box in collaboration with the coaching staff, identifying proper programming options. Finally, with signatures in the final box, the director of athletics commits to providing the funds necessary for such programming as well as the release time for participating coaches in the interest of professional development.

TEAM PROFILE for COACHING STAFF PROGRAMMING

TEAM: _____   YEAR: _____   DATE: _____

At first team meeting, students indicated participating in these other student organizations (enter # in each box):

☐ Band   ☐ Chess   ☐ Science Bowl   ☐ Math Club

☐ Theatre   ☐ FBLA   ☐ Robotics   ☐ HOSA

☐ Language Club ☐ LGBTQIA   ☐ Sci. Olympiad   ☐ Yearbook

☐ FFA   ☐ Student Council ☐ Anime   ☐ NHS

☐ _____   ☐ _____   ☐ _____   ☐ _____

* Coaching staff will post schedule of events for these groups alongside team schedule in locker room.
* Coaching staff will follow-up with each student throughout the semester about those experiences.
* Coaching staff will recognize achievements of participants in these activities alongside athletic achievements.

Upon completion of roster, Registrar provided the following self-reported demographics (enter # in each box):

☐ Am. Indian or Alaska Native   ☐ White   ☐ Qualifies for free or reduced lunch

☐ Asian   ☐ Two or more races   ☐ Does not qualify for free or reduced lunch

☐ Black or African-American   ☐ Non-Resident / International

☐ Hispanic   ☐ Other/Unknown   ☐ Parent / Guardian attended college

☐ Native Hawaiian or other Pacific Islander   ☐ No reply   ☐ Parent / Guardian did not attend college

* Counseling office will visit with coaches to discuss implications of the make-up of their team
* Administration will support efforts to incorporate cultural awareness based on these identifiers.
* Coaching staff will support school programs that might impact students from each group above.

This year, coaching staff will work with counseling staff and administration to attend the following events:

☐ Implicit bias training   ☐ Safe space training

☐ Anti-bullying program   ☐ Other: _____

☐ Cultural diversity: _____   ☐ Team research with local professor (contact info below):
                                    Professor: _____   Institution: _____
☐ Communication workshop: _____ Phone/email: _____

Signatures:

Head Coach   Director of Athletics   Counselor

Having completed the Team Profile Worksheet, the five recommenda-tions below offer practical suggestions for coaches and administrators who would like to enhance the experience of their student-athletes. These efforts can be undertaken with assistance and guidance from fellow school or district employees, as well as local nonprofit organizations.

1. *Assess the athletics department climate* by surveying students after each season. Engage professors from local colleges to assist in ana-lyzing this data. This will not only improve personal performance by revealing strengths and weaknesses, but will give coaches the opportunity to improve the profession by presenting findings at national conferences.

2. As part of their professional development, *provide a venue for coaches to discuss books and articles related to diversity and child devel-opment.* Administrators can provide reading materials and funding for expert facilitators, which often can be found through grants, especially when requested by an entire district. In the case of low-resource schools, non-coaching teachers and counselors in the dis-trict could be invited to host these discussions, making use of their knowledge base regarding content and their skill set regarding dialogue facilitation.

3. Once each week, during a team meeting, perhaps after a team prac-tice, *coaches can share a monthly calendar of school activities with the team* and encourage attendance of non-athletically related activ-ities. Such encouragement could introduce students to events they might not otherwise attend, thereby widening their comfort zone while enhancing campus camaraderie.

4. Decorate coaching offices and athletics facilities with a wide array of well-known and obscure athletic *role models representing diverse backgrounds*, nationalities, races, sexual orientations, gender iden-tities, abilities, and sport participation. Allowing a student to see a person from a group with which they identify who has been suc-cessful in a sport can provide confidence and motivation for a student who otherwise might not try out.

5. Cultural awareness training during in-service days or possible re-lease time for coaches can be provided to allow coaching staff members to *attend events in the communities of the students they serve.* Being physically present at events off the field of play is an out-ward sign of an employee's concern for and investment in the student. Teachers of students participating in service-learning ac-tivities in the communities in which their students live could invite coaching staff members to participate in these activities even if the activity is not related to the courses taught by the coach.

CONCLUSION

Although a coach in a K–12 school may not have been formally educated to place an emphasis on the nonathletic developmental or social concerns of students, athletics employees can lead a sea change along with counselors and teachers in developing the student as a whole person. This chapter provides a template for strategically, intentionally equipping coaches with the knowledge and skills necessary for awareness of developmental and societal concerns beyond the court that impact their students' experience.

As coaches often work long hours and are not necessarily compensated for all of their time on task, it might at first seem unrealistic to grow expectations of these hardworking professionals who already have the best interest of their students at heart. The processes and materials contained in this chapter, however, provide an athletics department a practical, collaborative strategy to help coaching staff members broaden their scope of considerations with very little impact on their regular work flow.

NOTES

1. Robert Simon, Peter Hagar, and Cesar Torres, *Fair Play: The Ethics of Sport* (New York: Westview Press, 2015).

2. Katie Griffith and Kristine Johnson, "Athletic Identity and Life Roles of Division I and Division III Collegiate Athletes," *University of Wisconsin—La Crosse Journal of Undergraduate Research* V (2002): 225–32; Frank Lu, Ya Hsu, Yuan Chan, Jang Cheen, and Kuei Kao, "Assessing College Student-Athletes' Life Stress: Initial Measurement Development and Validation," *Measurement in Physical Education and Exercise Science* 16, no. 4 (2012): 254–67; Lisa Wolf-Wendel, J. Douglas Toma, JD, and Christopher Morphew, "There's No 'I' in 'Team': Lessons from Athletics on Community Building," *Review of Higher Education* 12, no. 4 (2001): 369–96.

3. Erik Erickson, *Identity: Youth and Crisis* (New York: Norton, 1968).

4. Vivienne Cass, "Homosexual Identity Formation: Testing a Theoretical Model," *Journal of Sex Research* 20, no. 2 (1984): 143–67; Genny Beemyn and Sue Rankin, *The Lives of Transgender People* (New York: Columbia University Press, 2011).

5. Shawn Harper and Sylvia Hurtado, "Nine Themes in Campus Racial Climates and Implications for Institutional Transformation," in S. R. Harper and L. D. Patton, eds., *Responding to the Realities of Race on Campus, New Directions for Student Services* 120, 7–24 (San Francisco: Jossey-Bass, 2007); Sue Rankin and Robert Reason, "Differing Perceptions: How Students of Color and White Students Perceive Campus Climate for Underrepresented Groups," *Journal of College Student Development* 46, no. 1 (2005): 43–61.

6. Robert Crosnoe and Ruth Turley, "K–12 Educational Outcomes of Immigrant Youth," *Future of Children* 21, no. 1 (2011): 129–52.

7. Alexander Astin, "Student Involvement: A Developmental Theory for Higher Education," *Journal of College Student Personnel* 25 (1984): 297–308; John Gardner, "Building Community," *Kettering Review* (1989): 73–81; Nancy Schlossberg, "Marginality and Mattering: Key Issues in Building Community," *New Directions for Student Services* 1989, no. 48 (1989): 5–15.

8. Richard Keegan, Chris Harwood, Christopher Spray, and David Lavallee, "A Qualitative Investigation Exploring the Motivational Climate in Early Career Sports Participants: Coach, Parent and Peer Influences on Sport Motivation," *Psychology of Sport and Exercise* 10, no. 3 (2009): 361–72.

9. Nadine Mastroleo, Miesha Marzell, Rob Turrisi, and Brian Borsari, "Do Coaches Make a Difference Off the Field? The Examination of Athletic Coach Influence on Early College Student Drinking," *Addiction Research and Theory* 20, no. 1 (2012): 64–71; Dennis Scofield and Scott Unruh, "Dietary Supplement Use among Adolescent Athletes in Central Nebraska and Their Sources of Information," *Journal of Strength and Conditioning Research* 20, no. 2 (2006): 452–55.

10. Angela Cora Garcia, "Understanding High School Students' Sports Participation," *Sport Science Review* 24, nos. 3-4 (2015): 121.

11. Frank Aquila, *School Law for K–12 Educators: Concepts and Cases* (Thousand Oaks, CA: Sage, 2008).

12. Claude Steele, "A Threat in the Air: How Stereotypes Shape Intellectual Identity and Performance," *American Psychologist* 52, no. 6 (1997): 613–29.

13. Deborah Feltz, Richard Schneider, Seunghyun Hwang, and Nikolas Skogsberg, "Predictors of Collegiate Student-Athletes' Susceptibility to Stereotype Threat," *Journal of College Student Development* 54, no. 2 (2013): 184–201.

14. Virginia Huynh, "What Are Microaggressions?," 2016, http://link.springer.com/referenceworkentry/10.1007/978-3-319-32132-5_802-1; Derald Sue and Madonna Constantine, "Racial Microaggressions as Instigators of Difficult Dialogues on Race: Implications for Student Affairs Educators and Students," *College Student Affairs Journal* 26, no. 2 (2007): 136.

15. Ayana Allen, Lakia Scott, and Chance Lewis, "Racial Microaggressions and African American and Hispanic Students in Urban Schools: A Call for Culturally Affirming Education," *Interdisciplinary Journal of Teaching and Learning* 3, no. 2 (2013): 117–29.

16. Sabine Glock and Sabine Krolak-Scherdt, "Stereotype Activation versus Application: How Teachers Process and Judge Information about Students from Ethnic Minorities and with Low Socioeconomic Background," *Social Psychology of Education* 17, no. 4 (2014): 589–607.

17. See note 15 for reference.

18. Rita Kohli and Daniel Solórzano, "Teachers, Please Learn Our Names!: Racial Microaggressions and the K–12 Classroom," *Race Ethnicity and Education* 15, no. 4 (2012): 441–62.

19. See note 16 for reference.

SIX

Student-Athlete Identity Formation and the Relationship between an Athletic Subculture and Academic Success

De'Andre L. Shepard

The controversy surrounding the benefits of athletic participation for K–12 students is an ongoing conversation. An alarming amount of negative media attention has been given to certain school districts, coaching personnel, and organizations over their treatment of academically suspect athletes.[1] Thirty years ago, observers of scholastic sports were noting how high school athletics was becoming a training ground for stand-out athletes who showed the potential to participate in college and professional athletics,[2] a situation that seems little changed today. In fact, it has been institutionalized, with players ranked by their athletic ability and offered college scholarships while they are in junior high.[3] Furthermore, coaches and administrators sometimes have chosen to abuse the amateur athletic industry, as well as student-athletes, whose development has been entrusted to them.[4]

Supporters of K–12 athletics have long articulated and attempted to provide the public with meaningful ways of describing the benefits of athletic participation to offset the media frenzy. Research shows that sports-based extracurricular activities stimulate success in the classroom and spur progress in social environments.[5] In lower socioeconomic settings, where there is scarcity of resources, children are at higher risk of delinquent behavior without a positive outlet. Educational leaders now realize that in order for student-athletes to reach their full potential, the

77

entire district must function as one village. In particular, the cultural assumption that athletics exist and function as a separate entity within the district needs to be eliminated.

As most high school student-athletes understand, a doorway symbolizes the transition from the classroom to practice and a change in mind-set. The invisible line demarcated by the door divides the building into two sides with two sets of expectations. First is the *academic side*, which today's youthful minds arguably consider the most important as the gateway to college. But when the academic day is over, a select few make the journey to the *athletic side* or, as some may call it, the path to athletic success.

The presence of different leaders reinforces the division. The academic side of the building has an academic administrator—the principal—whereas the athletic side has an athletic administrator—the AD or athletic director. The principal depends on the teachers to develop relationships and educate students in the classroom; the athletic director relies on coaches, who sometimes are teachers, to develop student-athletes' athletic skill set. The principal sees the relationship between athletics as a privilege for those who maintain acceptable academic standing.

By comparison, the athletic administrator expects the principal and teachers to provide academic support to student-athletes so they can fulfill their athletic aspirations.[6] As such, they usually are wary to allow academics to limit athletes with extraordinary talent from reaching their full potential.

The result is one school, two leaders, two subcultures, and one student attempting to navigate a very complex system. Significantly, however, this divided model was not adapted to harm students; arguably, it was created to provide an alternative to traditional classroom instruction.

Indeed, K–12 schools never were intended to become a training facility for future college and professional athletes. Rather, schools developed sports-based extracurricular activities to teach things that are harder to teach in the classroom, including character development, sportsmanship, fair play, and teamwork. High school student-athletes take these lessons to heart and bear their membership with pride because it represents inclusion within a distinct group of students chosen to chase their athletic dreams. In practical terms, membership allows student-athletes the opportunity to work toward the goal of obtaining an athletic scholarship and, hopefully, a professional career. Even so, when on the "academic side," student-athletes often are mentally anticipating practice on the "athletic side" and therefore are not engaging in the classroom curriculum.[7]

Student-athletes can see the divide that exists between athletics and academics[8] and must decide which half is most beneficial to their identity and social status. Teachers, principals, and coaches can support student-athletes to navigate this tension if they understand what's going on developmentally and what's at stake. As this chapter reveals, elements of Erik Erikson's adult identity theory and Henri Tajfel's social identity theory can be useful for appreciating how young athletes form an identity and the importance of team membership, self-esteem, relationship-building, and social status in the formation of an athletic subculture in K–12 schools.

THE ATHLETE'S DILEMMA

Before proceeding, a brief portrait of student-athleticism is warranted, especially for readers who did not play sports in school. Those who did play sports no doubt will have different recollections of the standout moments from their athletic careers and have different understandings of those experiences, though they probably share some commonalities. Some former student-athletes might recall the joy of playing sports simply to socialize with close friends. As they excelled in sports, their popularity among peers, family, and friends may have grown. Indeed, being a recognizable middle and high school athlete, especially for those raised in urban communities, is a desired social status. Even those students who don't play ball want to be in the athletic social circle.

The athlete identity can be strong, and the young student-athlete often will acquire valuable lessons about who he is and is becoming. For many young athletes, participating in K–12 athletics is one of the few times they are able to be themselves. That version of the self receives daily reinforcement from an inner circle of coaches and teammates that offers a feeling of comfort and inclusion, even superiority. The more athletic praise received, the more loyal they become to the subculture of athletics.

By comparison, some student-athletes never develop this kind of close relationship with teachers. Athletes become so dependent on praise from coaches and teammates that off the field, court, or track, they often become withdrawn and resemble a person with no self-confidence.[9] That is, until game time; then, once again, the self-doubt leaves and is replaced with eagerness to display one's athletic ability.

This tacking between confidence and no confidence follows many student-athletes throughout their lives. The constant balancing act between an athletic and academic identity can lead to shaky and inconsistent self-esteem outside of athletic participation. A richer appreciation of what identity is, how it forms, and what it means in an athletic context sheds light on this balancing act and offers insights for those who support young athletes in K–12 settings.

IDENTITY PRIORITIES OF YOUNG ATHLETES

Broadly speaking, identity is useful for examining culture, social group identification, and how people navigate multiple roles and participation across groups and cultures.[10] Adult identity theory, in particular, spotlights the socialization process of individuals as they interact with peers and trains a lens on the transformation from adolescence into adulthood. The emergence of adolescent identity is important because it is the period during which youth can explore potential identity alternatives without having to assume permanent adult commitments.[11] Those identities are influenced by daily social interactions that determine how an individual adjusts to a given culture—in this case, how student-athletes adjust within the social and academic culture of the school.

The view of identity discussed in this section is rooted in Erik Erikson's foundational definition of identity as a process that unites personality and connects the individual to the social world.[12] In Erikson's view,

> the conscious feeling of having a personal identity is based on two simultaneous observations: the perception of the self-sameness and continuity of one's existence in time and space, and the perception of the fact that others recognize one's sameness and continuity.[13]

Erikson identified eight age-specific stages of development (see table 6.1).

Stage 4: Emergence of a Love of Sport

Much of the identity development that impacts school-age children occurs between Stages 4 and 5 (ages five through eighteen years). During this time, many young people are introduced to athletics and will begin

Table 6.1.   Table 6.1. Erikson's Eight Stages of Adult Identity Development.

Stage	Conflict	Age (years)
1	Basic Trust vs. Mistrust	Infancy (0 to 1)
2	Autonomy vs. Shame and Doubt	Early Childhood (1 to 3)
3	Initiative vs. Guilt	Play Age (3 to 5)
4	Industry vs. Inferiority	School Age (5 to 12)
5	Identity vs. Role	Adolescence (12 to 18)
6	Intimacy and Solidarity vs. Isolation	Young Adult (12 to 40)
7	Generosity vs. Self-absorption	Adulthood (40 to 65)
8	Integrity vs. Despair	Maturity (65+)

to develop an athletic identity. Within Stage 4 the child begins to recognize his ability to learn, to be creative, and to accomplish numerous new skills. It is also a point in time when the child begins to form the impulse to want to please others.

It is not surprising, then, that the fourth stage is when parents begin to introduce their children to youth athletics and other extracurricular activities, and children willingly comply.[14] These activities are used as a tool to teach children how to be competitive and the importance of physical exercise; participation also provides them with an opportunity to interact socially with their classmates outside of school. Parents must still monitor and help their child find a balance between time spent on extracurricular activities and ensure that such activities prove enjoyable. Whether parents and other influential adults, such as teachers or coaches, should use these learning experiences as opportunities to force children into making lifelong commitments to sports is debatable.[15]

In Stage 4, the process of balancing an athletic and academic identity still operates within the relative innocence of participation in sports for their own sake, rather than to explore a professional pathway. At this point, students are impressionable and are searching for social satisfaction and the comfort of building relationships with their teammates. Young athletes are not worried about statistics and fame but are more excited by being part of a team; they look forward to seeing their friends. Erickson explains that, developmentally, these experiences are critical to the identity the child will choose as she moves into adulthood.

The role of coach at this stage is different as well. The coach realizes that he has taken on the responsibility of introducing young athletes to competition, teamwork, communication, discipline, sportsmanship, and many important life lessons. Yet even as these skills are developed, the emerging adolescent still participates for the love of the sport. One day this love may turn into a lifelong obsession with athletics. Individual attention from a coach can fuel this obsession.

Coaches also are responsible for building a team's athletic culture, perhaps by acknowledging all victories, whether big or small. Indeed, feedback for young athletes will have more impact if it is positive. As adults, many athletes are likely to note how a coach's recommended improvements during childhood, though minimal, resonate years later. Likewise, a coach's genuine acts of love and affection can make youth at this stage want to participate in sports as they get older.

As a practice, both coaches and teachers are hired with the expectation that their guidance will have a lasting impact on their students. For children in Stage 4, the coach accepts the responsibility of creating an athletic culture that is engaging, focused on establishing relationships, and encouraging to athletes. This is where the teacher-coach relationship roles should coincide as both the teacher and the coach are expected to be motivators who will introduce and develop new skills to their students.[16]

In addition, they are expected to forge trusting relationships with students that will build self-confidence.

Stage 5: Emergence of an Athletic Identity

According to Erikson, Stage 5 involves role adoption as children, now adolescents, work to find an identity while considering their strengths, weaknesses, goals, and possible future occupations. At this stage of development, the adolescent's primary goal is to discover who he is as an individual apart from his family. The middle- and high-school-age student is consumed with identity and questions of *Who am I?* and *Who am I not?* Specifically, he explores ways of building relationships with peers and ways of gaining acceptance among those peers. Through this process, adolescents are preoccupied with who they appear to be in the eyes of others and how that compares to who they feel they are, or their self-perception. Erikson suggests that if this stage becomes too complex, children can withdraw and experience role confusion and turmoil.

For the student-athlete, growing up involves a pivot from a Stage 4 love of sports to a Stage 5 identification with sports. At this stage of development, young people want membership in a group that is well-respected throughout the school and the community. Playing a sport can fulfill this desire. Also, as in Stage 4, adolescent athletes tend to be less concerned about a professional athletic career. Instead, they are looking for comfort and acceptance, are generally self-absorbed, and may be prone to asking questions such as *How can I improve myself without dealing with stress?* For student-athletes, especially those who are exceptionally talented and possess a solid work ethic, this question often is directed toward improving athletic performance. In time, such individuals come to see themselves not only as loving sports, but as *athletes*.

A Difficult Balancing Act

The fact that the adolescent athlete—committed, hardworking, and capable of great things—often struggles in the classroom can be frustrating. Educators long have observed how student-athletes are willing to dedicate hours and hours to perfect their athletic skills but not to their studies. This is not true of all student-athletes, however, and reveals how such a work ethic, when applied to academics, can translate into classroom and career success.

Sometimes athletic participation positively impacts students' grades as well as their educational and occupational aspirations and attainment.[17] But a combination of factors, including increased social status in school, media attention, and moments of poor performance in the classroom, often result in declining commitment to academics among adolescent athletes.[18]

Framing the issue as one of identity development directs attention to where a young person is receiving affirming recognition of her emerging sense of self. Practically speaking, it is where she is experiencing the most success and praise. For athletes, affirmation often comes from teammates and their membership in the school's athletic subculture. Most athletes can recall memorable moments when the coach stopped practice to congratulate them on persevering to get a challenging move or technique right.

Public recognition also can come from the wider community. For example, schools have assemblies. The mere anticipation of being recognized and receiving support from peers for exhibiting excellence can be a motivator and build self-esteem for student-athletes. Former athletes may recall friendly competitions to see who on the team would receive the most awards at a given assembly. The public nature of such ceremonies can affirm the identity of athletes as they are put on display in a favorable light in the presence of family, friends, and teachers.

Young people in Stage 5 are likely to resist cultures that cause a lot of stress and communicate a lack of genuine concern about what matters to them.[19] In fact, the more stress or struggles that are present, the more the adolescent will run toward her comfort zone. Furthermore, an absence of a sense of belonging might have wider ramifications as the individual feels diminished interest and engagement not only in school but in ordinary life activities.[20]

It is worth asking, therefore, from the perspective of the student-athlete, which culture sounds more inviting and affirming of his emerging identity: one filled with seemingly insurmountable hurdles such as he finds in the classroom, or one filled with hurdles that have been overcome and celebrated, such as those he finds on the court, track, or field?

Teachers understand that classroom environments that provide students with self-confidence, attention, and recognition are critical in helping students develop an academic identity. Such environments offer affection, warmth, hope, and a sense of belonging and encouragement. Good teachers and coaches know that group membership matters, and young people need affirming social relationships.

The point at which the balance of the student-athlete identity tips toward the athletic component is when a young person begins receiving more recognition for athletic achievement than academic achievement. Schools do not necessarily mean for this to happen; it happens when classroom pedagogy fails to account for young people's need for social connection in the context of personally meaningful experiences.[21] Further consideration of identity and group membership reveals specific features of membership and areas for educators to make a difference.

GROUP MEMBERSHIP AND ATHLETES' SOCIAL IDENTITY FORMATION

Complementary to Erikson's adult identity theory is Henri Tajfel's framing of social identity theory, which is helpful for looking at individuals' sense of who they are based on their sense of belonging within the social world.[22] Significantly, the theory explains how people try to maintain a positive social identity by being part of an in-group, which elevates self-esteem.[23] As most educators know, students tend to crave the distinction that comes with belonging to certain social in-groups, especially being part of an athletic team.[24]

Tajfel offers four elements to explain how members choose their social groups and the impact it has on their development—categorization, consequence, social comparison, and psychological distinctiveness—that are described briefly with respect to student-athletes.

Categorization refers to the way in which people establish their place in society. The process involves defining groups and what membership means. Once a student-athlete commits to being an athlete, he already has begun defining his social identity and what it is and is not. As members of a particularly desirable group, student-athletes forge a social identity in part through a sense of superiority. Members will remain a part of the group and will not consider leaving unless an outside group proves to be more beneficial to their social identity.

Consequence refers to the tendency for individual members to leave a group if it does not satisfy personally valued requirements, including culturally significant goals or beliefs. Conflicts arise when individuals feel torn by the affirmation of some values but not others. Student-athletes, for example, understand the importance of an education, and academic success usually is a stated goal for the team.[25] Teammates' displays of anti-academic behavior might be reassuring for others struggling in the classroom but violate personal and team values. For many student-athletes, the consequences of fighting their team's anti-academic subculture can be risky. Thus, many student-athletes perform poorly in the classroom to maintain membership in their group, believing that their social identity is best served by athletic rather than academic achievement.[26]

Social comparison refers to how individuals often compare their group with other groups and feel a more favorable bias toward the group in which they have membership. Such comparisons are not objective realities but rather created from fantasy. As a result of their affiliation with the group, individuals tend to consider their social identity as superior, and they are willing to do whatever it takes to maintain that identity. Student-athletes, therefore, contribute in establishing the status of their group relative to other groups in the school and will police that hierarchy to maintain their high status.

Finally, *psychological distinctiveness* highlights how members of an in-group want their identities to be distinct and provide a positive identity when compared to other groups. This psychological distinctiveness can take many forms; in some cases, the superior group will create conditions that enable members to enhance their separation from other groups.[27] Also impacting the social identity of a given group is the desire for isola-tion from out-groups (e.g., from students who are not athletes) that may want their identities separated from that of the student-athlete. Indeed, given the negative academic statistics that follow student-athletes, non-athlete students may consider their social identity as superior to that of a student-athlete.

These four dimensions of social identity theory interact and explain how individuals both choose and reinforce group membership and iden-tity. The theory presents a vital question for educators: Is it possible to develop a classroom culture that mirrors athletic subculture? In other words, can teachers, attentive to identity development, increase class-room engagement, maintain student-athlete social status—and most im-portant—eliminate any self-confidence issues surrounding their academ-ic ability? The following case study explores this question through an application of social identity theory.

Case Study: The Leadership Games

In general, everyone struggles to commit and excel in environments where they do not feel appreciated or engaged.[28] Furthermore, the power of athletic subculture is the isolation it creates between student-athletes and non-student-athletes; students want their group membership to be exclusive and admired by their peers. In K–12 schools, a major conse-quence of such isolation is student-athletes failing to benefit from the complete educational experience.

This was the dilemma educators faced at an urban high school in Michigan where the student-athletes were isolated and had a sense of superiority and entitlement. Most troubling was how, once they were outside of athletics, they were non-contributors to the school. In re-sponse, several teachers decided to develop an after-school enrichment program that capitalized on students' desires to compete and be seen as leaders—desires especially strong among student-athletes. They named the effort the Leadership Games.

The teachers assumed that the competitive game format would attract students, but they also added an incentive to encourage participation by promising $50 per person to the winning team. The teachers recruited basketball players, who displayed amazing leadership potential on their athletic teams in ways that were less evident in the classroom. The teach-ers were strategic; they went for the students' Achilles heel: wanting money. But they also drew parallels between the recognition they would receive for dominating the Leadership Games and scoring the winning basket. They explained that the results of the games would be shared with the school in the same manner that athletic results were shared. After much persuading, they got a few of the star players to commit.

Just as the teachers envisioned, the athletes sparked interest in the initiative and made the enrichment program relevant. Through the lens of social identity theory, membership increased, as did *categorization* as students wanted everyone to know that they were part of the Leadership Games and affiliated with its high-status athlete participants. All participants benefited from the opportunity to forge new social identities. Importantly, the teachers were able to get student-athletes to leave the subculture of athletics for several hours per week and participate with non-student-athletes in an academic environment. As the club flourished, so did the members' self-esteem and social identity.

What happened next was as unexpected as the rapid increase in membership. The athletic coaches began to see the benefit of the games as their athletes displayed leadership qualities on and off the athletic field. Over time, coaches began to require participation in the leadership initiative for certain athletes. The games were also a great résumé builder for students expecting to participate in athletics beyond high school.

In many respects, the teachers were able to reform the athletic subculture of their school through the Leadership Games by developing a space for exploring another social identity without *consequence*. Student-athletes too often are willing to deal with the consequences of poor academic achievement in order to maintain group membership and identity with an athletic team. It isn't necessarily that they lack confidence in their ability to succeed in the classroom; rather, it's that they are willing to sacrifice academics to preserve time to improve their athletic skills, which hold greater value for their social identity.

The Leadership Games challenged this belief by establishing common ground between the athletic and academic subcultures through a new group that demanded academic effort that took advantage of skills valued in athletics. As a result, the student-athletes were able to maintain their preferred social status while learning to identify with and gain confidence within the academic subculture.

The Leadership Games also served to shift the landscape of intergroup *comparisons* within the school. A key component of the initiative's success was the teachers' recruitment of star student-athletes as participants. The membership of these students immediately provided the games with, in the language of social identity theory, in-group status.

The new group allowed the athletes and all participants to establish *psychological distinctiveness* as members of a novel club. But the social identity of group membership was built upon recognizable and valued components. The student-athletes not only maintained their social status, but they brought it with them, thus allowing non-athletes to attain membership within an in-group and distinctiveness among their peers.

The Leadership Games provided the high school students with enjoyment and self-esteem in an area outside their normal groups. The initiative became a blueprint in the school's district for a way to get student-athletes who were formerly isolated, entitled, and non-contributors to do something contrary to their social identity and obscure the invisible line between athletics and academics.

CONCLUDING THOUGHTS

For student-athletes, a lot is at stake in sustaining the line of separation between the athletic and academic sides of a school building. Too often educators question student-athletes' valuing of education; but the more important question to consider is what student-athletes do when they encounter academic struggle. Not surprisingly, they look for comfort within the athletic subculture. As the Leadership Games example illustrates, teachers do not need to break that yearning for comfort but can leverage it instead to develop opportunities for new social interaction and new identities to form. Good administrators and teachers make school an exciting and interesting place; they develop a personal and nurturing relationship with each and every student, even the athletes.

Attending to identity development reveals how fostering student-athletes' sense of belonging is critical to their ability to balance a meaningful high-status athletic identity, one built upon a love of the game and sustained through group membership, with an academic identity and all of the professional and personal rewards it affords. In the true essence of athleticism, faculty and staff are encouraged to support student-athletes by working as a team to bring both sides of the building together.

NOTES

1. See, for example, Mick McCabe's story from January 15, 2015, in the *Detroit Free Press*, "Oak Park Coach Resigns amid Grade Tampering Allegations," www.freep.com/story/sports/high-school/2015/01/28/oak-park-coach-resigns/22487061/.

2. Richard E. Lapchick, "The High School Athlete as the Future College Student-Athlete," *Journal of Sport and Social Issues* 11, nos. 1–2 (1987): 104–24.

3. A point Tim Casey makes in a recent article for *Bleacher Report* titled "When Will We Stop?" The Absurdity of Basketball Rankings," January 20, 2015, http://bleacherreport.com/articles/2308941-when-will-we-stop-the-absurdity-of-youth-basketball-rankings.

4. For more on this, see De'Andre L. Shepard's 2014 dissertation, "What Effect Does the Athletic Subculture at a Division I Institution Have on the Development of Adult Identity on Student-Athletes?" Oakland University, Rochester, MI.

5. For example, see Jennifer E. Bruening, Brianna S. Clark, and Michael Mudrick, "Sport-Based Youth Development in Practice: The Long-Term Impacts of an Urban

After-School Program for Girls," *Journal of Park and Recreation Administration* 33, no. 2 (2015): 87–103.

6.   Peter Adler and Patricia A. Adler, "From Idealism to Pragmatic Detachment: The Academic Performance of College Athletes," *Sociology of Education* (1985): 241–50.

7.   In fact, Na'ilah Suad Nasir and Victoria Hand, "From the Court to the Classroom: Opportunities for Engagement, Learning, and Identity in Basketball and Classroom Mathematics," *Journal of the Learning Sciences* 17, no. 2 (2008): 143–79, recommend that teachers could benefit from a better understanding of what students are learning outside the classroom on the court.

8.   See note 4 for reference.

9.   For more on this trend, see reference in note 4.

10.   Sheldon Stryker, "Identity Theory and Personality Theory: Mutual Relevance," *Journal of Personality* 75, no. 6 (2007): 1083–102.

11.   Seth J. Schwartz, James E. Côté, and Jeffrey Jensen Arnett, "Identity and Agency in Emerging Adulthood: Two Developmental Routes in the Individualization Process," *Youth & Society* 37, no. 2 (2005): 201–29.

12.   Erik H. Erikson, *Identity, Youth and Crisis* (New York: Norton, 1968).

13.   Ibid., 50–51.

14.   Caroline Payne and Kate Fogarty, "Importance of Youth Involvement in Sports," EDIS Document, FCS (2007).

15.   See note 4 for reference.

16.   Many educators view coaching and teaching as two distinct professions, but the distinction may do more harm than good, as Sheryle Bergmann Drewe explains in "An Examination of the Relationship between Coaching and Teaching," *Quest* 52, no. 1 (2000): 79–88.

17.   See Herbert Marsh and Sabina Kleitman, "Extracurricular School Activities: The Good, the Bad, and the Nonlinear," *Harvard Educational Review* 72, no. 4 (2002): 464–515.

18.   See note 2 for reference.

19.   See note 4 for reference.

20.   Robert S. Weiss, *Loneliness: The Experience of Emotional and Social Isolation* (Cambridge, MA: MIT Press, 1973).

21.   See note 16 for reference.

22.   See Henri Tajfel, "Social Identity and Intergroup Behavior," *Information (International Social Science Council)* 13, no. 2 (1974): 65–93; and Michael A. Hogg, "A Social Identity Theory of Leadership," *Personality and Social Psychology Review* 5, no. 3 (2001): 184–200.

23.   Rupert Brown, "Social Identity Theory: Past Achievements, Current Problems and Future Challenges," *European Journal of Social Psychology* 30, no. 6 (2000): 745–78.

24.   Beckett A. Broh, "Linking Extracurricular Programming to Academic Achievement: Who Benefits and Why?," *Sociology of Education* (2002): 69–95.

25.   See note 6 for reference.

26.   For more on this, see reference in note 4.

27.   See note 22 for reference.

28.   See note 23 for reference.

SEVEN

The Language of Teammates and Coaches in Action

Perspectives on Urban Girls' Volleyball and Basketball Teams

Antonio E. Naula-Rodríguez

Nec manus, nisi intellectus,
sibi permissus, multam valent:
instrumentis et auxilibus res perficture.

Neither the hand nor the mind alone,
left alone to themselves, would amount to much;
the tools and aids of culture render them perfect.
—Francis Bacon[1]

Urban schools can often struggle to offer students a wider range of extra-curricular or after-school opportunities[2] as they and their communities find themselves confronting a paucity of human resources and opportunities.[3] However, this is not for lack of effort, as these schools and communities endeavor to offer an array of activities, both academic and non-academic, to their students.[4]

A neighborhood recreation center may represent for youths of primary and secondary ages additional education or an alternative to academics—that is, an alternative to time spent in the classroom doing schoolwork. How youths interact in this alternate setting linguistically and nonlinguistically, how they groups themselves socially, and how they perceive and assume leadership roles from coaches and older, more experienced peers stand to be of interest to teachers, coaches, parents, and administrators.

The study discussed in this chapter grounds itself in praxis by bringing together theory and social practice as observed in two youth sports, volleyball and basketball, at Velázquez Recreation Center (a pseudonym). Of principal concern was how the coaches and youths at the center employed linguistic and other social implements to organize or mediate play during practices and at games.

As preteen and teenage girls outside their school day, these young athletes arguably were in the process of formulating their cultural and social identities. Because players and coaches alike were people of color, they may have grappled with issues such as gaining acceptance through sports in ways they may not have done in a more formal academic setting. The neighborhood recreation center where they practiced and played games was a locus for skill building and leadership via linguistic and social interplay. Multigenerational in nature, both practice sessions and games featured younger teammates associating with older players and coaches over the course of two seasons, volleyball in the fall and basketball in the winter.

A great deal is going on in a typical sports practice or competition. It is easy to take for granted the expectations one brings regarding the language and social practices in athletic settings. This chapter employs frame analysis to model how such expectations can be foregrounded alongside coaches' expectations and young players' interpretations of those expectations. Doing so evinces the hows and wherefores behind the linguistic and social choices that youths make, a useful exercise for educators serving underserved populations, especially young girls of color.

Indeed, the voices of Latinos and African Americans, especially preteen and teenage girls, are often left out of critical conversations and studies that have to do with them.[5] In addition, girls and women often struggle for acceptance as athletes.[6] In a recreation center that has long represented a community of color, Velázquez and its youth leagues could be viewed as bastions of this community and its history.

This study aims to give the community's youth and coaches a voice in how language in sport is developed and how they identify as athletes. As a historical ethnography, this study shows how youths, who are often more receptive to innovation,[7] can be leveraged by K–12 educators to become leaders of language use and social grouping in school.[8]

FRAME ANALYSIS AND LANGUAGE AS CAPITAL

Frame analysis focuses attention on the accepted conventions and protocols of the activities at hand as well as the participants and their language and actions.[9] More specifically, it frames what individuals (players) and groups (teams) say and do as written within the tacit rules and accepted norms of the observed activity (basketball and volleyball practices and competitions). This theory helps account for both macro (large-scale) linguistic considerations and large-scale forces at work,[10] as well as micro (local or small-scale) considerations. In this study, for example, the city government oversees a division called parks and recreation, which, in turn, administers various recreation centers, many of which form leagues in certain sports. The girls' volleyball and basketball teams at Velázquez Recreation Center operate within these frames.

For its part, analysis at a micro-level examines language and actions in three ways. First, it examines how coaches and administrators interpret large-scale rules and regulations of the recreation center and the league. Second, it looks at how coaches and players interpret the rules of play and practice. The third micro-level analysis is social interactional patterns (e.g., uttering a greeting that would be deemed appropriate to a familiar fellow player—"What's up?"—instead of "How do you do?"). Language, its lexicon (vocabulary words and phrases), and its grammatical structures all form part of this role. In short, local ad hoc interpretations of larger institutions make up the micro-level analysis. Linguistic analysis has shown, for example, how youth basketball coaches combine language and action via scripts as they explain to players the discrete skills involved in a sophisticated set of actions.[11]

Finally, language here is treated as a cultural implement. Aside from being a medium of communication, language reflects the culture in which it is embedded, while at the same time reifying or constituting that culture.[12] Furthermore, language can be viewed as a type of social asset to players and coaches, providing them with what scholars sometimes refer to as *cultural capital*. People accrue cultural capital by displaying resources—actions, objects, or other artifacts—to show valued knowledge that they have acquired and social practices that they have.[13] Young athletes, for example, often will mimic phrases popularized by professional athletes to signal their familiarity with the cultural values and preferences of their sports community.

When community members grant cultural capital to something, they are said to "buy in" to it, thereby matching personal values to those of a desired social system into which they want access and acceptance.[14] Lastly, the acquisition of linguistic cultural capital has implications for identity formation, as members come to view who they are in relation to their community and its culture.[15]

THE NEIGHBORHOOD RECREATION CENTER

Velázquez Recreation Center is located in a neighborhood in a rapidly growing city in the U.S. Midwest. The neighborhood is located close to the downtown area and within walking distance to restaurants and bars, office buildings, and a Major League Baseball ballpark; at the time of the study, it had recently undergone urban restructuring, housing construction, and gentrification. Perhaps as a result, the neighborhood's population changed from having more persons of color to having more white residents. It also included more couples with no children or with young children and fewer preteens and teenagers, especially those of color.

The recreation center itself is a red brick structure with parking spaces out front and a parking lot adjacent to the building. Across the street is a low-income health clinic. In the entryway, two information racks offer various free neighborhood publications. A plaque commemorates the construction of the old building, as well as its historic significance to the African American community as the city's first public recreation center for persons of color. A trophy case holds loving cups and other awards alongside photos of past coaches and teammates, both boys and girls, and in both basketball and volleyball.

The center features a pool, two weight rooms, and a gym with bleachers. The gym where the girls practiced and had home games is spacious, with bleachers that fold out where spectators can sit and observe. At practice, mostly parents would come and watch; during games, parents and other family members from both teams would fill the stands.

Other individuals, such as parents, siblings, and other family and community members, certainly were involved with the volleyball and basketball leagues. However, the principal participants observed were the adult coaches and their players, which included the 9 to 10-year-old and the 12 to 14-year-old girls who were the focus of this study. Coach Olivia (all coaches' names are pseudonyms) was the main coach, but two other coaches—Coach Valeria and Coach André—were observed interacting with the young athletes.

AN ETHNOGRAPHIC APPROACH

Various ethnographic studies have shown the value of examining a single local community.[16] Collectively, this body of work has expounded upon the importance of integrating oneself into a setting of interest in order to understand it more fully. Two pieces in particular stand out for their contributions to the approach used in this study. Penelope Eckert's landmark *Jocks and Burnouts*[17] chronicles through careful observation how categories and identities form based on age, popularity, and school-based and extracurricular activities. Shirley Bryce Heath's[18] use of frame analysis examines the language observed in youth basketball for clues to coaching techniques. Though admittedly older works, these seminal studies have remained quite relevant and served as conceptual and methodological resources.

Thick Description

In an effort to create *thick description*[19] of the athletic activity at Velázquez, detailed field observations were made of volleyball and basketball practices and games over the course of a year. Some interviews with coaches were also conducted, and several artifacts were collected. The aim was to capture as much detail as possible to ensure the accuracy of the representation of the site and its participants[20] and to use multiple data sources to triangulate for the sake of validity.[21]

Of particular interest were the linguistic data, which can assume many forms. Of course, it includes spoken words and phrases, but as with a declarative "We know the new mayor" vis-à-vis the declarative "We know the *new* mayor" (as opposed to the old mayor), intonation gives a layer of expression that often is crucial to understanding and communication.[22] Thus, paralinguistic features were captured in order to include word-level tone, sentence-level intonation, pauses, speech rate, and expressions such as sighs or gasps, as well as extralinguistic features, such as facial expressions, hand gestures, or gaze.[23]

In addition to linguistic data, players' and coaches' actions and physical positions and orientations were documented. Initially, much less language was being used than had been anticipated. That is, a coach would make a directive or request, and players would follow through without protest, make a counteroffer, or proceed to negotiate.

Compared with a typical classroom, players seemed more focused, perhaps because of the nature of the physical activity (with a lack of focus, they might take a basketball or volleyball to the face). As such, nonlinguistic behaviors such as social groupings or such subtleties also were accounted for. The company that the girls were assigned to (a basketball coach would say, "All forwards assemble on me.") and maintained, for example, showed a great deal about social groupings. In addition, looks directed toward or away from a coach appeared to reveal intentions or internal feelings of the players. Indeed, one could see how the linguistic and nonlinguistic dimension of social activity interplay, especially with respect to the formation of cultural and social identities.

INSIGHTS ON COMMUNITY AND IDENTITY BUILDING

At times Velázquez Recreation Center seemed idealized, with the coaches working amicably with the youths in their charge and everyone forming one cooperative group. Relationships formed in and out of the center had made a collective web, which in turn had germinated and strengthened over time to build a sports community. This sense of community building formed the essence of what it meant to operate as a team—a goal-oriented unit with strong leadership.

However, even though coaches ran the girls through practice drills or fostered winning or losing with grace, not all was as it seemed. Indeed, a richer inquiry reveals some insights into the nuances of this community of young athletes and their coaches.

Reinforcing Cultural Norms and Values

Youth athletics operates within a system of objectives bounded by the written and unwritten rules of specific sports and the cultural communities in which they are realized. In general, the explicit and overarching objective of team sports such as volleyball and basketball is to score more points and win. The individual sports themselves have their own documented and more explicit rules enforced by referees. In volleyball, a team may not volley the ball more than three times, and a volley must not be "palmed" by any player. "Palming the ball" is also not allowed in basketball. Unwritten rules, by comparison, represent the strategies and other subtleties of the game and include cultural rules, norms, and values of a given sports community. Through their language and actions, the coaches conveyed the unwritten "rules" to the girls.

The coaches seemed to use their feedback to direct the girls toward the community's cultural norms and values, which were considered different from those of other settings and communities. Coaches often were hard on the girls. For example, during a volleyball practice an exasperated Coach Olivia stressed to the girls at volleyball practice, "The ball does not touch the ground!" This rather direct and forceful manner of coaching (a form of instruction) may run contrary to how teachers—and coaches, for that matter—are expected to treat their students.

In many people's perspective, teachers and coaches alike tend to compliment more than Coach Olivia. In another instance, for example, she explained to the girls rather bluntly, "One thing you guys are doing wrong, is you're putting your back to [inaudible]. Why are you doing that?" Here, then, were manifestations of language used to remind their athletes of objectives, written rules, and unwritten rules of the sport.

It might have been that the coaches were more concerned with a different system of objectives and unwritten rules because, for them, both coaches and players already were practicing with a high-stakes situation in mind, namely winning a game. The issue of high versus low stakes can have a bearing on how coaches treat players and how players treat each other. In another revealing interaction between Coach Valeria and a group of older girls, the coach rebuked them: "You know why [inaudible]? 'Cause you don't have control of the ball. You know what that causes in games?" Some of the girls began to reply, "Turn-" and this coach chimed in (or outright interrupted), "Turnovers, right." Coach Valeria saw fit to address them all, even though just one player prompted this chastisement.

Coach Olivia was aware that she and the other coaches were perceived as harsh, but she felt they were justified on cultural grounds. Looking back at her athletic history to frame the harshness, she said of one of her revered coaches, "I really didn't *like* her [laughs]. We don't like our coaches." She went on to claim that different populations of girls required different approaches: "Yeah, you couldn't treat the girls at Wayne Park [another recreation center in an affluent part of town] the way I treat the Velázquez girls." Perhaps she felt she needed to speak more forcefully with them, that she had to exert authority in a way unnecessary with girls from a wealthier neighborhood. *The streets just outside Velázquez are tough,* she might be saying, *so I can't baby them.*

Despite condoning harshness in working with these young athletes of color, Coach Olivia also gave them positive reinforcement. The rules of play for volleyball and basketball do not require such reinforcement. However, because coaches in many respects are teachers, they operate within larger systems that contextualize how coaches use language and to what ends.

During a scrimmage in practice one evening, for example, more than one teammate on one side "went for the ball"—that is, two teammates dove for the ball, while another began to run toward it—even though no one saved the ball from being ruled out of bounds. Coach Olivia, however, took note, and her comment, "There ya go *ladies!*" with strong emphasis (i.e., high volume) and intonation (higher stress and pitch than normal on "*ladies*"), revealed as much. Comments that combine rules of a sport with language that is interpersonal (whether a rebuke or an approval) contextualize the activity itself. Moreover, they lead others to think, "Hey, our teammate looked really good (or bad) out there today."

Not all coaches gave feedback the same way. Whereas Coach Olivia often "shot from the hip," giving feedback while in the throes of the moment, Coach André was quieter and tended to lead with small directives. "OK," he once began a practice drill on layups, "How about two of y'all get over on this side and [you other three] get on the other side." He demonstrated how he wanted sides to pair up against each other and for one player to "cover" the offensive player before she shot a layup. His comments after the drill were calm but no less effective, "You can't be pushin', You can't be shovin', You can't be reachin' in." The girls' pensive reactions showed that they had understood.

Coach André seemed to be trying to effect behavior in line with the game's cultural norms via this string of negative directives; for their part, the basketball players seemed to take his advice to heart. It is in these moments of reflection that young athletes can learn to connect the physical (play) with the mental (the rules, norms, and values).

Social Group Dynamics and Formation

Certainly, the coaches were the primary leaders and authority figures at Velázquez; however, some of the girls from the older age groups also assumed the mantle of leadership, leading by example. This alpha group was the same group of girls who sometimes shared roles with the younger girls in being the followers and not the leaders, so they effectively were apprentices as leaders of the team during practices. Group membership and status reflected several factors. The following sections discuss *when* or *under what conditions* social groups formed and why some girls appeared to become leaders.

Inside Knowledge: The girls in the alpha group dressed the most like athletes, which served not only to identify them as basketball or volleyball players, but also to mark their position as members of the alpha group with insider knowledge of sports culture. On the court, this position was evidenced through style of dress and makeup that these girls wore.

During games alpha group members wore very loose shorts (*guangos*, they called them, taking the Mexican American term), a contrast to their tops, which were neither overly loose nor too snug. Jewelry was not allowed on the court during practices or games, but makeup was permitted and served as a marker of in-group status. Accessorizing also showed one's ability to dress the part of a teammate or just an athlete. These displays, it seemed, informed identity with the alpha group and signaled buy-in to a larger, more powerful athletic culture.[24]

Although capital can be gained by mimicking dress and behavior, it also can be gained by standing out from the crowd.[25] This was the case observed on one occasion with one of the younger volleyball players. Described as "taller than the others," she also accessorized with bike shorts (as opposed to *guango* shorts) and kneepads. At one point during practice, she clapped her hands together, then performed a "ghost serve," an advanced move in which the player makes the motions of serving the ball before doing so. This was a sign of athletic acumen as well as a way of emulating what she had seen older, more experienced players do—a way of showing her buy-in and, at the same time, standing out to her younger peers.

As this example illustrates, one's actions as well as style of dress—including makeup, accessories, and specific actions—can identify one as a player and prospective leader.

Outside Knowledge: These girls formed a team on the court during games, but their relationships extended beyond the court and did not include all team members. The alpha group invariably would enter the gym as a group already dressed or half-dressed for practice—that is, perhaps wearing sneakers and an athletic top but jeans, and they would go to the locker room shortly to change into shorts.

Even during downtimes at practice, they would "hang out" or socialize together. Once during practice, when the coaches were helping other groups and the alpha group was on the sidelines, a girl performed a funky dance step and jiggled her body, prompting another girl to comment, "Oh, that's mean." As she continued chatting with two other teammates, one of them feigned swinging a punch in slow motion, then feigned a head butt to a teammate nearby. Actions and comments such as these appeared to be artifacts from their time together outside the gym.

These girls, it seemed, had brought with them outside knowledge as tools of banter and actions as social cohesion. A combination of this banter and physical actions at practice indicated that they had brought these cultural tools to a place in which other talk (sports-related language) and other actions (practicing certain moves such as shooting, rebounding, or passing) were called for by the coaches and by the rules of practice and competition. Doing so signaled affiliations that were larger than the team but nonetheless had implications for the team and its social dynamics.

Leadership among Players: Leadership was a reflection of not only social group status, but also a reflection of athletic ability. The alpha group appeared to be the most socially influential and sometimes exhibited leadership through their use of language. At one point during a practice, for example, the girls were scrimmaging, and a player stopped in midplay. Coach Olivia rebuked her. The player took this rebuke hard. A short while later, Coach Olivia again critiqued the player, calling out, "Nope, that's a bad pass." She then substituted for this player. The girl began crying. In response, one of the girls from the alpha group called her over: "C'mere" (for "Come here"). When she received no response, she stamped her foot and reiterated more forcefully, "Come here!" The crying player consented and went over to the group, who consoled her.

The alpha group girl thus appeared to be taking a leader's role. Her "C'mere" was the utterance of a crony, but when she wanted to assert herself as a leader, perhaps also as a sort of caring older sibling, she repeated her demand, parsing each word. Ordinarily, an often-used phrase can run together, as represented by the hyposegmented "C'mere."[26] However, as she wanted to add emphasis, she no longer ran her consonants together in her enunciation of the phrase. Her demand belied her assuming a role of a leader in a salient social group, indeed, perhaps in the gym at the time. As a leader, perhaps she wanted to come across as caring but certainly not overly sensitive or coddling.

In addition to social group affiliation, athletic ability along with the appropriation of sports language and the tacit support of coaches seemed to confer leadership status. The girls who set and spike, who pass, dribble, and shoot with more prowess, were often the ones who gained approval—sometimes even a nonlinguistic nod or other subtle form of encouragement—or a "There ya go, ladies!"

But even without input from the coaches, the girls knew who was more athletically adept. These better players, whether part of the alpha group or not, formed a *jock* group, to use the categorical term from Heath's study,[27] which stood apart from the *non-jock* group. Then there were younger players whose future inclusion as a jock or non-jock was not always obvious.

Along with performances of athletic ability, jocks and prospective jocks signaled their group affiliation by demonstrating fluency with the language of their sport. It is in learning and using the language or jargon of a group to which one wants to belong that one can become an inducted member.

One form of interesting linguistic interplay arose from a younger player during a scrimmage in practice in the form of a purely back-and-forth verbal scuffle typical of volleyball and other sports. The ball had bounced out of play, but doubt remained whether a final significant bounce had been in bounds or out of bounds. At the time, a very distinct "'That was in' 'That was out'" interplay was heard from two different players. Then, a short while later, the same back and forth arose about a different play but much more loudly: "'That was in!' 'That was out!'"

Here, they showed how comfortable they were with language typical of their sport. In another instance, a girl called out, "Mine!" to claim an airborne ball. Although she no doubt used the word with just that intention, it is also worth noting how the language performed identity work and served to establish her social affiliation. In other words, by calling out "Mine!" she showed herself to be an authentic volleyball player and part of that select group.

Finally, coaches would sometimes affirm the relatively high status of the jock group through their language and behavior. At a volleyball practice, members of the jock group tended to gravitate to one side, while outsiders practiced on the other side of the net. Coach Olivia tended to command the attention of the jocks but not the others, even when addressing the entire group. Reacting to their inattentiveness, she admonished them once in practice by stating, "Ladies, I hope you're listening over there, 'cause I'm trying to get ya set up." Although it is understandable that the better athletes would gravitate toward each other, instances like this may have reinforced group divisions rather than promoting opportunities for mixing and leadership from the better players.

CONCLUSION

As the epigraph to this chapter intimates, people rely upon cultural implements to perfect, or at least improve, their cultures and their communities. Language, actions, and physical accoutrements can be seen working in concert, like a well-practiced team, to proffer value to that community itself. This was evident in the observations of the young athletes and their coaches at Velázquez Recreation Center. Together, they mediated the acquisition of new sports skills as they simultaneously appropriated linguistic interplay, mannerisms, and styles of dress that marked them as athletes and members of valued, self-identified social groups. The coaches played an important role in this effort by framing the rules and the cultural norms and values of the center's historically underserved community. In response, the girls became accustomed to the community and could be seen as attempting to buy in and gain acceptance to certain social groups within it.

At times it seemed that some girls were set up for athletic success whereas others were set up to remain middling players or quit sports altogether. Regardless, it should be noted that the girls of color at Velázquez were active rather than passive participants in the construction of their local community and their social identities. Recognizing this in their own educational settings, coaches, teachers, and administrators will be in a better position to hear the voices of marginalized students, see the important work they do, and leverage their leadership potential.

NOTES

1. Francis Bacon as cited in James V. Wertsch, ed., *Culture, Communication, and Cognition: Vygotskian Perspectives* (Cambridge, UK: Cambridge University Press, 1985), 23.

2. Linda Darling-Hammond, "Restructuring Schools for Student Success," *Daedalus* (1995): 153–62.

3. Fred M. Newmann, BetsAnn Smith, Elaine Allensworth, and Anthony S. Bryk, *School Instructional Program Coherence: Benefits and Challenges* (Chicago: Consortium on Chicago School Research, 2001).

4. Charles M. Payne, *So Much Reform, So Little Change: The Persistence of Failure in Urban Schools* (Cambridge, MA: Harvard Education Press, 2008).

5. Laura Azzarito and Melinda A. Solmon, "A Poststructural Analysis of High School Students' Gender and Racialized Bodily Meanings," *Journal of Teaching in Physical Education* 25, no. 1 (2006): 75–98. See also Susan C. Duncan, Lisa A. Strycker, and Nigel R. Chaumeton, "Sports Participation and Positive Correlates in African American, Latino, and White Girls," *Applied Developmental Science* 19, no. 4 (2015): 206–16.

6. See Marlene L. Mawson, "Sportswomanship: The Cultural Acceptance of Sport for Women versus the Accommodation of Cultured Women in Sport," and Jeffrey O. Seagrave, Katherine L. McDowell, and James G. King, "Language, Gender and Sport: A Review of the Literature," both chapters in Linda K. Fuller, ed., *Sport, Rhetoric, and Gender* (New York: Palgrave Macmillan, 2006).

7. Miguel Siguán, *Bilingüismo y Lenguas en Contacto* 177 (Madrid: Alianza Editorial, 2001).

8. Robert L. Trask, *Historical Linguistics* (London: Arnold, 1996).

9. Erving Goffman, *Frame Analysis: An Essay on the Organization of Experience* (Cambridge, MA: Harvard University Press, 1974).

10. Hank Johnston, "A Methodology for Frame Analysis: From Discourse to Cognitive Schemata," in Hank Johnston and Bert Klandermans, eds., *Social Movements and Culture* (Minneapolis: University of Minnesota Press, 1995), 217–46.

11. Shirley Bryce Heath, "'It's All about Winning!' The Language of Knowledge in Baseball," in Lauren B. Resnick, John M. Levine, and Stephanie D. Teasley, eds., *Perspectives on Socially Shared Cognition* (Washington, DC: American Psychological Association, 1991).

12. Miriam Meyerhoff, *Introducing Sociolinguistics* (New York: Routledge, 2007).

13. Pierre Bourdieu and Jean-Claude Passeron, *Reproduction in Education, Society and Culture*, vol. 4 (Thousand Oaks, CA: Sage, 1977). See also Lucia Tramonte and J. Douglas Willms, "Cultural Capital and Its Effects on Education Outcomes," *Economics of Education Review* 29, no. 2 (2010): 200–213; and Annie Tubadji, Masood Gheasi, and Peter Nijkamp, "Immigrants' 'Ability' and Welfare as a Function of Cultural Diversity: Effect of Cultural Capital at Individual and Local Level," *IZA Discussion Papers*, no. 8460 (2014).

14. Ronald S. Burt, "Structural Holes versus Network Closure as Social Capital," in Nan Lin, Karen S. Cook, and Ronald S. Burt, eds., *Social Capital: Theory and Research* (New Brunswick, NY: Transaction Publishers, 2001). See also Mark Granovetter, "Economic Action and Social Structure: The Problem of Embeddedness," *American Journal of Sociology* 91, no. 3 (1985): 481–510.

15. Julio A. Espinoza and Raymond T. Garza, "Social Group Salience and Interethnic Cooperation," *Journal of Experimental Social Psychology* 21, no. 4 (1985): 380–92. See also Michelle Chino, "Tribal Capacity Building as a Complex Adaptive System: New Insights, New Lessons Learned," in Rosemary M. Caron and Joav Merrick, eds., *Building Community Capacity: Minority and Immigrant Populations* (New York: Nova Science Publishers, 2012), 43–52.

16. Revered examples within the genre include Samuel G. Freedman, *Small Victories: The Real World of a Teacher, Her Students, and Their High School* (New York: HarperCollins, 1991); and Tracy Kidder, *Among Schoolchildren* (New York: Avon Books, 1989). More specific to a sports context is Gary Alan Fine, *With the Boys: Little League Baseball and Preadolescent Culture* (Chicago: University of Chicago Press, 1987).

17. Penelope Eckert, *Jocks and Burnouts: Social Categories and Identity in the High School* (New York: Teachers College Press, 1989).

18. See note 11 for reference.

19. Clifford Geertz, "Thick Description: Toward an Interpretative Theory of Culture," in *The Interpretation of Culture* (New York: Basic Books, 1973), 3–30.

20. Joseph A. Maxwell, *Qualitative Research Design: An Interaction Approach*, second edition (Thousand Oaks, CA: Sage, 2004).

21. Sandra Mathison, "Why Triangulate?," *Educational Researcher* 17, no. 2 (1988): 13–17.

22. Peter Ladefoged, *A Course in Phonetics*, 5th ed. (Boston: Thomson Wadsworth, 2006).

23. David Crystal, "The Linguistic Status of Prosodic and Paralinguistic Features," *Proceedings of the University of Newcastle-upon-Tyne Philosophical Society* 1 (1966): 93–108. See also Björn Schuller, Stefan Steidl, Anton Batliner, Felix Burkhardt, Laurence Devillers, Christian Müller, and Shrikanth Narayanan, "Paralinguistics in Speech and Language—State-of-the-Art and the Challenge," *Computer Speech & Language* 27, no. 1 (2013): 4–39.

24. See first reference in note 14.

25. Nathan C. Pettit and Robert B. Lount, "Looking Down and Ramping Up: The Impact of Status Differences on Effort in Intergroup Contexts," *Journal of Experimental Social Psychology* 46, no. 1 (2010): 9–20.

26. Joan Bybee, *Phonology and Language Use*, vol. 94 (Cambridge, UK: Cambridge University Press, 2003).

27. See note 10 for reference.

EIGHT

Race, Affect, and Running

A Decolonial Reflection on School Athletics

Michael Domínguez

This story begins on a rolling gravel road at 7 a.m., during a cross-country training camp in the middle of July. Barely awake, disrupted from their summer routines by a far too early wakeup call and a morning run more intense than expected, a group of high school athletes, shepherded by counselors and coaches, me included, grind along. As the sight of a creek emerges from the dense trees on the left, flowing parallel to the road on which we run, Noah leaps sideways out of the group and up onto a small boulder, laughing, yelling, "I'm on a boat!"—a joke from a recent *Saturday Night Live* episode—then leaping down, right back into the group, resuming his stride at six-flat per mile pace. The rest of the group shake their heads and laugh as best they can.

This was my first impression of Noah, and it remains the one that defines him in my mind, all joy and light and talent. An infectious smile and powerful laugh. On a boat. T-Pain in running shorts.

Over the next week of camp, as I worked with and coached Noah, we would connect, building a relationship that would last well beyond that week. Our discussions extended through and beyond running and sport, to questions of race, schooling, and identity—about what it meant to be in this place and space, he as a black African immigrant, myself as a Xicano, and to be engaged in school athletics as men of color. Yet looking back, the deep significance of what we were trying to make sense of in these conversations—the *affect* of colonization that permeates the intersection of athletics and schooling for youth of color—had not, even then,

101

several years on from my own years running in high school and the NCAA, been clear to me.

Now, in my relationship with Noah, in tragedy, that affect, and the importance of accounting for it, seem blindingly clear. This is Noah's story—our shared story, an athletic *testimonio*, in my voice—driven by my need to speak to the urgency of *witness* that we as educators must bring to sports, and our students' relationships to them.

In testimonio, we share our narratives to make sense of struggle, weaving personal experience together with analysis as a way to make sense of difficult and traumatic events and to illuminate how complicated theories *live* in the world.[1] In what follows, my hope is to illuminate how race, sports, and education come together for youth of color in ways that are often difficult and restrictive, but, when *decolonized*, can operate in culturally sustaining, ontologically productive ways.

COLONIALITY AND YOUTH OF COLOR

As you read this chapter and the story embedded within, I invite you to frame it conceptually through a decolonial lens—foregrounding the way racial and cultural difference have been historically constructed and received in the world, in schools, and sports. To do this, we must begin with the reality of *coloniality*, an understanding of which is vital to accurately naming the intense array of negative pressures from both in and beyond schools that youth of color in the present sociopolitical moment face. As Maldonado-Torres[2] explains, coloniality

> refers to long-standing patterns of power that emerged as a result of colonialism, but that define culture, labor, intersubjective relations, and knowledge production well beyond the strict limits of colonial admin-istrations. . . . It is maintained alive in books, in the criteria for academic performance, in cultural patterns, in common sense, in the self-image of peoples, in aspirations of self, and so many other aspects of our modern experience. (243)

Essentially, although the de jure systems of colonialism and racial/ethnic marginalization may have disappeared from view, something oppressive and colonial remains about how youth of color are positioned—for these differential "patterns of power" still fall along lines of racial, ethnic, and cultural difference. Implicitly, invisibly, whiteness is privileged, with profound negative consequences for the educational, athletic, and psychological success of youth and communities of color.

Coloniality lives on in disproportionate suspension/expulsion rates for youth of color[3] and the school-to-prison pipeline.[4] It persists in the achievement, or opportunity gap, documenting the institutional failure of schools to meet the academic needs of communities and youth of color.[5]

It is alive and well in the way static, often toxic, gender roles are replicated, particularly among youth of color,[6] particularly in sports.[7]

It is evident in the pressures on teachers to show narrow, quantifiable success, turning youth into commodities, while devaluing the interpersonal, intercultural work educators might otherwise do to promote student growth and development.[8] And it is apparent in the way curricula and policy bend themselves toward cultural erasure and English language hegemony,[9] creating conditions in which youth of color face intense identity struggles in the simple act of attending school.[10]

All of these things—as distinct statistics, policies, practices, realities—individually are fact. We know they exist. They have been documented by researchers. We observe them daily as teachers, coaches, and administrators. Though often misinterpreted, they are the root of the problems we deal with each day in schools and in society. They play out in the media, as experts weigh in on their causes, seeking to explain their persistence. And they play out in the lives of youth, shaping their relationships to school and their fundamental well-being.

> Noah is a young black man, a late-arrival immigrant from Africa—his father, Ethiopian; his mother, Moroccan. Even before he arrives in the United States, he lives straddling two worlds. Noah had arrived in ninth grade speaking Amharic before learning Spanglish in ESL courses dominated by Latin students. Only after this does he begin coming to grips with academic English. I joke with him that he is the only African I know who gets it when I shout "Orale!" His multilingual and multicultural dynamism is hugely impressive, but no one is even looking for these types of competencies, not when such ingenuity doesn't register on assessments of his academic English ability.
>
> Now heading toward twelfth grade, Noah tells me, as we add additional miles onto a run, just the two of us, that he is living mostly with his uncle, whose schedule and frequent long absences have meant that Noah had to move in temporarily with friends at times, once with his track coach. With his parents and the rest of his family still overseas, Noah continues to struggle with language in a school where no one speaks Amharic, and his ESL services have run out. His life is turbulent and, at times, culturally opaque. He makes friends easily, but he is confused by the hostility he so often faces. He confesses that he still is learning what it means to be black in America.

What coloniality, as a conceptual frame, offers is a cohesive and historical view of the interconnections between ostensibly independent issues. It helps us see that things such as achievement gaps, disproportionate discipline rates, and Eurocentric textbooks do not appear from nowhere. They do not happen by chance. The individual difficult experiences youth of color have are not isolated, but linked; related elements coalescing into a treacherous *affective geography*[11]—a realm of socio-emotional intensities and assaults—that youth of color must navigate, striving and struggling for agency in a hostile institutional landscape.

COLONIZING AND DECOLONIZING SPORT

This chapter, however, is not just about education, and the influence of coloniality does not end at the classroom door. Rather, as something "we breathe . . . all the time and everyday,"[12] coloniality lives equally in the daily workings of sport, both at and beyond its intersections with schools.

Indeed, sport has operated as a racial project for centuries,[13] using the ostensible equality of the sporting endeavor to mask divergent, racialized life experiences, institutional privileges, and assimilative pressures. This is a functionalist view of sport,[14] promoting athletics as a neutral, character-building, socially productive, and culturally unifying endeavor,[15] while obscuring the ways sports, from professional leagues to school and youth organizations, are dominated, culturally, disproportionately—in their norms, rules, expectations, administration—by whiteness.[16]

The result is a colorblind[17] narrative of sport in our popular consciousness; in the feel-good stories of blockbuster movies such as *We Are Marshall*, *Remember the Titans*, or *McFarland U.S.A.*, whose plots romanticize overcoming difference through unity on the field, glossing over white-savior motifs, and downplaying the divergent systemic realities that persist once the game is over.

It lives in the ways Jackie Robinson, John Carlos, Tommie Smith, and Muhammad Ali (among others) have been glorified in retrospect for their courage and character, while conveniently neglecting to recall the backlash they received in the moment, or recognize the persistence of systemic racism.[18] It lives on in the way those athletes' present-day counterparts are being met with the same vitriol and racism they sought to protest decades ago, still being directed at politically conscious athletes from the highest reaches of institutional power.[19] In short, coloniality permeates sport too,[20] contributing to the hostile *affect*—or socio-emotional intensity—youth of color must contend with each day in school, sport, and beyond.[21]

Yet this chapter is not a condemnation of sport—quite the opposite— and a de-colonial perspective is not a pessimistic way to view the world. Rather, coupled with all of this tension, always, are hope and possibility. Despite the ways coloniality still flows through our lives, athletic endeavor remains a powerful space for stability and culturally sustaining[22] possibility, particularly in schools.

> Camp is drawing to a close, and Noah and I are racing down a narrow trail, completing a workout the other youth were not up to. As we climb a steep hill, Noah and I speak of our reasons for running. We talk

of ancestry, of the blood pumping through our veins—Oromo, Mexica, Berber, Tarahumara—runners not just for ourselves, but for our gente. Noah tells me how when he is running, he feels like himself; it is the only time he feels stable, confident in being African, his Ethiopian and Moroccan selves converging, doing something reflective of his own complicated heritage. And running, he says, is his way to remain attached to all of this, to a life and culture that seem so painfully distant.

I tell him about my own Xicano identity and running. How in indigenous practice, running matters; it is a living prayer. And though the specificity of my own ancestry has been lost in centuries of colonial mestizaje, running, I tell him, is like a thread to the past, a way to honor an inheritance of struggle and possibility.

This conversation leaves us both quiet, ponderous for a moment. Our breathing, and the sounds of the woods around us, takes on new depth. For both of us, this is more than an extracurricular activity. Running here together, we are each working at the uncovering of a self who belongs, who contributes, and whose histories can live meaningfully in the present and into the future.

As the run continues, so does our discussion; of our shared feeling of how important this is, running, not just because of competition or ambition or team camaraderie (though those motivations surely exist), but because this is who we are. This is how we connect and how we balance ourselves.

As we depart that summer, we exchange contact info, connect on Facebook, and plan to be in touch. I can help with his writing, his college plans. And I give him my stretching rope, red and white, eight feet long, three-quarter-inch braided nylon. Keep stretching, I tell him. Stay healthy. This rope got me through my injuries. This rope brought me to my greatest races. It's a simple thing, but it is imbued with history and meaning. Use it as a lifeline. Use me as a lifeline. Call when you need to. This rope connects us as I return home across the country, and he to this last, most vital year of school.

When we extricate the athletic and sporting endeavors of youth from the ways they are so often framed—as fitness, competition, or character development—what emerges are spaces in which powerful forms of divergent ingenuity and cultural production are occurring.[23] Where schools and institutions always have been anchored to countless, layered cultural expectations, social rules, and bodies of knowledge that reproduce dominant cultural repertoires and institutional power,[24] sport, despite its many constraints, has remained less restrictive.[25]

Even a marginalized community can pick up and transform a game, suit it to its own needs, shape it in its own image.[26] Soccer has had profound sociopolitical and ontological meaning and importance across the racial and ethnic diversity of Latin America and beyond.[27] Basketball, particularly, has a powerful sociopolitical history as a site of expression, agency, and cultural creativity in many black American communities.[28]

In indigenous and First Nations communities worldwide, colonial sports, including rugby in Maori communities,[29] skateboarding,[30] and basketball[31] in some American reservation communities, have become sites of active resistance, ways to preserve and affirm identity by actively contesting cultural erasure and misrecognition.[32] And running, to both East African[33] and indigenous American populations,[34] is a practice of far more cultural and historical significance than simple participation in track and cross-country can capture.

In this way, even as the racial project of sport unfolds, and the global world participates in "colonial" sporting activities (i.e., sports whose form and rules have been crafted by European nations and spread through settler-colonialism, such as football/soccer, cricket, and basketball), or heritage sporting activities now governed by colonial rules and culture (e.g., track and field, wrestling, and mountaineering), sport remains culturally sustaining. It is an enterprise, taken up and shaped by communities of color in ways that reflect their own ingenuity,[35] as ways to claim agency,[36] and to define and affirm positive community identity.[37]

For youth of color, participation means more than building character and teamwork skills, excelling in competition, or seeking scholarships; participation in sport is an ontological, spiritual endeavor.[38] The rich community histories attached to sport make it a site full of possibility for ontological healing[39]—healing related to one's sense of self, agency, and identity—and a space and source of stability through which to transcend the hostile affective geographies of schooling.

> "Mike!" Noah's Facebook messages and texts always begin like this, in the same way he spoke, punctuated with enthusiasm and joy: "I am healthy! I placed top 10 in state! School is going ok, not great, but ok . . . but I am running fast!"
>
> Running is Noah's respite from struggle, from failure. It is a place to be proud of himself, a place for stability. It is equally a place where his intelligence can shine in ways that may never be possible in the Eurocentric curricula I know he is working with: schooling that seeks to subtract and erase his culture, his perspective, his Amharic language. Though he struggles with academic, disciplinary vocabulary in his school subjects, he doesn't in track; he understands and speaks thoughtfully about PRs, periodization, the distinction between tempos and intervals, aerobic and anaerobic training. Driven by passion, by a welcoming, patient community unconcerned with his mispronunciations, welcoming his cultural self, his ingenuity shines, his identity thrives.
>
> We continue to exchange Facebook messages and phone calls. We workshop his essays. We discuss his running, and we talk, realistically, about how he might keep running, what to tell the coaches who are now calling with some frequency; about the different types of schools

and collegiate athletics, and where he might be comfortable, successful, stable.

Though not always acknowledged in schools, for some youth—particularly youth of color—sport is often a space of incredible ontological importance. It represents a facet of institutional life in which they can belong, contribute, and feel valued. It is a rare space in which identity, stability, and agency can be found, and sustained, in ways that otherwise elude them and that are culturally affirming, patient, welcoming.

COLONIALITY, SPORT, AND SCHOOLS

Unfortunately, far too often in schools, these positive, culturally sustaining, and ontologically significant elements of sport are ignored or warped. The functionalist, colorblind view of sports and athletics dominates our conception of sport in its intersection with school, operating in profound and insidious ways, amplifying the forces of marginalization and exclusion that already are present.

In schools, the colonial commodification of youth in academic terms, as empty vessels, products, collides with narratives of sport as a colorblind means of social mobility. School sport becomes a post-racial fantasy, a character-building, extracurricular indulgence, but one that in reality occurs *on the terms of the school*, on the terms of whiteness. Participation is imbued with promise, as a way to achieve higher—academically, economically, socially—than one might otherwise hope, but these hopes remain linked to normative views of cultural capital.[40]

Youth of color are at once valorized for their athletic prowess and skill—often cultivated by their unique heritage cultural practices and identity-building experiences in racialized communities—and granted some limited agency, but then chastised and disciplined when this focus on sport is judged to be too consuming.[41] In this way, sport becomes an affective, socio-emotional double bind. We position sport as commendable and full of promise on one hand, yet simultaneously as a peripheral indulgence, a luxury that only matters insofar as its lessons eventually translate into more "significant" endeavors (as defined by colonial aspirations of self and criteria for advancement) on the other.[42]

> Noah rides waves of highs and lows, praise and critique. He runs fast, and is a credit to his school, a wonderful example of its diverse community. He struggles in class and is told to work harder, show more perseverance, more "grit"—an ironic demand given what he accomplishes each day while running and while navigating a cultural world and life far more complex, difficult, and cognitively demanding than anything his teachers could imagine. Is it not "grit" to be nearing graduation from an institution that operates in his third language, one

learned only three years ago? All of this wears on him, he writes. It's becoming a battle.

I read over his papers, and we edit together. We continue to talk about colleges. There's hope, but there's also tension; something heavy is setting in. I worry, for he has flirted with academic ineligibility in the past.

During these conversations, I regularly think of my own struggles, of days when I leaned heavily into running, the weight of navigating the affective terrain getting to me. I share this with Noah, about days in elementary school, high school, and college, when the affect of being Xicano, of my name being mispronounced, of hearing teachers and peers laugh at jokes about Mexicans, built up, and I would just go run—alone, harder than I was supposed to—because I had to. I wanted him to know he wasn't alone in the affect he was experiencing, but there's only so much you can convey over the phone, through an email. I wonder, and worry, because this can lead equally to injury—the existential need to run, balanced with the physical reality that our bodies can only take so much.

When we reject what athletics and physical endeavor might *mean* across difference, and to cultural and racialized experiences beyond the colonial sphere, sport becomes dispossessed of its community histories. The resulting dissonance between the coloniality of school culture and the possibility present in the freedom of sport is difficult to navigate. Certainly learning happens in sport that can enrich academic development, but as with all learning, it is contextual. The culturally and socially connected passion, engagement, community identity, and spiritual meaningfulness youth of color may find in learning and doing sport cannot simply be translated directly to academic endeavors that often involve a dehumanizing, Eurocentric, culturally irrelevant curricula hostile to their very existence.[43]

My point here is not to dismiss the importance of academics, or suggest that athletics should take precedence over academic goals. Our expectations must be rigorous, particularly for youth and communities of color who have been historically, and continue to be disproportionately, underserved. The reality is that few will make a living from playing sports, and even those who will deserve a robust, critical education.

Rather, I want to suggest that the productive socio-emotional, ontological aspects that might be present in athletics—the ways it can operate as a site of ingenuity, creativity, resistance, and culturally sustaining identity development—become too easily consumed by the externally imposed, culturally myopic expectations of what sport *should* be to youth. Moreover, these expectations themselves, criteria for success, for knowledge production, defined by whiteness and coloniality, are presented far too uncritically, with little regard for their colonial origins or the ontological rift they can impose on youth of color.

The school year goes on, and the turbulence in Noah's schooling and life continues. He is once again bouncing among homes week to week. He has hit a rocky patch in school. Then, in the depths of winter, near the end of the indoor track season, Noah is felled by an injury. It lingers, and his one source of stability, connection, meaning, is untethered.

Yearning to run, Noah attempts a premature comeback and exacerbates the injury. Just stop, his teachers tell him. This is taking too much time, they say; focus on your studies instead. It isn't that simple. To be himself, to be present, to cultivate the resilience he needs to do what they ask, he needs to be running. So he tries again, breaks again, and the cycle repeats. He is left only with training room rehab and the unrelenting reality of institutional struggle.

Things happen quickly, or seemingly so, from there. Noah becomes difficult to get in touch with. The exclamation point has fallen away from his greeting when we do connect. I know he is injured. I know he is struggling. His reports on school grow increasingly pessimistic, but all we can do is retread the same conversations, try to focus on the positives, look to the promise of running again soon, of running as a collegiate athlete sometime in the future.

Each time we do speak, I'm poignantly aware of what's happening, the depression, the turbulence, the longing to run. I'm left wondering at the intensity of the storm he is weathering, hoping he can hold on.

Put in other terms, "hoop dreams" (understood as the athletic aspirations youth harbor, which extend across all sports, not just basketball) are not just the capitalist fantasies of youth of color, desires for wealth and prestige, but ontological yearnings; dreams of being able to pursue a practice that feels congruent—culturally, ontologically, ancestrally—with who they see and feel themselves to be.

When educators maintain a functionalist stance in regard to sport, choose to ignore how coloniality shapes the expectations schools construct around what youth are meant to take from participation, they exacerbate the affective hostility of the geographies youth find themselves in. What may be a central element of their cultural and personal identity, an ontological pin that holds their lives together, offering stability and focus, becomes always and necessarily subservient to others' approval, yet another realm of their identity colonized and controlled.

THE PSYCHOLOGICAL TOLL OF AFFECT

The systemic things—achievement gaps and disproportionate discipline rates, monolingual and monocultural curricula, functionalist approaches to school sport—these are merely the facets we can see on the surface. It is the deeper, lingering psychological and ontological impacts that are most jarring: the toll colonial affect takes on youth.

The effects are well documented. Even for the most successful students of color, those who can find ways to navigate hostile schooling and societal terrain, retaining some semblance of agency, their experiences are marked by racial battle fatigue.[44] To maintain stability, a cohesive sense of agency and identity, youth of color face either cultivating oppositional identities that affirm their racial and cultural selves, but distance them from the possibility of institutional success and acceptance,[45] or the prospect of assenting to covering demands,[46] achieving success and acceptance, but at the expense of their racial and cultural identities, thus losing something of themselves in the process.

The impact is draining. As *allostatic load*—a measure of stress chemicals in the brain—increases, then remains high from the socio-emotional toll of dealing with racism, trauma, and hostile affect on a daily basis, well-being and health on many dimensions are eroded in a process that psychology has described as *weathering*.[47] But these clinical realities are only part of the story; living constantly with these affective pressures are challenges of emotion, sensation, and experience,[48] *soul wounds*[49] that linger and accrue beyond any one incident, speaking themselves into existence in ways that rarely are acknowledged or understood in schools.[50]

If we can appreciate and accept sport as an ontologically important, culturally sustaining, and even spiritual pursuit for youth of color, then it should be an easy step to understand that when the relationship youth have with that endeavor is distorted, limited, or restricted in ways that feel oppressive and dehumanizing, ignoring what it might and does mean to youth, the affective impact goes well beyond disappointment or frustration; it can be ontologically crushing.

The trauma of all of this, of living in a world hostile to one's existence, wears on the soul.

> April rolls into May. I am sitting in the back of a classroom, a research-observer, taking notes on how students with difficult relationships to school are being invited into this classroom. My pocket vibrates; another athlete from camp texts me, cryptically. It has been weeks since I have spoken with Noah, and my heart races as I excuse myself to text back. After receiving no reply, I call my old coach, and now coaching-partner at camp, needing to know more. He relates to me devastating news.
>
> Many of the details remain unclear, but what we know is this: the previous day, almost to the end of the school year, Noah is told by a teacher, bluntly, that he won't graduate.
>
> Did he really expect to, given his writing and English abilities? No, they don't have any solutions for him. No next steps either. That's it.
>
> This news crushes a slender dream—not just to run and compete, not just to further his education, but to fulfill what is most true about himself, to pursue and revel in those connections to his heritage and

identity, to continue to engage in this thing that gives him stability and meaning in an otherwise tumultuous, hostile world. After this, still injured but on the mend, he goes briefly to practice. Then home. Late in the evening, in a park where he had once regularly practiced, full of life, blazing intervals around the grassy fields, he hangs himself. His body is found that next morning, and the news now reaches me, several times zones distant.

Walking silently out of the school, I cannot stop seeing Noah with my, his, our stretching rope tangled around his neck, a lifeline that failed to deliver on its promises.

I sit in my car in a school parking lot, thousands of miles away, and I cry.

WITNESSING IDENTITY FOR YOUTH OF COLOR IN SPORT

I want to be clear on this point: I do not blame the teachers. I cannot imagine what they must have felt. I do not know them. I have never met them. But I know that they were devastated, as was the entire school and community, in the wake of Noah's suicide. I cannot count how many stupid, hurtful things I uttered in my years in the classroom—things that come spilling out of us without thought because of the systemic pressures and colonial ideologies that invisibly surround us and shape our expectations for students—and that in an instant can negatively change a student's trajectory, or shape a relationship with schooling.

And that, perhaps, is the point: to call attention to the ways that we operate in institutional systems with a troubling history—a system that works to marginalize, to create *ontological distance* between youth of color, schools, and educators.[51] This is not a phenomenon limited to sport, but unwittingly, we have allowed sport, as it has lived in schools, to become a part of it; positioned in ways that obscure the significance and value sport might have to youth, instead imposing on them external, colonial values and criteria for what it should mean. For all of its potential to encourage personal, cultural, and academic growth for youth of color in schools, sport easily becomes yet another tool of dehumanization.

There is tension in my telling of this story, because our engagement with youth of color should not focus solely on damage-centered narratives.[52] That too is limiting, dehumanizing: they are not victims. Yet I feel an urgency to tell this story, to articulate what the lived effects of coloniality and affect look like, because although this degree of tragedy is not the norm, it insists on action.

Stories such as this encourage us to reframe our conceptual lenses and our engagement with youth of color, both around sport and beyond it. They demand that we consider—with humility and honesty—the influence of coloniality on our perspectives, our practices, and hopefully, to adjust, and engage in the process of *witnessing*,[53] which involves seeing youth of color *on their terms*, rather than our own, and recognizing that trauma often exists not as some specific, explosive event, but in the "relationship between some students' difficult positioning in schools and . . . the ongoing, accruing impact and consequences of social malignancies such as racism, sexism, and homophobia,"[54] in the affect of coloniality.

It is easy to see the challenges of school, the struggles of youth of color, and attribute them to an individual's lack of ambition or aptitude. This attitude maintains our emotional distance; it keeps us safe. What is less easy is to be a *witness*, to reflect on how systemic realities, the accumulating, difficult experiences students of color face, are less idiosyncratic, individual factors and more likely related to practices and institutions we may be complicit in. Witnessing calls for this difficult introspection: for engaging with how the affective geography of coloniality has simply made it difficult, challenging, to *be* of color in school, in sports, in the world, and how our mundane practices may be contributing to that.

This realization can be painful, but it opens the door for hope and possibility, for us to take de-colonizing action. When we see youth of color in new ways, full of promise, ingenuity, creativity, and agency, and witness, recognize, trauma in the mundane, we can transform our relationships and understandings of youth. We can begin to imagine ways our work in and around sport might support youth to go beyond just competitive and social goals: how we might offer the possibility of ontological healing, stability, and culturally sustaining identity development in their athletic and academic endeavors.

> Several months on from that day, I am out on a trail, running. Normally my running is systematic, compulsive. Lately, it had been sporadic and reckless. Some days I can't run. It feels too close. Other days, full of grief and rage and regret, I find myself unable to stop, running far longer than I should.
>
> Today is one of those days. In two weeks, I will return to camp, to coach more young athletes, some new, some returning, many who knew Noah. My arm carries a new tattoo, an archive to Noah's life and spirit, which I am sure I will be asked about. Today, I think about our conversations on running as identity and connection. I find myself coherently reflecting on this piece of our relationship for the first time in months, and it brings my emotions into some degree of focus. Maybe sharing these conversations anew, acknowledging the trauma with new athletes likely struggling with the same things, may lead us toward healing.
>
> Running may not be the focal point of my life anymore—indeed, two years in the future from that day of clarity, an injury would end my own waning competitive career—but it matters, as it mattered to Noah. It is the fulfillment of who I see myself to be, the time I am most truly myself, most safely Xicano. I run less now, but that run, and every run since, has been a living prayer for Noah—a fleeting chance to hon-

or him by connecting to something beyond what we could articulate, embodying an affective experience we shared once, and share still.

CONCLUSION: HOPE, AND AN ATHLETE'S RAGE

Decades ago, Renato Rosaldo[55] detailed the ways in which seemingly mundane, arbitrary activities can have untold significance within the ontological and epistemic practices of cultures different from our own, significance that goes unnoticed, or feels peripheral from the perspective of observers. For youth of color, sport can be such a practice—often seen as peripheral, trivial—but rich with meaning to its participants.

Read this story in decolonial terms; what follows is a decolonial challenge: As educators, it is not our place to determine what meaning or significance sport should hold for youth, or what should matter most to their identity development. Rather, our task is to be culturally sustaining and revitalizing in our orientation toward youth of color, to *witness* what sport and other social and cultural practices (music, art, and more, for sport will not be of significance to all youth) might mean to them, on *their* terms, to encourage the ingenuity and competency that might not be measured or valued by our present institutions, and to support them as they navigate hostile affective geographies composed of traumas both exceptional and mundane.

Our worlds are shaped by our own cultural and racialized experiences. A decolonial lens helps us see that for youth of color, marginalized from institutional power by complex sociopolitical histories, their experiences, identities, and valued practices will not easily align with those we educators often hold so dear, accepting as fact, as normative, as obvious, for these "norms"—as jarring as it can be to hear and recognize this—are the legacies of a violent and dehumanizing colonization. As educators— teachers, administrators, coaches—the question we face is whether we are willing to listen, to witness, to appreciate, and to leverage the untold significance that arbitrary activities and diverse practices—sport included—might have to youth whose lived affective realities are different from our own. It is an important question. And let us make no mistake: lives depend on how we choose to answer.

NOTES

1. Lindsay Pérez Huber, "Disrupting Apartheid of Knowledge: Testimonio as Methodology in Latina/o Critical Race Research in Education," *International Journal of Qualitative Studies in Education* 22, no. 6 (2009): 639–54.

2. Nelson Maldonado-Torres, "On the Coloniality of Being: Contributions to the Development of a Concept," *Cultural Studies* 21, nos. 2–3 (2007): 240–70.

3. Russell J. Skiba, Robert H. Horner, Choong-Geun Chung, M. Karega Rausch, Seth L. May, and Tary Tobin, "Race Is Not Neutral: A National Investigation of

African American and Latino Disproportionality in School Discipline," *School Psychology Review* 40, no. 1 (2011): 85.

4. Maryam Adamu and Lauren Hogan, *Point of Entry: The Preschool-to-Prison Pipeline* (Washington, DC: Center for American Progress, 2015).

5. H. Richard Milner IV, "Rethinking Achievement Gap Talk in Urban Education," *Urban Education* 48, no. 1 (2013): 3–8.

6. Patricia Hill Collins, *Black Sexual Politics: African Americans, Gender, and the New Racism* (New York: Routledge, 2004).

7. Jacco Van Sterkenburg and Annelies Knoppers, "Dominant Discourses about Race/Ethnicity and Gender in Sport Practice and Performance," *International Review for the Sociology of Sport* 39, no. 3 (2004): 301–21.

8. Henry A. Giroux, *Disposable Youth: Racialized Memories, and the Culture of Cruelty* (New York: Routledge, 2012).

9. Antonia Darder, *Culture and Power in the Classroom: A Critical Foundation for Bicultural Education* (Boulder, CO: Paradigm Publishers, 2012).

10. John U. Ogbu, "Collective Identity and the Burden of 'Acting White' in Black History, Community, and Education," *Urban Review* 36, no. 1 (2004): 1–35. See also Beverly Daniel Tatum, *"Why Are All the Black Kids Sitting Together in the Cafeteria?": And Other Conversations about Race* (New York: Basic Books, 2017).

11. Sara Ahmed, *Cultural Politics of Emotion* (Edinburgh, UK: Edinburgh University Press, 2014).

12. See note 2 for reference.

13. Ben Carrington, *Race, Sport and Politics: The Sporting Black Diaspora* (Los Angeles: Sage, 2010); Ben Carrington, "Assessing the Sociology of Sport: On Race and Diaspora," *International Review for the Sociology of Sport* 50, nos. 4–5 (2015): 39–396.

14. Jay J. Coakley, *Sport in Society: Issues & Controversies*, 12th ed. (New York: McGraw-Hill, 2017).

15. Jay J. Coakley, "Youth Sports: What Counts as 'Positive Development'?," *Journal of Sport and Social Issues* 35, no. 3 (2011): 306–24; Bonnie Sierlecki, "Grit and Graciousness: Race and Rhetoric in Barack Obama's 2008 Presidential Campaign," in *Sports and Identity: New Agendas in Communication*, edited by Barry Brummett (New York: Routledge, 2014), 106–26.

16. Kevin Hylton, *"Race" and Sport: Critical Race Theory* (New York: Routledge, 2008); C. Richard King, David J. Leonard, and Kyle W. Kusz, "White Power and Sport: An Introduction," *Journal of Sport & Social Issues* 31, no. 1 (2007): 3–10.

17. Eduardo Bonilla-Silva, *Racism without Racists: Color-Blind Racism and the Persistence of Racial Inequality in America* (New York: Rowman & Littlefield, 2017); Douglas Hartman, *Race, Culture, and the Revolt of the Black Athlete: The 1968 Olympic Protests and Their Aftermath* (Chicago: University of Chicago Press, 2003).

18. See second reference in note 17.

19. Abraham Iqbal Khan, "Michael Sam, Jackie Robinson, and the Politics of Respectability," *Communication & Sport* 5, no. 3 (2017): 331–51; David Remnick, "The Racial Demagoguery of Trump's Assaults on Kaepernick and Steph Curry," *New Yorker*, September 23, 2017.

20. Brian Stoddart, "Sport, Colonialism and Struggle: C. L. R. James and Cricket," in *Sport and Modern Social Theorists*, edited by Richard Giulianotti (New York: Palgrave-McMillan, 2004), 111–28.

21. Jen Skattebol, "Affect: A Tool to Support Pedagogical Change," *Discourse: Studies in the Cultural Politics of Education* 31, no. 1 (2010): 75–91.

22. Django Paris, "Culturally Sustaining Pedagogy: A Needed Change in Stance, Terminology, and Practice," *Educational Researcher* 41, no. 3 (2012): 93–97.

23. Todd Boyd, *Am I Black Enough for You?: Popular Culture from the 'Hood and Beyond* (Bloomington: Indiana University Press, 1997); Harry Edwards, "Black Youths' Commitment to Sports Achievement: A Virtue-Turned-Tragic-Turned-Virtue," *Sport* 85, no. 7 (1994): 86.

24. Henry A. Giroux, *Education and the Crisis of Public Values: Challenging the Assault on Teachers, Students, and Public Education* (New York: Peter Lang, 2012).

25. Thabiti Lewis, *Ballers of the New School: Race and Sports in America* (Chicago: Third World Press, 2010).

26. Stuart Hall, "What Is This 'Black' in Black Popular Culture?," *Social Justice* 20, nos. 1/2 (1993): 104–14.

27. Eduardo Galeano, *Soccer in Sun and Shadow* (New York: Nation Books, 2013).

28. See note 23; Jabari Mahiri, *Shooting for Excellence: African American and Youth Culture in New Century Schools* (Urbana, IL: National Council of Teachers of English, 1998).

29. Brendan Hokowhitu, "Tackling Maori Masculinity: A Colonial Genealogy of Savagery and Sport," *Contemporary Pacific* 16, no. 2 (2004): 259–84.

30. *Apache Chronicle*, directed by Nanna Dalunde (Rossette Film Company, 2010).

31. Sherman Alexie, "Why We Play Basketball," *College English* 58, no. 6 (1996): 709–12; Sherman Alexie, *Blasphemy: New and Selected Stories* (New York: Grove/Atlantic, 2012).

32. Eric D. Anderson, "Using the Master's Tools: Resisting Colonization through Colonial Sports," *International Journal of the History of Sport* 23, no. 2 (2006): 247–66.

33. John Bale and Joe Sang, *Kenyan Running: Movement Culture, Geography, and Global Change* (Portland, OR: Frank Cass, 2003); Grant Jarvie, "The Promise and Possibilities of Running in and out of East Africa," in *East African Running: Towards a Cross-Disciplinary Perspective*, edited by Yannis Pitsiladis, John Bale, Craig Sharp, and Timothy Noakes (New York: Routledge, 2007), 24–39.

34. Peter Nabokov, *Indian Running* (Santa Barbara, CA: Capra Press, 1981).

35. See second reference in note 31.

36. Harry Edwards, "The Decline of the Black Athlete," *Color Lines* 3 (Spring 2000): 20–29.

37. John Edgar Wideman, *Hoop Roots* (New York: Houghton Mifflin Harcourt, 2002).

38. Francesc Torralba and Ismael Santos, *Inteligencia Espiritual y Deporte* (Barcelona: Plataforma Editorial, 2016).

39. Sonia Abigail Sánchez, Michael Domínguez, Andrew Cory Greene, Elizabeth Mendoza, Michelle Fine, Helen A. Neville, and Kris D. Gutiérrez, "Revisiting the Collective in Critical Consciousness: Diverse Sociopolitical Wisdoms and Ontological Healing in Sociopolitical Development," *Urban Review* 47, no. 5 (2015): 824–46.

40. Joshua Dubrow and Jimi Adams, "Hoop Inequalities: Race, Class and Family Structure Background and the Odds of Playing in the National Basketball Association," *International Review for the Sociology of Sport* 47, no. 1 (2012): 43–59; Tamela McNulty Eitle and David J. Eitle, "Race, Cultural Capital, and the Educational Effects of Participation in Sports," *Sociology of Education* (2002): 123–46.

41. See note 24 for reference.

42. See first reference in note 13.

43. See note 9 for reference.

44. William A. Smith, Tara J. Yosso, and Daniel G. Solórzano, "Challenging Racial Battle Fatigue on Historically White Campuses: A Critical Race Examination of Race-Related Stress," in *Covert Racism*, edited by Rodney Coates (Boston: Brill, 2011), 211–38.

45. See note 10 for reference.

46. Kenji Yoshino, *Covering: The Hidden Assault on Our Civil Rights* (New York: Random House, 2007).

47. Arline T. Geronimus, Margaret Hicken, Danya Keene, and John Bound, "'Weathering' and Age Patterns of Allostatic Load Scores among Blacks and Whites in the United States," *American Journal of Public Health* 96, no. 5 (2006): 826–33; Wendy Kliewer, Kathryn Reid-Quiñones, Brian J. Shields, and Lauren Foutz, "Multiple Risks, Emotion Regulation Skill, and Cortisol in Low-Income African American Youth: A Prospective Study," *Journal of Black Psychology* 35, no. 1 (2009): 24–43; Wendy Kliewer,

"Violence Exposure and Cortisol Responses in Urban Youth," *International Journal of Behavioral Medicine* 13, no. 2 (2006): 109–20.

48. Megan Watkins, "Pedagogic Affect/Effect: Embodying a Desire to Learn," *Pedagogies* 1, no. 4 (2006): 269–82.

49. Marcos Pizarro, *Chicanas and Chicanos in School: Racial Profiling, Identity Battles, and Empowerment* (Austin: University of Texas Press, 2009).

50. Elizabeth Dutro and Andrea C. Bien, "Listening to the Speaking Wound: A Trauma Studies Perspective on Student Positioning in Schools," *American Educational Research Journal* 51, no. 1 (2014): 7–35.

51. Michael Domínguez, "Se Hace Puentes al Andar: Decolonial Teacher Education as a Needed Bridge to Culturally Sustaining and Revitalizing Pedagogies," in *Culturally Sustaining Pedagogies: Teaching and Learning for Justice in a Changing World*, edited by Django Paris and H. Samy Alim (New York: Teachers College Press, 2017), 225–45.

52. Eve Tuck, "Suspending Damage: A Letter to Communities," *Harvard Educational Review* 79, no. 3 (2009): 409–28.

53. Michalinos Zembylas, "Witnessing in the Classroom: The Ethics and Politics of Affect," *Educational Theory* 56, no. 3 (2006): 305–24.

54. See note 49 for reference.

55. Renato Rosaldo, "Grief and a Headhunter's Rage," *Death, Mourning, and Burial: A Cross-Cultural Reader* (2004): 167–78.

Part III

Sports, Media, and Schools

Sports, Media, and Schools

Sports, Media, and Schools

INTRODUCTION

What messages are conveyed through popular media about sports and athletes? It is an understatement at this point in human history to claim that media matter. The volume of media formats and venues has exploded as communication technologies have advanced rapidly over the past century. The internet quickly has become the major conduit of information, and a generation of students has emerged that not only has not known life without the World Wide Web, but also has not known life without quick and easy access to it through smartphones. Media literacy is undoubtedly a vital skill not only for students, but also for those who educate them.[1]

Sports media are no longer confined to television broadcasts of games and the sports section of the local newspaper or *Sports Illustrated*. Countless Web resources disperse scores, players, teams, and editorial opinions. Along with such resources, fictional materials such as young adult literature, film, and television must be included in the basket of influential media that shape cultural understandings of sports in schools and society. Part III models a few ways of engaging critically and constructively with a range of sports media.

In the ninth chapter, Crystal L. Beach and Katie S. Dredger extend Part II's identity discussion to the construction of gendered identities by foregrounding troubling representations of female athletes in news reports, postgame interviews, and popular Twitter hashtags. They show how such portrayals are used to reduce female athletes to fashion symbols and objects of unwanted sexual attention. Beach and Dredger's analysis points to the urgency of educators dispelling gendered myths about athletes that are common in schools.

Those myths arguably are interwoven with broader narratives of what it means to be a young person who identifies closely with athletics. In chapter 10, Mark A. Lewis and Luke Rodesiler spotlight adolescent-athlete characters in young adult literature to illuminate how harmful notions of the "good" athlete can be challenged. The selected texts, which include Sherman Alexie's *The Absolutely True Diary of a Part-Time Indian* and Lisa Luedeke's *Smashed*,[2] provide nuanced portrayals of students who play sports. Lewis and Rodesiler's discussion of fictional students reveals ways in which popular perceptions of teenagers as always rebellious and attention-seeking might be reframed by educators to better serve student-athletes.

An invitation to reframe common understandings is likewise offered by Ian Parker Renga in the eleventh chapter. Instead of focusing on students, however, Renga considers teachers' perceptions of their instructional practice. He observes how sports commentators and athletes have little trouble talking about athletic performance as beautiful, but the same cannot be said for teachers. Drawing upon the humanities, Renga goes on to argue that sports values, rooted in the nature of competition, are readily apparent in the media and are widely accepted beyond the athletic arena. He wonders if teachers struggle to see the beauty of their work because the values informing their work are more debatable and less celebrated in society.

NOTES

1. For conceptual insight, see David Buckingham, *Media Education: Literacy, Learning and Contemporary Culture* (Cambridge, UK: Polity Press, 2003); for a sense of the issue's enormous scope, see Julie Coiro, Michele Knobel, Colin Lankshear, and Donald J. Leu, eds., *Handbook of Research on New Literacies* (New York: Routledge, 2014).

2. Sherman Alexie, *The Absolutely True Diary of a Part-Time Indian* (New York: Little, Brown, 2007); Lisa Luedeke, *Smashed* (New York: Margaret K. McElderry Books, 2012).

NINE

Sporty Girls and Tomboys

Negotiating the Rhetoric Surrounding Female Athletes

Crystal L. Beach and Katie S. Dredger

Female athletes learn early about the power of language.[1] The authors, experienced high school English teachers, have watched the changing language that has been used to refer to athletes in their adolescent years and beyond. The language surrounding female athletic bodies is one that deserves to be unpacked as teachers and school leaders negotiate the ways in which they can become better supporters of young women who are getting mixed messages on the worth of their bodies and minds in our media-rich culture.

Crystal grew up identifying as a "tomboy" playing every sport she could. She then went on to play Division I softball. Today, she coaches high school girls because she's experienced the positive influence athletics have had throughout her entire life and hopes to help young women develop a passion for sports through her mentorship and dedication to living a healthy lifestyle. Others have told her that she's "intense, strong, and hard working," which are characteristics that have helped her lead teams to state championship titles over the years. These characteristics, nurtured on the field, translate to the classroom, where she manages and encourages adolescents relentlessly and enthusiastically to be better readers and writers.

Katie grew up as a rural millennial, at the nascence of Title IX, captaining her high school cheerleading team and tennis teams but not identifying as an athlete. She has experienced, as a teacher and coach, and then as a soccer parent, the value in opportunities that are now afforded to her daughters that weren't available to her.

Ultimately, the authors both have found the ways in which females have navigated the labels that have been projected onto their bodies and roles by those around them. They have supported students and players as they resist the idea of being only one thing in school cliques and as they grow to be seen as multifaceted individuals in a complex society.

In projecting these lessons onto the discussion of female athletes, teachers can mitigate the too often reduction to labels that can be limiting, even damaging. Chimamanda Adichie's TED Talk, the "Danger of a Single Story,"[2] espouses the ways in which students can learn about others, particularly those in other cultures, in order to shed stereotypes and one-dimensional representations.

For this reason, through the study and use of effective rhetorical techniques, adolescent girls can be empowered by their allies in K–12 schools—teachers, coaches, administrators, peers, and parents—as they move into traditionally male-dominated spaces. Likewise, male students can look at authentic ways that rhetoric can be used to empower, persuade, defend, or marginalize as allies from a place of power, using what Alan Brown and Luke Rodesiler have termed "critical sports literacy."[3]

Educators can explore ways that language is used in the discussions by and of female athletes within popular media. This chapter seeks to share relevant examples of the ways language is used to demean or empower groups and individuals, relevant in many classrooms and beyond. Language has been used to reduce female athletes to fashion symbols, to objects of sexual attention, and to divide women. In response, language can empower. Female athletes need to be seen as more than one thing, and our language about them can do more than reduce. As an answer to the reduction, the language that the athletes choose in response can serve as models for others as we guide our adolescents into a more equitable world.

UNDERSTANDING DISCOURSES

This chapter focuses on the following examples of rhetoric concerning female athletes with James Gee's notion of *Discourses*. Gee's description of Discourses includes "ways of behaving, interacting, valuing, thinking, believing, speaking, and often reading and writing, that are accepted as instantiations of particular identities."[4] In fact, Discourses are "always and everywhere social products of social histories" and are "always more than just language."[5] Language, in other words, is never apolitical; this is especially true in advertising and sports media coverage.

Furthermore, Gee helps educators understand how Discourses are practiced in and out of school by differentiating between *acquisition* and *learning.* Acquisition as he defines it "is a process of acquiring something (usually subconsciously) by exposure to models, a process of trial and error, and practice within social groups, without formal teaching . . . This is how people come to control their first language."[6]

By comparison, Gee argues that learning is "a process that involves conscious knowledge gained through teaching (though not necessarily from someone officially designated a teacher) or through certain life-experiences that trigger conscious reflection." Acquisition thus is what helps educators lay the foundation for understanding the language surrounding female athletes. Learning, then, is what we hope students will do when beginning to understand the rich complexities of how society reads female athletes.

Language, symbolic expressions, beliefs and values, or other forms of meanings influence how female athletes are understood through thoughtful reflection of the examples provided in this chapter. Yet, it is important for educators to remember that these influences tie into the bigger picture of representations based on sociocultural and historical influences. Especially today, through various technologies, these meanings can quickly disseminate and change in the time that it could take for someone to retweet, share, or remix within social media. For those unfamiliar with the term, *remix* "means to take cultural artifacts and combine and manipulate them into new kinds of creative blends,"[7] which can be seen through many of the examples outlined below. For this reason, understanding the intricate connections behind how Discourses shape representations is especially important when analyzing the rhetoric surrounding female athletes.

The following rhetorical lenses can help educators understand these connections as they consider what these examples mean for the K–12 classroom: rhetoric used to define female athletes as more than fashion; rhetoric used to define female athletes as sexual objects; rhetoric used to divide and label female athletes; and rhetoric used to justify and challenge inequities in female sports.

RHETORIC USED TO DEFINE FEMALE ATHLETES AS MORE THAN FASHION

The purpose of the female body should not be to please others aesthetically, but instead to perform under the athlete's own terms. Yet, history has recorded many times when this was not the case. In 1896, for example, Ellen Parkhust defended female bicyclists against those calling them immoral for wearing pants, promoting instead the benefits of exercise and fresh air.[8] Helen Wills Moody, tennis Olympic gold medalist in 1924, was dubbed "Queen Helen" because she wore makeup in order to defy stereotypes that sports were unfeminine.[9]

Babe Didrikson Zaharias, one of the greatest female athletes in modern history, is perhaps the first well-documented, multisport female athlete publicly to negotiate the language of femininity in regard to athletics.[10] In the 1930s, she told stories of the fisticuffs that marked her early years, but she was advised to transform herself to be more feminine to appease her fans and critics. Discussing the implications for this transformation, Susan Cayleff states:

> Babe's successful ascension to femininity is hailed as an applaudable accomplishment, not the tumultuous, contrived, and limiting self-molding that it really was. Portrayed as a win-win situation, the toll taken on self-esteem, individuality, and difference is ignored. Even for many years after her transformation, it remained standard fare for interviewers to spend as much time describing her physicality as her sports accomplishments. In doing so, they reassured themselves and their readers of Babe's acceptability.[11]

As one can see, these women's stories across time show how language used to define female athletes' physical appearances, based on their attire and other characteristics, has been problematic.

Unfortunately, though many years later, not enough has changed in the demands of what society expects female athletes to look like in their appearance and dress to remain "feminine." After all, "Twirlgate"[12] reminded the world that once again female athletes' bodies are only viewed as ornamental and adorned by fashionable clothing. Here, Eugenie Bouchard, Canadian tennis star, questioned why she was asked to twirl during her Australian Open match when men would not be asked to do the same. Fashion questions typically are directed more toward women and posed even before the women are asked about their athletic achievements, whereas some men are asked about their clothing only when it is considered not ordinary.[13]

Another example of how women are subjected to comments about their appearance and fashion stems from the commentary surrounding Olympic athletes.[14] From gymnast Gabby Douglas's hair to volleyball players described as "semi-naked women . . . glistening like wet otters,"[15] it is clear that female athletes too often are judged by their looks before their athletic abilities. For this reason, the Representation Project established the #AskHerMore campaign to challenge media outlets to reconsider their coverage of amazing female athletes when they are on the performance stage or the medal platform.[16]

Yet, what happens when some readers see a representation of a female body in one way and the publisher or athlete sees it in another? This discussion or perspective and interpretation tie into critical reading skills that can be encouraged in K–12 classrooms and beyond to confront the danger of a single story as a way to combat stereotypes of all stripes.

The development of critical literacy in the areas of perspective, reduction, and marginalization are relevant to students and can have immediate effect on the female athletes negotiating these issues, often alone. These are complicated layers of understanding that need to be unpacked to thoroughly analyze the message being spread. For example, Lindsey Vonn's images in *ESPN*'s "Body Issue" brought into play these very complications. As Braverman writes,

> The *ESPN* Body Issue's "athletic nude" imagery has become almost instantly recognizable as a symbol of empowerment: muscled bodies chiseled from stone, as perfect as classical Greek statues. It's still radical for a magazine to photograph its male and female models in the same way, and a large part of the Body Issue's significance is that it celebrates athletes of all genders and shapes, including paralympians. Still, any so-called empowerment is granted almost exclusively to female athletes; men, and especially male athletes, are assumed to have all the power they need.[17]

With this point in mind, readers can begin to understand how Vonn perhaps garnered a sense of empowerment with her images, and yet, the sociocultural and historical notions of what men and women can and cannot do are deeply embedded in the experiences that readers bring with them to the text.

Significantly, women continue to challenge the model of being seen only as fashion symbols or ornaments, thus empowering themselves in a variety of ways. For example, when Serena Williams was asked why she wasn't laughing and smiling during a press conference, she reminded the press, with a very direct tone, that it was 11:30 p.m., and she really didn't want to be there because she would rather be in bed getting ready for her early morning practice the next day.[18] Her honesty resonates with adolescents and their perceptions of athleticism depicted in photographs when their energy is on what their body can do while viewers bring attention to how the body should look.[19]

An athlete's attention before a competition is on the contest and not on others' perceptions of them. Requested smiles and commentary on fashion don't resonate with the athletes competing. For example, Jen Kessy made it clear that they were comfortable wearing bikinis, and comfort should be a choice for all athletes, despite controversy surrounding beach volleyball attire.[20] Here, women are using empowering language to challenge the traditional model of defining women by their fashion. After all, their fellow male colleagues could only stare, laugh, and walk away when the media asked female athletes ridiculous questions instead of focusing on their successes,[21] reminding us all to #CoverTheAthlete, or pay attention to the athlete's achievements instead of the fashion.

In the words of Babe Didrikson Zaharias, "It's not enough just to swing at the ball. You've got to loosen your girdle and let 'er fly."[22]

Fashion cannot restrict performance, and neither can the sexist expectations of others. Historically, great female athletes have had to defend
their femininity and sexual identity to their fans and critics. They have
done this with their dress, their actions, and their words. Classroom
teachers and coaches see the ways that student athletes in their classrooms may be negotiating identity in terms of athleticism, femininity,
and image *if* they are attuned to see it.

RHETORIC USED TO DEFINE FEMALE ATHLETES AS SEXUAL OBJECTS

When reports of the 2012 "scouting report" published in a Google document by male soccer players at Harvard University hit mainstream media
in 2016, the Harvard athletic director initially chose to dismiss it as an
anomaly. Later it was revealed that this report, rating the sexual attrac-
tiveness of incoming freshman female recruits, assigning each a sexual
position and dubbing each with a nickname, had been a staple of the
men's team for some time.[23]

The apology that came after sanctions from the university, including
the loss of the season, was not enough to some. In the apology, male
athletes acknowledged that no women should be treated that way, as
they wouldn't want their mothers, sisters, or peers to be subjected to such
treatment. Expressed respect for women sounds nice, but more arguably
is needed. Phyllis Thompson, a lecturer in gender studies at Harvard,
suggests that "[a] commitment to equality requires shifting this mindset,
so that a man can imagine *himself* in the role of the target—that is, to
empathize with women not as potential sisters and daughters but as
potential selves."[24]

This sentiment is one way that classroom teachers and coaches can
frame discussions about women and their objectification. The language
used about female athletes should be the same whether one is speaking in
public or in the locker room. There is no place for private injurious talk. A
woman should *not* be only valued in relation to her brother, her father,
her son, or any other man, but also valued, treated, and referenced as the
male athlete traditionally has been, in all facets of life.

The study of women's responses to objectifying language is valuable
for all, from classrooms to courts, tracks, mats, pools, and fields, until this
equality of public and private language is realized. The rhetorical response of the Harvard women, published in the school paper, *The Harvard Crimson*, is powerful because of the arc of the language; it begins
with the team stating their feelings with bravery and honesty, then they
refuse to excuse the behavior, and finally they rise as the fighters that
their years of athletic training have empowered them to be.

The women begin by stating feelings of anger and sadness. They are clearly shocked, noting that they "feel hopeless." They are "appalled . . . [and] distraught."[25] The Harvard women give all athletes a model response to follow. They acknowledge the pain and refuse to mitigate the transgressions of their male counterparts. Using active voice, the women call the men "careless, disgusting, and appalling," their words an "aberrant display of misogyny."[26]

They say "locker room talk is not an excuse."[27] The letter ends with hope, sharing the sentiments of a team that has survived together. They are "stronger together." The Harvard women remind the team and the readers that they "are human beings and should be treated with dignity."[28] This last line is important, because objectification is insidious in its positioning of the victims as forgotten as people; the Harvard women empower all victims to see the larger implications of words that hurt.

RHETORIC USED TO DIVIDE AND LABEL FEMALE ATHLETES

The Harvard women made a point of concluding their response with words of unity, answering as a team, and explicitly stating their refusal to be divided against one another. However, this is not always the case in a world where the discourses of misogynistic systems pit the oppressed against each other. Language is used to divide and label groups without equal power. Like the Harvard women's team, language of unity emboldens and strengthens the collective argument against division.

Perhaps one of the most noticeable divisions stems from the "strong versus skinny" argument. Crystal remembers struggling with the idea that her athletic build was not like others. It was commonplace to find young men working to become stronger in the weight room; however, not many young female athletes could be found.

In college she and her teammates joked about their strong, thick legs, broad shoulders, or large(r) trapezius and forearm muscles, jokes she still makes with her adult athletic peers. Yet, she still catches herself thinking about athletic bodies and what that means for a female, worried that she'll look "too big." And she hears that constant concern expressed by today's younger female athletes as some worry, as she did, about getting bigger. These same young women joke with their fellow male peers, who are going to play Division I athletics, too, about their "trap game," or how large their trapezius muscles will get once they go off to school. They realize that a strong body is what will help them perform at a high level within their sport, but they're afraid of what that strong body will say to the rest of society in other areas of their multifaceted lives.

Sadly, these young women's concerns about their body shapes are not new. Katherine Switzer, famously assaulted by race official Jock Semple as she ran as the first registered female competitor in the Boston Marathon, describes how it felt to be a distance runner in the 1960s:

> When I was first running marathons, we were sailing on flat earth. We
> were afraid we'd get big legs, grow mustaches, not get boyfriends, not
> be able to have babies. Women thought that something would happen
> to them, that they'd break down or turn into men, something shadowy,
> when they were only limited by their own society's sense of limita-
> tions.[29]

Switzer's comments remind all, even today, that so often what is defined as feminine is what men want, including an either/or discourse on bodies and beauty,[30] and usually never includes the amazing things that a body can do. Instead, the shape of the body is critiqued.

Thus, it is important to acknowledge that this critique still pervades much of society, especially on social media.[31] For this reason, UFC bantamweight fighter Ronda Rousey has pushed readers to consider how #StrongIsBeautiful in her recent advertisement campaign with Pantene hair products.[32] In her advertisement, posted on Twitter, she states, "I'm not one without the other." Here, the directors juxtapose Rousey with loose hair and light flowing garments (physically) versus braided hair and dark sportswear (her physicality) showcasing her boxing prowess.

It has been said that society should not worry so much that adolescents do not listen to what adults say because youth are watching what adults do. Yet, although these messages of strength are important in and of themselves, money, fame, and respect are beginning to follow these females who are reminding those consuming the media that they are more than beautiful bodies.

As shown with #StrongIsBeautiful, social media are used to spread sentiments quickly and effectively in the form of memes.[33] These messages can be analyzed critically in classrooms and in locker rooms. When Maria Kang, fitness consultant and mother of three, posted a picture of her perfect abs with the question, "What's your excuse?" less-fit women responded.[34] Feeling body shamed for their genetics and life choices, they photographed themselves prioritizing what mattered to them, pointing out that women can choose how to spend their time without expecting others to do the same.[35]

Although this example focuses on a demographic older than adolescents, it speaks to the danger of a single story when it comes to women and the changing attitudes toward one ideal female body, and the focus on empowering all people for the ways the body can be used for healthy physical activity on one's own terms instead of for the gratification of others.

In classrooms today, educators have to be wary of the way girls are labeled—and the way they label themselves. Young female athletes may be described to each other as either tomboys or sporty girls, as skinny or strong.[36] Babe Didrikson Zaharias, when giving advice to others in 1934, suggested that they should "get toughened up by playing boys' games, but don't get tough."[37] And though this advice is memorable, how often are boys warned against getting tough? Indeed, these false dichotomies may be presented to female athletes at crucial stages in their identity growth, and are indicative of the ways that girls have had to define themselves while resisting others' labels.

RHETORIC USED TO JUSTIFY AND CHALLENGE INEQUITIES IN FEMALE SPORTS

Rhetorical analysis of the fight for equal pay and working conditions is perhaps the hot-button topic of modern times in regard to text analysis. Molly Fletcher's viral letter encompassed the heart of the message that athletes give to those who follow: keep going, even in the face of adversity.[38]

It seems that change is happening slowly, and better outcomes for each subsequent generation are being realized. Women have drawn attention to inequities in resources while demanding change for years. Title IX legislators such as Birch Bayh and activist athletes such as Billy Jean King, the 2016 women's U.S. soccer team, and Serena Williams have leveraged language to effect change and to challenge the status quo in regard to equality in sports with their reasoned arguments and strong evidence. In analysis of argument, students in today's classrooms can be taught to be perceptive about language used toward female athletes and the ways that, over time, women have used the power of language to change their circumstances, for themselves and for those who will come after them.

Congresswoman Edith Green, a former teacher, began the fight for equality for girls' education in the 1960s. In her argument, one echoed in the U.S. women's soccer team's request of 2016, she states "that if two individuals, a man and a woman . . . have equal credentials . . . they should be treated as equals."[39] As Karen Blumenthal documents, in 1971, boys participating in varsity sports in high schools outnumbered girls 3,666,917 to 294,015, and female athletes were clamoring to join boys' teams.

She highlights how Senator Bayh of Indiana suggested "little girls needed strong bodies to carry their minds around like little boys do." By 1973, girls in varsity sports had increased to 817,073, showing how influential those who argued for Title IX were to the athletes who would benefit from the law. Old attitudes persisted even as the passing of Title IX allowed for equality in funding for girls.

A study of the rhetoric of a few of the influential battles can show how hard advocates had to work to win over avowed misogynists. In the early

1970s Billy Jean King served as the voice for the formation of the Women's Tennis Association (WTA). She took on the establishment by valuing unity of women and, in 1973, by agreeing to play Bobby Riggs in a televised tennis match. Through such highly publicized acts she was instrumental in advocating for the sport as the men had done: together with other athletes. Reflecting on her advocacy, King said, "That's the way I want the world to look: men and women working together, championing each other, helping each other, promoting each other—we're all in this world together."[40] And reformed chauvinist Bobby Riggs advocated with King for equality until he died. Maya Angelou captured the essence of such transformative possibilities when she said, "I did then what I knew how to do. Now that I know better, I do better."[41]

Doing better by standing united is what the 2016 women's U.S. soccer team did as they filed a federal complaint against U.S. Soccer for equal pay. An analysis of their argument, summarized on CBS's *60 Minutes*, begins with their perceptions of being treated as less than, to an objective argument about the reality of their pay and working conditions in direct comparison to the men, and concludes with the threat of a strike if demands of absolute equality were not met in 2017.[42] One of the ways that they work to gain support for their cause is by noting the importance of making the sport better for the young girls who look up to them. Here, audience members can see hope for their own daughters.

Most recently, Serena Williams's open letter titled "To all incredible women who strive for excellence" reminded readers that they should always be judged by their actions and achievements. She writes, "As we know, women have to break down many barriers on the road to success. One of those barriers is the way we are constantly reminded we are not men, as if it is a flaw."[43] Like the Harvard women, many athletes are finding the strength to call out insidious but often overlooked sexism in language. In fact, Williams spoke out about being considered one of ESPN's greatest athletes ever. She said, "I think if I were a man, I would have been in that conversation a long time ago."[44] Ultimately, in pressrooms and classrooms, a first step is calling out sexism when it happens.

The more female athletes and their allies become more critically conscious of the weight of the rhetorical devices levied against women who are striving simply to hone their craft, the less these transgressions will occur. After all, the pervasive reminders of being the best "female athlete" and not just the best "athlete" is yet another way language is used to undermine female bodies and their athleticism.[45] Yet, Williams's ability to call out the inequity is one that she hopes, and we believe, will help pave the way for younger athletes "to dream big" in order to "empower the next generation of women to be just as bold in their pursuits."[46] For this reason, athletes, coaches, parents, and other allies of female athletes should strive to be inclusive with the language they use to discuss young athletes' achievements.

IMPLICATIONS FOR K–12 CLASSROOMS

The examples discussed in this chapter show how popular culture demands a certain literacy for identity work within athletics because it has the "power to shape beliefs and behaviors,"[47] on screen broadcasts, in print texts, and online.[48] Thus, rhetorically analyzing the ways in which female athletes are represented within society today is especially important when unpacking the sociocultural and historical layers that often influence the reading of texts.

Tying back to Gee's notion of *learning*, one must remember that one cannot look at "learning and language spaces separately as they both influence each other."[49] Digitally mediated spaces in particular often create meanings that our students need to unpack more thoroughly when it comes to female bodies. For example, as noted above, Serena Williams felt that if she were a man, her name would have been included in the discussion about best athletes years ago.

Yet, many people still point to the fact that others are stuck on her body, and flawed understandings at the intersections of gender and race could be keeping them from seeing her as one of the best.[50] Whether the texts are physical bodies or bodies represented by varied media, they "need to help students move past the obvious meanings and work on a deeper level with the texts in front of them."[51]

In the classroom, educators can rhetorically present these examples for student analysis through a different perspective to help all students garner a better understanding of the world around them. After all, "we have to navigate these mediated intersections with our students if we are to ensure that our pedagogical strategies and classrooms remain relevant for them."[52] Students surely will be able to supply their own examples of times when female athleticism was valued less than female appearance, or follow social media hashtags during professional sporting events to examine critical responses to media coverage or advertisements, acting as participants in activism if they so choose.

Educators should invite students to view these examples of female athletes through feminist, narrative, visual, or media-centered perspectives. For example, students begin to understand, through a feminist perspective, that it is not about men oppressing women, but instead how hegemony "is reinforced and reproduced *by both women and men*—[which] simultaneously empowers men and oppresses women."[53] One can see how language surrounding female athletes' bodies, performances, and successes is nuanced and supports the dominant, male point of view in many of the examples outlined here.

A narrative perspective also helps readers make sense of the world around them, but reminds readers that they "can't experience all of life first hand, so we learn from the stories told by others about how we *ought* to believe and behave."[54] These stories break down stereotypes and teach beyond the limited experience of one.

It is important for all stakeholders to ensure that all voices are valued and shared with inclusive language to foster a culture of allies of female athletes in schools. It must be acknowledged that the female athletic body should only be controlled by the athlete herself and not by corporations determined to make money on her body. Finally, a media-centered approach focuses on the rhetorical strategies often used to convey messages through different mediums to various audiences. Specifically, Sellnow notes that "media logic focuses on the degree to which viewers tend to take the medium and its social uses for granted and, thus, fail to realize how it influences us to believe and behave about what is *normal, good, desirable,* and so forth."[55]

This is where developing critical sports literacy is vital.[56] Today's students must understand that even at a young age they already are positioned in society, and their positioning influences how texts are introduced to them.

Although consuming media and images critically is reflected in all ELA state and national standards, this work also is important for coaches, parents, and other allies of female athletes. Gatorade's commercial "Keep Her in the Game" challenges gender norms and encourages the benefits of physical activity, team play, and the ways that language can be used to manipulate, label, or empower.[57] Avoiding labels and sweeping generalizations with careful word choice can avoid the danger of a single story and uphold moral obligations to understand how, through language, all can have "effects on people, sometimes harmful, sometimes beneficial, sometimes a bit of both, and sometimes neither."[58]

By avoiding and challenging labels, everyone can work to dispel myths of females without divergence or nuance, as only a single thing: the stereotype of a sporty girl or tomboy. Instead, educators work together in and outside their classrooms, creating a space where boys and girls see strength in what their bodies *can* do instead of serving as an ornament for the visual satisfaction of others.

NOTES

1. Elizabeth Daniels, "Sex Objects, Athletes, and Sexy Athletes: How Media Representations of Women Athletes Can Impact Adolescent Girls and College Women," *Journal of Adolescent Research* (2009): 399–422.

2. Chimamanda Adichie, "The Danger of a Single Story," video file, 2009, https://www.google.com/webhp?sourceid=chrome-instant&ion=1&espv=2&ie=UTF-8#q=chimamanda%20adichie%20the%20danger%20of%20a%20single%20story.

3. Alan Brown and Luke Rodesiler, *Developing Contemporary Literacies through Sports* (Urbana, IL: NCTE, 2016).

4. James Gee, *Social Linguistics and Literacies: Ideology in Discourses* (New York: Routledge, 2012), 3.

5. Ibid., 151.

6. Ibid., 167.

7. Michele Knobel and Colin Lankshear, "Remix: The Art and Craft of Endless Hybridization," *Journal of Adolescent & Adult Literacy* 52, no. 1 (2008): 22–33. doi:10.1598/JAAL.52.1.3. 22.

8. Sue Macy, *Wheels of Change: How Women Rode the Bicycle to Freedom (with a Few Flat Tires along the Way)* (Washington, DC: National Geographic, 2011).

9. Penny Hastings, *Sports for Her: A Reference Guide for Teenage Girls* (Westport, CT: Greenwood Publishing Group, 1999), 12.

10. Russell Freedman, *Babe Didrikson Zaharias: The Making of a Champion* (New York: Houghton Mifflin, 2014).

11. Susan E. Cayleff, *Babe: The Life and Legend of Babe Didrikson Zaharias* (Chicago: University of Illinois Press, 1995), 133.

12. ABC News, "Tennis Twirl: Eugenie Bouchard Asked to Spin," video file, January 23, 2015, https://youtu.be/bekZR7pNYug.

13. Jim Caple, "Why Twirlgate Is So Much More Interesting Than Deflategate," *ESPNW*, January 24, 2015, http://www.espn.com/espnw/news-commentary/article/12220097/why-twirlgate-much-more-interesting-deflategate.

14. J. A. Carter, Erynn Casanova, and David J. Maume, "Gendering Olympians: Olympic Media Guide Profiles of Men and Women Athletes," *Sociology of Sport Journal* 32, no. 3 (2015): 312–31. Also see Margaret C. Duncan, "Sports Photographs and Sexual Difference: Images of Women and Men in the 1984 and 1988 Olympic Games," *Sociology of Sport Journal* 7, no. 1 (1990).

15. "ATTN: Female Athletes Should Be Asked about Their Athletic Ability, Not Their Looks," video file, August 5, 2016, https://www.facebook.com/attn/videos/1104268306275294/.

16. The Representation Project, #AskHerMore at the Olympics, 2016, http://therepresentationproject.org/the-movement/askhermore/.

17. Blaire Braverman, "Lindsey Vonn's Body Politics," *Outside*, October 7, 2016, https://www.outsideonline.com/2123541/lindsey-vonns-body-politics.

18. Helena Horton, "A Journalist Asked Serena Williams Why She Wasn't Smiling, and She Gave Quite a Shocking Response," *Telegraph*, September 11, 2015, http://www.telegraph.co.uk/sport/tennis/usopen/11858581/A-journalist-asked-Serena-Williams-why-she-wasnt-smiling-and-she-gave-quite-a-shocking-response.html.

19. Vikki Krane, Sally Ross, Montana Miller, Kristy Ganoe, Cathryn Lucas-Carr, and Katie Barak, "'It's Cheesy When They Smile': What Girl Athletes Prefer in Images of Female College Athletes," *Research Quarterly for Exercise and Sport* 82, no. 4 (2011): 755–68. See also Elizabeth Daniels and Heidi Wartena, "Athlete or Sex Symbol: What Boys Think of Media Representations of Female Athletes," *Sex Roles* 65, nos. 7–8 (2011): 566–79.

20. Lawrence Bonk, "Here's Why the USA Women's Volleyball Team Refuses to Stop Wearing Bikinis," *Independent Journal Review*, August 2016, http://ijr.com/2016/08/670528-heres-why-the-usa-womens-volleyball-team-refuses-to-stop-wearing-bikinis/.

21. Rachel Moss, "What If Male Sports Starts Were Asked the Same Questions as Female Athletes?," *HuffPost Women*, April 11, 2015, http://www.huffingtonpost.co.uk/2015/11/04/cover-the-athlete-sexist-questions-women-in-sport_n_8470420.html.

22. See note 11 for reference, 164.

23. Phyllis Thompson, "The Dehumanizing Sexism of the Harvard Men's Soccer Team's 'Scouting Report,'" *New Yorker*, November 8, 2016, http://www.newyorker.com/culture/culture-desk/the-dehumanizing-sexism-of-the-harvard-mens-soccer-teams-scouting-report.

24. Ibid., paragraph 7.

25. Kelsey Clayman, Lauren Varela, Brooke Dickens, Alika Keene, Haley Washburn, and Emily Mosbacher, "Stronger Together," *Harvard Crimson*, October 29, 2016, para. 5, http://www.thecrimson.com/article/2016/10/29/oped-soccer-report/.

26. Ibid., paragraph 9.

27. Ibid., paragraph 10.

28. Ibid., paragraph 12.

29. Jane Gross, "Women's Old Images Fading Rapidly," in *A Kind of Grace: A Treasury of Sportswriting by Women*, edited Ron Rapoport (Berkeley, CA: Zenobia, 1994), 29.

30. Toni Bruce, "New Rules for New Times: Sportswomen and Media Representation in the Third Wave," *Sex Roles* 74, nos. 7–8 (2016): 361–76.

31. Emma Sherry, Angela Osborne, and Matthew Nicholson, "Images of Sports Women: A Review," *Sex Roles* 74, nos. 7–8 (2016): 299–309.

32. . Ronda Rousey, "Partnering w/ @Patene to Show How Beautiful Strong Women Can Be. Don't Hate Me BC I'm Strong," December 7, 2016, https://twitter.com/RondaRousey/status/806518733111889920/video/1.

33. Crystal L. Beach and Katie S. Dredger, "Living the YOLO Lifestyle: The Rhetorical Power of Memes in the Classroom," in *Deconstructing the Education-Industrial Complex in the Digital Age*, edited by D. J. Loveless, P. Sullivan, K. Dredger, and J. Burns (Hershey, PA: IGI Global, 2017).

34. Tracy Miller, "Mom of 3 Called a Bully for Posting 'What's Your Excuse?' Fitness Photo," *New York Daily News*, October 16, 2013, http://www.nydailynews.com/life-style/health/mom-3-called-bully-excuse-fitness-photo-article-1.1487278.

35. Dionne Ford, "We Don't Need an Excuse," *Huffington Post*, May 18, 2014, http://www.huffingtonpost.com/dionna-ford/we-dont-need-an-excuse_b_4937228.html.

36. Elizabeth A. Daniels, "Sexy versus Strong: What Girls and Women Think of Female Athletes," *Journal of Applied Developmental Psychology* 33, no. 2 (2012): 79–90.

37. See note 11 for reference, 132.

38. Molly Fletcher, "My Letter to Every Girl Who Plays Sports—and Her Parents," *Linkedin*, 2016, https://www.linkedin.com/pulse/my-letter-every-girl-who-plays-sportsand-her-parents-molly-fletcher?platform=hootsuite.

39. Karen Blumenthal, *Let Me Play: The Story of Title IX, the Law That Changed the Future of Girls in America* (New York: Atheneum, 2005), 43.

40. Paul Gittings, "Pioneer Billie Jean King Championed Equality in Women's Tennis," *CNN*, 2013, http://edition.cnn.com/2013/08/20/sport/tennis/tennis-billie-jean-king-wta-equality/.

41. Oprah Winfrey, "The Powerful Lesson Maya Angelou Taught Oprah," *Oprah's Lifeclass*, October 2011, http://www.oprah.com/oprahs-lifeclass/the-powerful-lesson-maya-angelou-taught-oprah-video#ixzz4UeaRsfM9.

42. CBS News, "Team USA Members on Historic Fight for Equal Pay in Women's Soccer," *60 Minutes*, 2016, http://www.cbsnews.com/news/60-minutes-women-soccer-team-usa-gender-discrimination-equal-pay/.

43. Serena Williams, "'We Must Continue to Dream Big': An Open Letter from Serena Williams," *Guardian*, November 29, 2016, https://www.theguardian.com/life-andstyle/2016/nov/29/dream-big-open-letter-serena-williams-porter-magazine-incredible-women-of-2016-issue-women-athletes.

44. The Undefeated, "Serena Williams Sits Down with Common to Talk about Race and Identity," December 19, 2016, http://theundefeated.com/features/serena-williams-sits-down-with-common-to-talk-about-race-and-identity/.

45. Emily R. Kaskan and Ivy K. Ho, "Microaggressions and Female Athletes," *Sex Roles* 74, nos. 7–8 (2016): 275–87.

46. See note 45 for reference.

47. Deanna D. Sellnow, *The Rhetorical Power of Popular Culture* (New York: Sage, 2010).

48. Donna E. Alvermann, "Why Bother Theorizing about Adolescents' Online Literacies for Classroom Practice and Research?," *Journal of Adolescent & Adult Literacy* 52, no. 1 (2008): 8–19. doi:10.1598/JAAL.52.1.2. See also Donna E. Alvermann, "Is There a Place for Popular Culture in Curriculum and Classroom Instruction?," The Point Position in *Curriculum and Instruction*, edited by A. J. Eakle (Thousand Oaks, CA: Sage, 2012), no. 2, 214–20, 227–28. doi:10.4135/9781452218465.n13.

49. See note 4 for reference, 3. Also see Crystal L. Beach, "Making Sense of Authors and Texts in a Remixed, Participatory Culture," in *Deconstructing the Education-Industrial Complex in the Digital Age*, edited by D. J. Loveless, P. Sullivan, K. Dredger, and J. Burns (Hershey, PA: IGI Global, 2017).

50. Zeba Blay, "When We Attack Serena Williams' Body, It's Really about Her Blackness," *Huffington Post*, July 13, 2015, serena-williams-policing-of-black-bodies_us_55a3bef4e4b0a47ac15ccc00.

51. Donna E. Alvermann, Crystal L. Beach, and George L. Boggs, "What Does Digital Media Allow Us to 'Do' to One Another?: Economic Significance of Content and Connection," in *Handbook of Research on the Societal Impact of Digital Media*, edited by B. Guzzetti and M. Lesley (Hershey, PA: IGI Global, 2016), 1–23.

52. Crystal L. Beach, "Media, Culture, and Education: One Teacher's Journey through the Mediated Intersections," *Journal of Media Literacy Education* 7, no. 2 (2015): 77–80.

53. See note 47 for reference, 89.

54. Ibid., 88.

55. Ibid., 162.

56. See note 3 for reference.

57. Gatorade, "Keep Her in the Game," video file, June 19, 2012, https://www.youtube.com/watch?v=URVYgTbbryE.

58. See note 2 for reference. Also see note 4 for reference, 3.

TEN

Between Being and Becoming

The Adolescent-Athlete in Young Adult Fiction

Mark A. Lewis and Luke Rodesiler

Athletes continually are examined and critiqued by the public, the media, and fans for their actions inside and outside the arena. Like athletes, adolescents are typically viewed as egotistical, adrenaline-driven, and immature (if not downright dumb). When considered together, these stereotypical characterizations work to create a monolithic "adolescent-athlete." Moreover, literature, movies, and television shows often work to manifest but also complicate how adolescents and athletes are perceived by the viewing public.[1] For example, in the young adult (YA) text *Inexcusable*,[2] the football-playing protagonist is portrayed as a monster on and off the field—he severely injures an opponent and sexually assaults his girlfriend, apparently without regret—which works to corroborate a view of the adolescent-athlete as violently out of control.[3] In other words, this story feeds into a caricature of the adolescent-athlete that unfortunately is accepted as truth by the larger public.

Such a portrayal is categorically unfair: adolescents and athletes are as complex and diverse as any other community member. Further, other YA literary texts include alternative portraits of the adolescent-athlete that deserve to be highlighted as well.

Therefore, this chapter presents an examination of the complex ways a set of YA texts represent the adolescent-athlete. This examination stands to expand how these common characters are understood; that is, complicating literary representations has the potential to broaden how adolescent-athletes in schools are viewed by teachers and teacher educators, coaches and administrators, as well as the larger community. Before illustrating several representations of and tensions felt by fictional adolescent-athletes within YA literature, two critical perspectives are established to help frame this study: critical youth studies and sports culture within literacy learning. Then, based on this framework, a "youth lens" is employed to analyze the selected set of texts.

DISRUPTING COMMONSENSICAL UNDERSTANDINGS OF ADOLESCENTS

First, this analysis draws on scholarship in critical youth studies that aim to trouble notions of being versus becoming. It is common for adults to worry over the lives of young people, especially those identified as adolescent, in terms of what they should become. This adult gaze functions to the point that the current lives of youth—including their actions, ideas, beliefs, desires, and interests—tend to be devalued.

As Kate Tilleczek explains, contemporary educational practices have set aside previous forms of individualized and narrative understandings of youth for standardized and statistical ways of discerning youth, which have led to a perspective of being "as a hollowed-out and simplified form of preparation for becoming. If young people are deemed to be incapable now of meeting standardized and statistical form of self, they are then also deemed to be incapable of becoming adults."[4] In other words, if a young person is viewed as not meeting a standard of what it means to be an adult—as determined by adults—then she is failing at being and will fail at becoming.

Not only does this perspective place an undue burden upon youth, it debilitates any decisions they can make in their current lives, because each decision might somehow derail their entire future existence.[5] Therefore, the adolescent who does not fit into a normed set of "confident characterizations," such as peer-oriented or rebellious,[6] is viewed as "delayed, aberrant, deviant, or simply queer."[7] Similarly, the athlete who does not demonstrate positive development of sport skills is relegated to the margins, or the "good" athlete who does not mature into a leadership, captaincy role can be viewed as selfish or failing a team-before-me mentality.[8]

A more critical understanding of youth, however, seeks to disrupt such incapacitating conceptions through a sociocultural constructionist lens. This lens contends that social, cultural, and political contexts influence how youth are viewed and fabricated[9] as much as biological and psychological developmentalist paradigms. A sociocultural perspective insists that notions of "adolescence" highly depend on external factors surrounding youth that are draped on young people as they work, live, and play. For example, an African American urban adolescent most likely experiences a much different reality during her teen years than a white suburban adolescent does during his teen years.

This view does not mean to imply that internal factors related to biological and cognitive changes do not matter, as important changes certainly occur between the ages of twelve and eighteen; rather, it complicates the idea that such changes have the same effect for *all* youth. Indeed, it would be wise to be careful about using generalized characterizations to describe all members of an entire age group, similar to how we should be careful about essentializing members of any social or cultural group.[10] This critical perspective of youth is a more productive way to discern the lives of adolescent-athletes.

CONCEPTUALIZING THE PLACE OF SPORTS CULTURE IN LITERACY LEARNING

Second, this analysis relies on an understanding that sports culture plays a central role in the lives of many adolescents. With nearly eight million boys and girls participating in high school sports[11] and countless more engrossed as members of sports fandom, the prevalence of sports culture in the lives of today's youth cannot be overstated. Research and scholarship suggest that immersion in sports culture stands to foster a range of literacy practices among adolescents.[12] Therefore, rather than dismiss students' interests in and passion for sports as extraneous to literacy learning and of little relevance in the English language arts classroom, scholars advocate for teachers tapping students' funds of knowledge,[13] the cultural knowledge and experiences students have constructed and accumulated beyond the classroom walls, to maximize student learning.

By taking into account students' knowledge of popular cultures, including sports culture, teachers can provide students with resources and frames of reference that support literacy learning.[14] In fact, scholars argue that failing to account for students' cultural knowledge stands to undermine a teacher's efforts because it devalues students and the knowledge they bring to the classroom.[15] When approaching sports and other popular cultures from a "cultural capital model"[16] — that is, when recognizing the connections between popular cultures and students' lived experiences — teachers position themselves to honor the wealth of knowledge and experiences students have cultivated over time through extended engagement with their passions and personal interests.

When immersed in sports culture, adolescents may find themselves carrying out literacy practices not unlike those teachers seek to foster in the English language arts classroom. For example, Jabari Mahiri reports that adolescent boys participating in a youth basketball program engaged in a host of literacy events as they analyzed, synthesized, and evaluated various texts outside the traditional school setting.[17] Informed by their readings of sports-based newspaper articles and diagrams, video game instruction manuals, magazines, and trading cards, participants launched discussions and debates around a topic that held significant cultural value: basketball.

Similarly, Ernest Morrell describes student-athletes employing literacy practices as they read sports pages, media guides, and how-to books; as they wrote goal sheets, notes based on game tapes, and arguments based on insider knowledge about sports; and as they deconstructed stereotypes of athletes as ignorant, volatile, and unmotivated to succeed in academic pursuits.[18]

In light of this and related research documenting the potential for advancing literacy learning through students' participation in and passion for sports culture, scholars have presented methods for engaging students in the study of various types of sports-based texts, including memoirs,[19] short and feature-length documentary films,[20] graphic novels,[21] and satires.[22]

Further, scholars have encouraged teachers and students to consider, from a critical perspective, representations of figures, events, and norms associated with sports culture.[23] Reading any text critically entails examining issues of power, identity, and difference and weighing how actors are positioned by social constructions of the word and the world.[24] Accordingly, when applying a critical lens to the sports world, students can, for example, disrupt normalized beliefs about athletes,[25] question common perceptions of what counts as sport,[26] and reconsider narrow representations of women in sports culture.[27]

This chapter continues building on such scholarship by inviting teachers and other educational leaders who guide curricular decision making to consider how sports-related YA literature might be used to discuss alternative understandings for what it means to "grow up" in and out of the athletic arena.

ANALYZING REPRESENTATIONS OF THE ADOLESCENT-ATHLETE WITHIN YOUNG ADULT LITERATURE

With these two overarching perspectives in mind, the selected texts are analyzed through a "youth lens,"[28] which relies on a sociocultural constructionist view of adolescence. Any analysis through this lens begins with two questions: How do texts represent adolescence and youth? And how might these representations reify and/or disrupt stereotypical views of adolescence and youth? These foundational questions have been augmented to inform the current analysis:

- How does sports-related YA literature represent the adolescent-athlete?

- Within this literary subgenre, what tensions between being and becoming must adolescent-athletes navigate inside and outside the sports arena?

The focal texts include stories with female and male protagonists, extended sports-action scenes, and a history of positive reviews as quality YA literature. The selections also include sports beyond the most popular, such as football and baseball. They feature award-winning authors and stories, and they also represent varied settings across the United States. Although not exhaustive of the genre, these particular stories provide emblematic cases of how sports and youth are often written about within the subgenre.

These analyses demonstrate how these authors, and the characters living in their stories, disrupt common and stereotypical perspectives of the adolescent-athlete. Most important, these analyses and critiques provide opportunities for teachers, coaches, and other educational leaders to learn and expand their perspectives on the role of athletics in education. However, any critiques included in this discussion should not be understood as an overall negative view of these particular authors and texts, as they are often used in teacher education courses to demonstrate the usefulness of including sports-related YA literature in a secondary English language arts curriculum.

From Cheerleaders to Hoopsters: Sports-Related Young Adult Literature

The first of the five texts is from Sherman Alexie, *The Absolutely True Diary of a Part-Time Indian*,[29] which was honored with a National Book Award. Alexie tells the story of an American Indian high school basketball player, Junior, who lives on the Spokane Indian Reservation and has high academic aspirations. However, upon entering the reservation high school, he realizes that educational opportunity is limited by the impoverished resources available to him. Therefore, he decides to transfer to the predominantly white high school off the reservation, where he joins the basketball team and must face his old friends on the court.

Second, this study focuses on the short story "Montana Wild,"[30] from Chris Crutcher's collection *Angry Management*. Crutcher is an esteemed, award-winning author who received an ALAN Award for Significant Contribution to Adolescent Literature, and this story represents his authorial skill. In the story, Montana, an ex-cheerleader, takes on a West Texas school board over her first amendment rights because they blocked her attempt to publish an article about medical marijuana in the school newspaper. To make matters more stressful, her father is the school board chairman. On her side are the newspaper teacher-mentor, her classmates, and the grandmother of her new boyfriend.

The third text is *Ball Don't Lie* by Matt de la Peña,[31] who recently was honored by the National Council of Teachers of English with the Intellectual Freedom Award. *Ball Don't Lie* is a "street ball" story focusing on Sticky, who grew up in the foster care system in Los Angeles, endures an obsessive-compulsive disorder, and loves to play basketball. He spends most of his free time playing at Lincoln Rec Center, where he is the only white guy in the gym, and his fellow players give him advice (both verbal and physical) about how to play ball and how to navigate life off the court. Sticky's mother had substance abuse issues and died when he was very young. He bounces between possible foster homes and child services, mainly because he rebels against the foster families and the system.

Also included is *Smashed* by Lisa Luedeke,[32] a story about Katie, captain of her high school field hockey team in a small town in Maine. She has a serious drug and alcohol addiction, exacerbated by her family situation. Katie's father abandoned the family when she was young, leaving her mother to support her and her brother. Her mother provides this support by working as a nurse, but her job is in another city, and she chooses to spend many nights with her boyfriend, basically leaving Katie to raise her brother on her own. Her addictive behaviors spiral during her senior year as she sporadically dates a popular football player, which leads to a series of poor decisions and horrifying consequences. Yet, her play on the field has led to a possible college scholarship and her team vying for a state championship.

The final selection is *The Running Dream* by Wendelin Van Draanen,[33] which received the Schneider Family Book Award by the American Library Association for children's or adolescent literature that presents positive representations of disability experiences. The protagonist, Jessica, primarily identifies as a runner and is an all-star on her high school track team. Tragically, after a track meet, her school bus is hit by a truck, and her leg is so badly damaged that it must be amputated. Forced to think about her life with a prosthesis, she finds solace in a friend, Rosa, enduring cerebral palsy, which leads to a new focus in her running life.

ADOLESCENCE AND ATHLETICISM IN YOUNG ADULT LITERATURE

Drawing from these texts, the two research questions on the representations of the adolescent-athlete and the tensions the characters face between being and becoming are addressed first. Then, the chapter closes with implications these analyses hold for various constituents.

Representations of the Adolescent-Athlete

In light of the first research question, two representations of adolescent-athletes emerged consistently from the analyses of the five selected texts. Both representations stand in contrast to popular views of adolescents and athletes. First, adolescent-athletes were routinely depicted as caring for others to such a degree that they disregarded their own well-being. Second, adolescent-athletes were often represented as having artistic and intellectual talents that matched or exceeded their athletic abilities, suggesting that figures had more than just their athletic prowess. This subsection explores each representation and, as appropriate, addresses a non-example from the chosen texts to further illuminate the findings.

The Adolescent-Athlete as an Altruistic Figure

Adolescents often are characterized as being considerably more concerned with their own self-interests than the well-being of others.[34] However, this analysis revealed representations that depict adolescents as altruistic figures, as individuals so concerned about the well-being of others that they are willing to forsake their own security, wellness, and success.

Though much of Chris Crutcher's "Montana Wild" revolves around Montana West's clash with her father, the schoolboard chairman, over the censoring of an article she wrote about medical marijuana, that conflict is not what drives Montana from her home. Depicted throughout the story as caring for Tara, a foster child living with the Wests, Montana is devastated to learn that her father directed a social worker to remove Tara from their home. Caring deeply for Tara, in part because she knows firsthand the challenges of living in foster care, Montana attempts to stop the removal with threats of her own departure: "If she goes, I go!"[35] And when Tara does go, Montana is true to her word; she packs her bags and moves out of the West home.

But even when living separately, Montana goes to great lengths to care for Tara. For example, she visits a social worker to ensure Tara's well-being and provides advice for the new foster parents. Montana's dedication to Tara extends to making room for her on visits to the home of Trey and his grandmother, where Montana now resides, and babysitting for Tara's new foster parents. Between caring for Tara and championing medical marijuana for cancer victims such as Trey's grandmother, Montana's altruism disrupts narrow depictions of the self-absorbed adolescent-athlete.

In *The Running Dream*, after losing her lower right leg and befriending Rosa, a peer with cerebral palsy, track star Jessica Carlisle recognizes the importance of seeing others for who they are instead of foregrounding their conditions or circumstances. To help others see Rosa too, Jessica sets out to complete the River Run, a ten-mile race, while pushing Rosa in a specially designed wheelchair: "'[T]his is not about me. I'm doing this for Rosa. . . . Her biggest wish isn't to cross a finish line or have people cheer for her. It's to have people see *her* instead of her condition."[36] A grueling race on its own, the River Run is made that much more difficult with the added challenge of pushing Rosa's wheelchair. With arms aching, hips knotting up, legs growing heavy, and a prosthesis irritating her amputated leg, Jessica endures and pushes her friend across her first finish line. Jessica's refusal to give in to her body's own pleas for self-preservation reflects a selflessness not commonly associated with adolescence/ts.

Another adolescent-athlete prone to selflessness is featured in *The Absolutely True Diary of a Part-Time Indian*. Junior Spirit is a freshman on the varsity basketball team at Reardon High School who constantly questions whether his decision to leave the reservation was a selfish act. This struggle is exemplified on the court when playing his former teammates.[37] Though Junior and his teammates took their lumps the first time they competed against Wellpinit High School and his friends from the reservation, Reardon upended Wellpinit in the rematch, a forty-point blowout. Rather than revel in the celebration of his team's victory, Junior found himself overcome with concern for his friends and feeling shame for leaving them behind. Junior explained his feelings as he looked down from atop the shoulders of his jovial teammates:

> I knew that two or three of those Indians might not have eaten breakfast that morning.
>
> No food in the house.
>
> I knew that seven or eight of those Indians lived with drunken mothers and fathers.
>
> I knew that one of those Indians had a father who dealt crack and meth.
>
> I knew two of those Indians had fathers in prison.
>
> I knew that none of them were going to college. Not one of them.
>
> And I knew that Rowdy's father was probably going to beat the crap out of him for losing this game.[38]

Junior's capacity to show empathy for his friends from the reservation during his team's season-defining moment undermines traditional views that paint adolescents *and* athletes as, above all else, self-serving individuals who have yet to develop the means of looking beyond themselves and showing concern for others.

The Adolescent-Athlete as a Multidimensional Talent

The dumb-jock stereotype has roots dating back as far as the days of Socrates.[39] It suggests that athletes lack intellectual abilities and interests and are defined solely by their physical feats and capabilities. The dumb-jock stereotype has persisted over time as reports of academic misconduct within collegiate athletic programs have reinforced the generality, and caricatures have recurred in popular culture, including YA literature.

Smashed's Katie Martin, for example, reflects the stereotype. In Luedeke's novel, Katie has two primary interests: playing field hockey and partying with her teammates. Even her job teaching swimming classes speaks to her interest in athletics. Whereas Katie's friends have artistic and intellectual interests (i.e., Matt has a passion for photography, and Cassie is headed to Brown University), Katie's interests do not move far beyond playing and partying. It is little wonder, then, that Matt and Cassie are there to pick up Katie when she falters and not the other way around.

Though Katie and many of the minor characters in the novel stand as negative cases, adolescent-athletes in the other selected YA texts examined are consistently depicted as multidimensional talents. In *The Absolutely True Diary of a Part-Time Indian*, Junior's athletic abilities are on full display in chapters detailing his basketball games, yet Junior's talents as an artist are featured even more prominently in his drawings scattered throughout the book. From Junior's self-portrait in the opening pages to a sketch of him and his best friend Rowdy holding hands while jumping into Turtle Lake, Junior's artwork provides readers with a steady source of levity, insights into his worldview, and a look at the multiple talents he possesses.

Readers learn about Junior's artistic abilities well before they discover his prowess shooting hoops. The book's first visual is accompanied by Junior describing how often he draws—"all the time"[40]—what he draws—"cartoons of my mother and father; my sister and grandmother; my best friend, Rowdy; and everybody else on the rez"[41]—and the reasons he draws—"I think the world is a series of broken dams and floods, and my cartoons are tiny little lifeboats."[42] Such reasoning underscores the value of Junior's artistic talents, for it is in his abilities as a cartoonist that he finds salvation, not in his skills as an athlete.

The Running Dream's Jessica is another adolescent-athlete represented as a multidimensional talent. Rather than depicting Jessica as a flat caricature of the dumb jock, Van Draanen presents Jessica as a true student-athlete. The accolades Jessica earned before her accident and the subsequent amputation of her lower right leg are well documented in the book. But her persistence studying mathematics and ultimately succeeding in the classroom also are featured prominently. Despite struggling to manage her coursework upon returning to school, as any student might, Jessica persists and enlists Rosa, whom she describes as "a math genius,"[43] to support her cause. Following tutoring sessions in Room 402 and review sessions at Rosa's house, Rosa congratulates Jessica for earning her first "A" on a test in Ms. Rucker's math class. Lest readers discount the weight of Jessica's high mark, it is noted that classmate Eric Hollander earned a "D" on the same test. With Jessica reaping both athletic and academic rewards, her narrative runs counter to those that narrowly define adolescent-athletes by their athletic abilities alone.

Montana's talents away from the sports arena are foregrounded in Crutcher's story, making her another adolescent-athlete whose depiction defies the dumb-jock stereotype. Described as having "the lean, muscular body of a dancer,"[44] Montana is a cheerleader-turned-writer, a prolific contributor to the school newspaper. Through Montana's discussion with Dr. Conroy, her journalism teacher, readers learn that Montana uses writing to shine a light on various social issues: hunting, subjecting animals to scientific experiments, gay marriage, and medical marijuana. Though Montana's articles are consistently shut down by forces that oppose her liberal contributions (i.e., conservative school-board members, including her father), her writing is described by Dr. Conroy as "A work."[45]

Moreover, by the end of "Montana Wild," readers learn that such success in the classroom has helped Montana secure a full academic scholarship. Juxtaposed with *Smashed*'s Katie Martin, Montana West shows that college scholarships are not just awarded for one's talents on the field; they can be earned in the classroom, too.

The stereotype of athletes as less than interested in intellectual pursuits or endeavors beyond the realm of the athletic arena endures. Still, characters from YA literature such as Junior, Jessica, and Montana serve as models of adolescent-athletes who are more than simply athletes; they are multidimensional talents whose stories disrupt the dumb-jock stereotype.

Being and Becoming

Analysis revealed two primary tensions between being and becoming that manifest across these five texts. First, adults tend to worry more about expectations and potential than the current lives of youth. This worry stems from an adult gaze and evaluation of the decisions made by adolescent-athletes. Second, the adolescent-athlete is afforded the opportunity to simply *be in the moment* when playing a sport and can forget about any pressures of *becoming*. This second tension most often reveals itself during extended scenes in which the protagonist is on the court or field.

Adult Gaze and Worry over Becoming

Junior in *The Absolutely True Diary of a Part-Time Indian* expresses a central aspect of living as an adolescent and as an athlete—that others' expectations drive behavior outcomes. As an adolescent, he constantly resides within a tension of living in the moment and moving across school and society spaces toward a future self.[46] This tension is highlighted by his math teacher in the reservation school who demands that Junior leave the reservation because of the teacher's worry that he will not be able to meet his potential if he remains there. As an athlete, Junior also is emerging as a "good" player, particularly in his understanding of how a coach and team affect his performative role:

> I suppose it had something to do with confidence. I mean, I'd always been the lowest Indian on the reservation totem pole—I wasn't expected to be good so I wasn't. But in Reardan, my coach and the other players wanted me to be good. They needed me to be good. They expected me to be good. And so I became good. I wanted to live up to expectations. I guess that's what it comes down to. The power of expectations.[47]

In addition, this adult worry over expectations arises in a scene with a reporter before the basketball rematch with his reservation school, and it reveals different perspectives of adults and youth. The adult reporter calls the game a "major deal in [Junior's] life"[48] because of the repercussions of the outcome for the league and for his relationship with his former teammates. Junior also responds by admitting that the situation has made him feel like he has had to "grow up really fast, too fast, and that I've come to realize that every single moment of [my] life is important. And that every choice I make is important."[49] In other words, he did not need an adult reporter to tell him that the game is a "major deal" because he already knows. He already knows that he can never "quit playing hard,"[50] both on the court and in life.

In *Smashed*, the youth with a "strong" and "stable" adult presence and surveillance make better decisions (from the adult gaze) on and off the field. Cassie and Matt, Katie's closest friends, do not get into trouble, and Matt does not drink. Cassie gets a college scholarship, which is a stark contrast to Katie's loss of her scholarship due to her fall into deep addiction. Also, Cassie and Matt try to protect Katie, presumably because their parents have tried to protect them.

On the other hand, the youth in the novel without a strong adult presence (i.e., Katie's abusive boyfriend, Alec, and her field hockey teammates, Marcy, Megan, and Cheryl) attempt to peer pressure Katie into substance abuse. Marcy is a hothead on the field, often getting penalized for misconduct, including earning a five-minute suspension during a regular season match and directing a racial slur at an opponent during the state championship. Of course, Katie greatly illustrates this tension due to the literal and figurative abandonment of her father and mother, respectively. The implication of this tension is that youth without adult surveillance will end up hurting themselves.

Finally, in "Montana Wild," the entire fight over freedom of speech between Maxwell West (and the school board) and Montana (and her journalistic mentors) exemplifies the clear presumption that adults know what is best for youth. The "rights" discussion reveals an ageism stance by Maxwell and the school board because they believe that youth are not "ready to take *responsibility* for what they express [in the school newspaper]."[51] However, some adults support Montana, mainly because they trust her to make choices that will benefit her future, a stance vindicated when she founds a newspaper, the *Bear Creek Barb*, and publishes within it the very article supporting medical marijuana that sparked the original censorship fight with the school board.

Being in the Arena

The tension between being and becoming was in stark contrast for the adolescent-athlete when he took the court or the field. For example, Sticky in *Ball Don't Lie* believes that forgetting about any issues of becoming is imperative to his on-court success: "The more a player thinks about the game—what setting they're in, who they're running against, what folk *will say* depending on whether or not they hook up a decent showing—the more messed up that player is gonna play. *It's unnatural.*"[52] In an attempt to explain his athletic prowess, he describes having a mind-set focused on living in the moment—a pejorative descriptor of adolescents who, adults often assume, are not worrying sufficiently about the future.

Elite athletes often discuss how time "slows down" when they are playing, which happens to Sticky repeatedly when he is playing basketball, such as when he lists all of the different options of beating an opponent one-on-one while playing at Lincoln Rec. Jessica, in *The Running Dream*, also eventually understands that her present condition (losing her leg) does not necessarily ruin her future, which she believed immediately after the accident. Rather, she must "hold the baton" and win her "leg" of the race.[53] In other words, if one constantly worries about the future (and past), then she will lose the present, which means she will lose the "race" of life anyway.

Yet, these adolescent-athletes realize that they must find a balance between being and becoming. As Rosa reminds Jessica, she shouldn't "look so far ahead"[54] when worrying over getting her prosthetic running leg. However, her parents must worry about the future because of the overwhelming medical bills they are facing due to the school's insurance company delaying financial reimbursement, which Jessica just assumed would "go away." Junior, while playing basketball with his old friend from the reservation, also realizes that it is important to think and talk about the future, but it is also perfectly acceptable to live in the moment of the arena:

> I hoped and prayed that they would someday forgive me for leaving them.
>
> I hoped and prayed that I would someday forgive myself for leaving them.
>
> "Ah, man," Rowdy said. "Stop crying."
>
> "Will we still know each other when we're old men?" I asked.
>
> "Who knows anything?" Rowdy asked.
>
> Then he threw me the ball.
>
> "Now quit your blubbering," he said. "And play ball."[55]

IMPLICATIONS AND CONCLUSION

Though adolescents often are assumed to be more selfish than selfless and more single-minded than multitalented, adolescent-athletes examined in these five texts were often depicted in ways that run counter to such stereotypes. This analysis found that these texts provide richer and perhaps more accurate depictions of adolescent-athletes than the stereotypical representations adults working with youth might have in mind.

By considering depictions of adolescent-athletes in sports-related YA literature, teachers, coaches, and school administrators stand to shift from narrowly conceptualizing what it means to be an adolescent-athlete to embracing a broader, more nuanced view of adolescent-athletes and the role of athletics in the lives of youth. For example, the protagonists from these five texts—through their altruism, thoughtfulness, and diverse talents—clearly demonstrate how the representation of the "dumb jock" stereotype is overplayed in fiction.

In addition, teacher education settings are primed for inviting prospective and practicing teachers to broaden their understandings of the youth they serve. In such settings, discussions around sports-based YA literature can challenge narrow perspectives on the role of athletics in schools, illuminating the potential for sports to enrich the lives of youth, such as how Sticky used basketball as a form of therapy for his personal pain. Many teacher candidates may end up coaching, and sports-related YA literature can complicate their understandings about the roles available to and relationships between coaches and young athletes. Therefore, teacher educators should be encouraged to consider how they might weave into their curriculum the study of texts such as those featured in this chapter.

For teachers serving in secondary classrooms, studying fictional adolescent-athletes such as Jessica, Junior, and Montana can help students question how they, their peers, and other adolescent literary characters are typically positioned. Alongside fictional depictions, teachers can present stories about real-life adolescent-athletes who defy stereotypes, such as Hunter Gandee, the 2015 Sports Illustrated High School Athlete of the Year.[56]

In a story not unlike Jessica and Rosa's, Gandee has carried his sibling Braden, who has cerebral palsy, while walking upward of one hundred miles to inspire acceptance of those with disabilities.[57] As supplements or as stand-alone texts, stories such as Gandee's can help students reconsider narrow depictions of adolescence/ts. Therefore, this implication argues that including examinations of civic-minded adolescent-athletes would add dynamism to any secondary curriculum aimed at demonstrating to youth that they can be change agents working toward a more socially just community.

Most important, this examination of sports-related YA literature reminds adults that placing too much emphasis on what adolescent-athletes might become (i.e., their potential—as athletes, as human beings) detracts from all that they are in the present day. Whether in the arena or out, as educators, as administrators, or as coaches, we can learn from fictional adolescent-athletes such as Sticky, Jessica, and Junior, who have come to recognize that sometimes just *being* is more than good enough; it can be advantageous to one's success.

NOTES

1. See Mark A. Lewis, "Illustrating Youth: A Critical Examination of the Artful Depictions of Adolescent Characters in Comics," in *Teaching Comics through Multiple Lenses: Critical Perspectives*, edited by Crag Hill (New York: Routledge, 2016), 49–61. See also Mark A. Lewis and Ian Renga, "(Re)Imagining Life in the Classroom: Inciting Dialogue through an Examination of Teacher-Student Relationships in Film," in *Exploring Teachers in Fiction and Film: Saviors, Scapegoats, and Schoolmarms*, edited by Melanie Shoffner (New York: Routledge, 2016), 65–75.

2. Chris Lynch, *Inexcusable* (New York: Altheneum Books, 2005).

3. See Mark A. Lewis and E. Sybil Durand, "Sexuality as Risk and Resistance in Young Adult Literature," in *The Critical Merits of Young Adult Literature: Coming of Age*, edited by Crag Hill (New York: Routledge, 2014), 38–54.

4. Kate Tilleczek, "Theorizing Young Lives: Biography, Society, and Time," in *Critical Youth Studies Reader*, edited by Awad Ibrahim and Shirley R. Steinberg (New York: Peter Lang, 2014), 20.

5. See Susan Talburt and Nancy Lesko, "A History of the Present of Youth Studies," in *Keywords in Youth Studies: Tracing Affects, Movements, Knowledges*, edited by Nancy Lesko and Susan Talburt (New York: Routledge, 2012), 11–23.

6. Nancy Lesko, *Act Your Age!: A Cultural Construction of Adolescence*, second edition (New York: Routledge, 2012), 2–3.

7. Michael O'Loughlin and P. Taylor Van Zile IV, "Becoming Revolutionaries: Toward Non-teleological and Non-normative Notions of Youth Growth," in *Critical Youth Studies Reader*, edited by Awad Ibrahim and Shirley R. Steinberg (New York: Peter Lang, 2014), 48.

8. See Tracy D. Keats, "We Don't Need Another Hero: Captaining in Youth Sport," in *Critical Youth Studies Reader*, edited by Awad Ibrahim and Shirley R. Steinberg (New York: Peter Lang, 2014).

9. See Thomas S. Popkewitz, "Research and Regulation of Knowledge," in *Keywords in Youth Studies: Tracing Affects, Movements, Knowledges*, edited by Nancy Lesko and Susan Talburt (New York: Routledge, 2012), 59–71.

10. See Kris Gutiérrez and Barbara Rogoff, "Cultural Ways of Learning: Individual Traits or Repertoires of Practice," *Educational Researcher* 32, no. 5 (2003): 19–25.

11. National Federation of State High School Associations, "High School Sports Participation Increases for 28th Straight Year, Nears 8 Million Mark," September 6, 2017, http://www.nfhs.org/articles/high-school-sports-participation-increases-for-28th-straight-year-nears-8-million-mark.

12. See Jabari Mahiri, *Shooting for Excellence: African American and Youth Culture in New Century Schools* (Urbana, IL: NCTE, 1998). See also Ernest Morrell, *Linking Literacy Learning and Popular Culture: Finding Connections for Lifelong Learning* (Norwood, MA: Christopher-Gordon, 2004).

13. See Luis C. Moll, Cathy Amanti, Deborah Neff, and Norma González, "Funds of Knowledge for Teaching: Using a Qualitative Approach to Connect Homes and Classrooms," *Theory into Practice* 31, no. 2 (1992): 132–41.

14. See Anne Haas Dyson, *The Brothers and Sisters Learn to Write: Popular Literacies in Childhood and School Cultures* (New York: Teachers College Press, 2003).

15. Henry A. Giroux and Roger I. Simon, *Popular Culture: Schooling and Everyday Life* (Granby, MA: Bergin & Garvey, 1989), 3.

16. Margaret C. Hagood, Donna E. Alvermann, and Alison Heron-Hruby, *Bring It to Class: Unpacking Popular Culture in Literacy Learning* (New York: Teachers College Press, 2010), 29.

17. See first reference in note 12.

18. See second reference in note 12.

19. See Ryan Skardal, "Power, Authorship, and Identity in Texts by and about High-Profile Athletes," in *Developing Contemporary Literacies through Sports: A Guide for the English Classroom*, edited by Alan Brown and Luke Rodesiler (Urbana, IL: NCTE, 2016), 55–59.

20. See Luke Rodesiler, "Teaching with and about Sports-Based Documentary Films to Address Core Standards," *English Journal* 104, no. 1 (2014): 31–36. See also Luke Rodesiler, "Quick Plays: Studying Short Sports-Based Documentaries," *Screen Education* 79 (2015): 26–31.

21. See David M. Pegram, "Baseball and Graphic Novels: An Effective Approach to Teaching Literature," in *Developing Contemporary Literacies through Sports: A Guide for the English Classroom*, edited by Alan Brown and Luke Rodesiler (Urbana, IL: NCTE, 2016), 37–42.

22. See Luke Rodesiler, "Satiric Remixes: Crafting Commentaries about Sport and Society," in *Developing Contemporary Literacies through Sports: A Guide for the English Classroom*, edited by Alan Brown and Luke Rodesiler (Urbana, IL: NCTE, 2016), 152–58.

23. See Alan Brown and Luke Rodesiler, *Developing Contemporary Literacies through Sports: A Guide for the English Classroom* (Urbana, IL: NCTE, 2016).

24. See Hillary Janks, "Critical Literacy in Teaching and Research," *Education Inquiry* 4, no. 2 (2013): 225–42.

25. See Danielle M. King, "Disability and Athletics: (Re)defining 'Typical,'" in *Developing Contemporary Literacies through Sports: A Guide for the English Classroom*, edited by Alan Brown and Luke Rodesiler (Urbana, IL: NCTE, 2016), 173–79.

26. See Robert Petrone, "Is Skateboarding a Sport? Inquiring into Non-School Sports," in *Developing Contemporary Literacies through Sports: A Guide for the English Classroom*, edited by Alan Brown and Luke Rodesiler (Urbana, IL: NCTE, 2016), 506–33.

27. See note 19 for reference.

28. See Robert Petrone, Sophia Tatiana Sarigianides, and Mark A. Lewis, "The Youth Lens: Analyzing Adolescence/ts in Literary Texts," *Journal of Literacy Research* 46, no. 4 (2014): 506–33.

29. Sherman Alexie, *The Absolutely True Diary of a Part-Time Indian* (New York: Little, Brown, 2007).

30. Chris Crutcher, "Montana Wild" in *Angry Management* (New York: Greenwillow Books, 2009).

31. Matt de la Peña, *Ball Don't Lie* (New York: Delacorte Press, 2005).

32. Lisa Luedeke, *Smashed* (New York: Margaret K. McElderry Books, 2012).

33. Wendelin Van Draanen, *The Running Dream* (New York: Ember, 2011).

34. For example, see Jean M. Twenge, *Generation Me: Why Today's Young Americans Are More Confident, Assertive, Entitled—and More Miserable Than Ever Before* (New York: Atria, 2006).

35. See note 30 for reference, 121.

36. See note 33, 306–7. Emphasis in original.

37. See Sophia Tatiana Sarigianides, Robert Petrone, and Mark A. Lewis, *Re-thinking the "Adolescent" in Adolescent Literacy* (Urbana: NCTE, 2017) for an extended discussion on how race intersects with adolescence in this scene.

38. See note 29 for reference, 195–96.

39. Gregory M. C. Semenza, *Sport, Politics, and Literature in the English Renaissance* (Newark: University of Delaware Press, 2003), 34.

40. See note 29 for reference, 5.

41. Ibid.

42. Ibid., 6.

43. See note 33 for reference, 176.

44. See note 30 for reference, 89.

45. Ibid., 86.

46. See note 4 for reference.

47. See note 29 for reference, 180.

48. Ibid., 183.

49. Ibid., 184.

50. Ibid., 186.

51. See note 30 for reference, 141. Emphasis in original.

52. See note 31 for reference, 92. Emphasis added.

53. See note 33 for reference, 78.

54. Ibid., 203.

55. See note 29 for reference, 230.

56. Ali Fenwick, "High School Athlete of the Year: Hunter Gandee," *Sports Illustrated*, December 14, 2015, films.si.com/high-school/video/2015/12/14/high-school-athlete-year-hunter-gandee-wrestling?rs=.

57. "Monroe County Boy, 16, Finishes 111-Mile Trek with Brother on His Back," *Detroit Free Press*, April 25, 2016, http://www.freep.com/story/news/local/michigan/2016/04/25 /hunter-gandee-braden-gandee-cerebral-palsy-brother-back/83525112/.

ELEVEN

Beautiful Quarterback Passes, Golf Swings, and . . . Teaching Moves?

Ian Parker Renga

> Unless all ages and races of men have been deluded by the same mass hypnotist (who?), there seems to be such a thing as beauty, a grace wholly gratuitous.
> —Annie Dillard[1]

> First thing about it, and this seems so obvious that maybe we overlook it, baseball is a beautiful thing. It's more beautiful than an old park that's asymmetrical and quirky . . . even in a dome with artificial turf it's beautiful. The way the field fans out. The choreography of the sport. The pace and rhythm of it. The fact that pace and rhythm allows for conversation and reflection, opinion and comparison.
> —Bob Costas[2]

Sports media personalities such as Bob Costas have little trouble waxing eloquently about the beauty in the games they love. The internet is replete with videos and articles featuring pundits highlighting the beauty they find in exhibitions of athletic skill, whether it is a golfer's swing, the elusiveness of a quarterback, or a footballer's fulfillment of Pelé's "Beautiful Game" on the pitch.[3]

Ideally, such beauty reflects not only individual performance, but also the masterful coordination of practice between teammates. Writing about professional basketball for the *New Yorker*, Nicholas Dawidoff suggests that the Golden State Warriors' fluid ball movement is beautiful in a way that should please the game's purists, unlike the disgustingly selfish play of his hometown Knicks.[4] Indeed, poor performances often are labeled in beauty's opposite terms. The Denver Broncos won the 2015 Super Bowl through masterful defensive play that produced what some considered a "maddeningly ugly" game.[5] The fact that beautiful defensive play tends to produce ugly offensive play is an odd quirk of team sports that calls to mind the popular maxim of beauty being in the eye of the beholder.

Drop into any pub, sports bar, or social club the world over, and you are likely to hear fans arguing over the beauty (or ugliness) of athletic performance. The same is true in schools as young sports fans engage in similar arguments. Students may even prove their point by mimicking a favorite athlete by doing a quick juke move around a classmate or by launching a piece of crumpled paper at the recycling bin with a smooth flick of the wrist (followed by the mandatory hushed crowd roar). Educators, although perhaps less likely than their students to perform a juke move, can still be found in the break room exchanging aesthetic judgments of the local team or star athlete's recent performance.

Educators will sometimes share with each other snap assessments of their instruction, saying things such as "I nailed it today!" or "I totally messed up that lesson." Encoded within these proclamations is a sense of awe or disgust regarding one's practice, yet educators seem less likely than sports pundits to talk of their exhibitions of practice in aesthetic terms, as beautiful or evidence of beauty.[6]

Months of documenting the talk of teacher educators and trainees from an intensive teacher training program, for example, yielded only one excerpt mirroring how sports media talks of beautiful practice. In that instance, beginning teacher Mark (pseudonym) began by passionately imitating his mentor teacher's method of keeping students engaged: "OK, everybody hands up, stretch! Okay, hands down on the table! You're tracking me." He then added:

> And it's very intentional without being, *Your eyes on me!* You know? And it's just this beautiful thing, because when she goes through it it's like, like as I was watching I was like, Damn! That is what I want to be!

In professional education settings, it is more common to overhear instructional performance discussed with reference to norms, standards, and academic outcomes. All of this is fine and certainly important. But listening to the poetic way pundits such as Costas talk of sports, one yearns for more. The language of beauty seems to come easier in discussions of athletics than in discussions of teaching. Why?

The obvious answer is that sports are entertaining. Talk of sports can offer a welcome distraction from talk of thornier social issues. Sports are also big business, with profits sustained by holding the public attention through nonstop ad blitzes, op-eds, talk shows, magazine profiles, documentaries, and Hollywood films of beloved coaches or players. As a large and entrenched social institution, sport culture arguably assaults the senses through the media in ways education never will. The persistent visual presence of sports in daily life begs for aesthetic judgment, and it thrives by ensnaring fans in perpetual and irresolvable debates over what counts as beautiful performance.

By comparison, exhibitions of teaching are not intended to entertain a wider audience. Much of what teachers do, therefore, is less visible than what athletes do. But that does not mean that teaching lacks beauty or defies aesthetic evaluation. To appreciate the beauty of practice, it is helpful to understand what it means to see something as beautiful and name it as such. "Beauty has a thousand names," explains the philosopher Crispin Sartwell, so "[t]he point, obviously, is not to nail it down or make it ours . . . but to expand into it. That is an exercise in awareness, a way to keep finding what we've lost."[7] Following Sartwell, what can teachers, coaches, and those who support them rediscover in teaching by expanding into its beauty? To answer this question, it helps to understand a little more about beauty and what it means to find something beautiful.

BEAUTY IN CULTURALLY RICH, EVERYDAY PRACTICE

Simply framed, what one finds beautiful reflects what one values. Because those values are rooted in culture, beauty is inherently cultural. Sartwell notes how the ancient Greeks valued adherence to ideals (*kalon*) and saw beauty in the perfection of mathematics, architecture, and sculpture. The ancient Japanese, by comparison, valued a close relationship with nature and saw beauty in the perfect imperfection (*wabi-sabi*) of flowers leaning with the breeze and the grit of raw earthen materials. Other cultures, Sartwell notes, valued and continue to value spirituality, transformation, or harmony; their sense of beauty can only be appreciated by seeing the world with these ideas in mind.

Sartwell suggests that beauty in the United States and much of Europe is tightly linked with desire. Objects that are highly visible but out of reach such as new cars, big homes, fancy vacations, or famous actors are considered beautiful. The consumer-driven gaudiness of it all, it would seem, has produced a widespread belief that claims of beauty are nothing more than sales pitches. Seeing our wide eyes trained on the latest smart phone, the salesman swoops in and gives voice to our desire: "Yes, it's definitely a beautiful piece of technology. Go ahead and try it out." From this stilted perspective, sports pundits' incessant talk of beautiful shots, swings, and passes become nothing more than signs of a sports-industrial complex hawking its wares for profit.

Although it is hard to deny the big business of sports, the skeptical stance toward beauty it has engendered has helped divorce Western society from the richness of aesthetic experience. As a remedy, Sartwell calls for renewing a poetic and spiritual conception of beauty that allows for its nuance and subtlety, where the aim of a beautiful thing is "never to impress you, only—quietly—to affect you."[8] This begins with training one's gaze down from distant horizons and outward, away from the ego to appreciate the beauties of daily practice and the crafting of useful things. Reoriented in this way, the creative process itself becomes a source of profound beauty.

Seeing beauty in the craft of teaching enriches the significance and pleasure of the work. Jim Garrison proposes that beauty is a bridge to the good, spurring teachers to seek the happiness of bringing goodness into the world. That goodness reflects a teacher's adherence to culturally rooted, deeply held values. "Watch the eyes of a good teacher in action," he suggests:

> Note how easily he sees a discipline problem before it occurs, how he looks away from minor transgressions so as not to interrupt a group's enjoyment in rehearsing a dramatic story. The left arm embraces the child needing the hug, while the right hand confiscates the baseball cards being traded during class time. More deliberately, the teacher rearranges class seating or reorganizes small group participants to reduce cruel teaching. All these acts establish good, harmonious social relations conducive to learning, and that is beautiful.[9]

Garrison notes how John Dewey, the great pragmatist philosopher of education, joined his classical Grecian predecessors in seeing harmony and beauty as the same thing. But Dewey disagreed that beauty should be judged against divine perfection or rest upon how well an earthly object expressed godly ideals. Rather, he saw beauty in the imperfect process of seeking harmony—in teachers persisting to create order from chaos, attracted by the promise of creating newer, more beautiful worlds through their work.

Following from Dewey's line of thinking, ugly practice is not teaching that fails to achieve harmony but teaching that achieves it by betraying core values. Take, for example, a teacher who values caring relationships. Such a teacher is likely to feel uncomfortable at a school that requires her to force student compliance through threats of punishment. Although such threats might achieve obedient, productive students and an ordered classroom, such harmony will have been bought at the expense of the kind of relationships she values having with students.

Sartwell and Garrison both agree that the seemingly mundane activity of daily life holds underappreciated beauty. They observe how one of art's virtues is its tendency to reveal subtle beauty and the truths it contains about everyday practice. Garrison observes that "teaching is a lovely art whose beauty is often concealed beneath bureaucratic forms, teacher-proof curricula, and tests."[10] Denying the artfulness of teaching sustains this concealment. It forecloses the search for truth and possibility in teaching, or at least bounds it within the strictures of science, policy-making, and a narrow band of cultural values.[11] Seeing teaching as beautiful can expand these boundaries.

VALUES OF COMPETITIVE PERFORMANCE

To appreciate beauty, then, requires understanding the values of a given community and its culture. Examining media portrayals of "beautiful" sports performances reveals several values that help explain the perception of beauty among sports pundits, fans, and participants. Take, for example, a moment from a pivotal American football game from the 2015 season:

> It is a snowy night in Colorado. A growing layer of white conveys how cold it is on the football field. The hometown Denver Broncos are sixteen long yards from the New England Patriots' end zone; a touchdown is essential to surmount a two score deficit and have a chance of winning the game. Quarterback Peyton Manning snaps the ball and hands it off to running back C. J. Anderson. The Patriots defense is ready, and defenders break quickly to bring down the smallish runner. Undeterred, Anderson nimbly jumps left to dodge his assailants and then sprints his way to the end zone. The crowd roars. A reporter quickly posts a video of the move online and labels it "an absolute thing of beauty," [12] adding the comment that this how a running back is "supposed" to run.

So what made the play beautiful for the reporter and, presumably, many of those who watched the game or highlight reel? Answering this question requires teasing out and appreciating how the performance exemplified some of sports culture's cherished values, four of which are highlighted here:

Excellence. Anderson's exhibition reflected an ideal of athletic excellence, or near perfection of practice—in this case, an ideal for how the football can be run with masterful skill. Comparing his performance to an envisioned image of great running—what it is *supposed* to look like on game day—made it pleasing to behold. Dimensions of that ideal tend to include elusiveness, speed, and toughness, all of which could be seen in the performance.

Merit. The running back's achievement was earned and could be viewed as beautiful in its exemplification of meritorious performance. The Patriots did not let him stroll casually into the end zone; he had to fight his way in. Anderson had struggled earlier in the season, eventually losing his job to a teammate. This moment arguably capped the running back's dogged persistence to earn back the starting role.

Glory. The masterful performance brought glory to the team and its fans. Skilled athletic exhibitions that lead to wins are perceived as more beautiful than those accompanying losses. The performance that wins the game or captures the medal leaves a memory that continues to elicit awe in fans for years to come. Comparable performances that do not produce wins may be remembered, though often with head shaking at the wasted opportunity for glory. [13]

Honor. Anderson's touchdown run was accomplished in accordance with the rules and, significantly, with respect to the game's social norms. He briefly celebrated the touchdown but avoided taunting the Patriot defensive players. Such honorable demonstrations of sportsmanship and respect for rules and norms can contribute to a sense of beauty, or at least prevent an otherwise beautiful play from being negated and recast as ugly.

These are not the only values that can be teased out from the example (some will notice that teamwork, for example, is missing); nor are they the sole purview of sports culture. In many ways, sports culture mirrors military culture, which is built around the assumed necessity of competition within ranks and against opponents. A case can likewise be made that competition is threaded through the culture of contemporary schooling as students vie for limited opportunities and resources, jockeying to position themselves favorably in the classroom and eventually in the job market.[14]

Values evident in sports culture can thus be seen in many K–12 schools as well. Within much of Western society, schools are expected to establish a fair playing field built around clear and ambitious standards (excellence) where students must earn their marks of accomplishment and advancement (merit); it is assumed that rules and codes of conduct will be enforced to ensure the integrity of the effort (honor); and it is expected that achievement will be marked with a graduation ceremony where celebrated victors—usually the valedictorian and successful alumni—make speeches connecting their accomplishments to the school community (glory).[15] If beautiful teaching *is* good teaching in the sense that it is the enactment of communal values, then beauty in such an environment is to be found in instruction that upholds the goodness of fair competition.

The appeal of this vision of good teaching is evident in Hollywood depictions of great teaching performances. In many heroic teacher films, teachers are shown dispensing tough love to students while demonstrating a firm and unyielding commitment to merit and the rewards of academic achievement. Jaime Escalante in *Stand and Deliver*, for example, stands sternly before his class of mostly Latino students and proclaims:

> There will be no free rides, no excuses. You already have two strikes against you. There are some people in this world who will assume you know less than you do because of your last name and your complexion. But math is the great equalizer.[16]

He then proceeds through some trial and error to teach them algebra and calculus. Whether it's passing the AP calculus exam or graduating from high school, the viewer is supposed to be moved when teachers such as Escalante succeed through gritty resolve in finding the instructional moves that ultimately help students to overcome the odds and beat low expectations. Swap out the teacher for a coach, and the script fits most popular sports films.

Some educators, no doubt, are drawn to the competitive narrative and buy into its resulting vision of good and beautiful teaching. They prefer learning environments where, as with points or wins in sports, the measures of success are clear—where the beauty of instructional moves is in their execution of coherent, prestructured game plans for learning; or, when things go awry, in steering wayward students back to that plan. They seek to excel and promote excellence, and they accept the premise that it's a dog-eat-dog world.

Educators who are less taken in by this narrative and the values it engenders may find this vision of good teaching less appealing—necessary within a climate stressing teacher accountability, perhaps, though not exactly beautiful. They might prefer school cultures built around alternative formulations of goodness that emphasize equity, cooperation, or care and will look for beauty in instructional moves that reflect these values.

EXPANDING INTO THE LOVELY ART

Returning to the initial question of why it seems easier to talk of beauty in sports than in teaching, it is not because what teachers do is inherently less beautiful than what athletes do. Rather, it is because values in K–12 education arguably are more contentious and harder to agree upon than those preoccupying the world of sports. A pundit can give his two cents about an athlete's elegant performance and safely assume his audience shares the values informing his opinion; this is not always true for teachers.

Significantly, what Dewey called the *ends-in-view*[17] of education are more varied and debatable than they are in sports. Although both athletic performance and instructional performance are bounded by rules and realities, athletics is more limited by its emphasis on beating opponents or setting new records. As such, novelty in sports tends to come in the form of technological innovation (e.g., better shoes, instant replay, narrowing the goalposts) or perhaps new approaches to training. This limitation may be part of the appeal; it avoids the messiness of moral deliberation around what counts as the good so energy and resources can be expended on fulfilling the good.

In some sense, standardized testing and efforts to develop uniform measures of teaching quality are driven by a desire to make education more like sports by creating clarity of purpose for the sake of efficiency, comparison, and progress. Similarly, then, novelty is sought in new educational technologies or the search for best practices rather than in wholesale interrogation or change in philosophy. Narrowing the aims of education is a reasonable response to the complexity of such an ambitious endeavor. However, it risks shutting down crucial discussions about what matters in teaching and why. These delicate and often frustrating conversations can be slow going, but they serve to revive and renew commitments and establish common values.

Teachers are engaged in such efforts every day in their schools as they negotiate desired aims and outcomes with students; they are also negotiated with parents, colleagues, and other stakeholders in brief chats after class and during formal meetings. These interactions build relationships that can produce results.

Even so, their impact always will remain somewhat hazy. Jim Garrison notes how good teachers learn to live with uncertainty and doubt regarding what their work ultimately accomplishes. In a given classroom, students might achieve many things: learning to write, mastering a concept, maturing emotionally, or finding their political voice. But they inevitably leave the classroom as time passes and life's currents sweep them along. Years later, a few of them might reach out in gratitude and recount indelible classroom memories. Yet it's hard to predict which instructional moments will really matter, for whom they will matter, or why. To teach, then, is to have faith that one is making a difference.

A common refrain in teaching is to celebrate the little victories—the seemingly infrequent moments where students show growth. Doing so sustains the faith. Further nurturing that faith in the face of so much uncertainty, however, involves something more that keeps academic outcomes in mind without imbuing them with too much significance.

This chapter suggests something more: a capacity to expand into the loveliness of teaching, which requires a willingness to see beauty in its mundane and often ephemeral moments—in the teacher's intentional forging of a bond between students by pairing them together; in the posing of a thought-provoking question at the right moment during class discussion; in the last-minute modification of an assignment to enable access to learning; or in the quick aside to give students appropriate language for talking about race. Doing so draws attention to the various ways in which teachers not only enact values, but also craft them through their instruction.

FINAL THOUGHTS

It may be a stretch for some to find teaching as beautiful as sports. Appreciating how a teacher's moves in the classroom can be as awe-inspiring as a running back's dogged persistence to score a touchdown may entail a reimagining of the role. Too often teachers are asked to see themselves as technicians or learning managers; seeing them as artists who ply their craft toward the production of goodness enlarges the educational imagination.

Sports media fuel a popular narrative that goodness is the pursuit of excellence, achievement, honor, and the glory of victory. It is a narrative not uncommon in schools. Yet sitting in a classroom and simply observing teachers as they work with children reveals more to the story. Empathy, care, and compassion often are present in the many small acts of teaching and don't so much impress as *subtly affect* the observer. This makes the acts beautiful to behold. The fact that such beauty is less appreciated publicly than the beauty of athletic performance suggests a woeful overestimation of competitive values compared to the caring values enacted daily by millions of teachers. Educators, thus, are encouraged to look at their work as Bob Costas looks at baseball and take note of its understated loveliness.

NOTES

1. Annie Dillard, *Pilgrim at Tinker Creek* (New York: HarperCollins, 1974), 9.

2. Geoffrey C. Ward, writer, and Ken Burns, writer and director, "Inning 1: Our Game," in Ken Burns and Lynn Novick, producers, *Baseball*, Florentine Films, United States, September 18, 1994.

3. Some examples include Michael Shamburger, "Butch Harmon Still Has a Beautiful Golf Swing at 72-Years-Old," *thebiglead.com*, December 23, 2015, http://thebiglead.com/2015/12/23/butch-harmon-still-has-a-beautiful-golf-swing-at-72-years-old/; and Yael Averbuch, "Recognizing Art in the Other Side of the Beautiful Game," *New York Times*, June 3, 2015, www.nytimes.com/2015/06/04/sports/soccer/recognizing-art-in-the-other-side-of-the-beautiful-game.html.

4. Nicholas Dawidoff, "The Golden State Warriors' Beautiful Game," *New Yorker*, February 3, 2016, www.newyorker.com/news/sporting-scene/the-golden-state-warriors-intricate-approach-to-basketball.

5. Justin Peters, "One of the Worst Super Bowls Ever," *Slate.com*, February 7, 2016, www.slate.com/articles/sports/sports_nut/2016/02/the_denver_broncos_win_one_of_the_worst_super_bowls_ever.html.

6. It bears mentioning that some traditions, such as the Reggio Emilia approach to early childhood education, are built explicitly around aesthetics, the arts, and imagery in ways that seem likely to render beauty as an appropriate descriptor of teaching. Also, a few scholars, including Maxine Greene and Dan Liston, have explored the contours of beauty in teaching.

7. Crispin Sartwell, *Six Names of Beauty* (New York: Routledge, 2004), 152.

8. Ibid., 65.

9. Jim Garrison, *Dewey and Eros: Wisdom and Desire in the Art of Teaching* (New York: Teachers College Press, 1997), 80–81.

10. Ibid., 84.

11. Some education scholars, such as Deborah Ball, take issue with characterizing teaching as an art on the grounds that it permits teachers to evade systematic, scientific scrutiny of their practice. This view helpfully brings thoughtful inquiry to teaching. But advocating for the scientific study of teaching need not undermine the artistry involved in enacting teaching practice. Also, artistic inquiry into teaching (i.e., portraiture, fiction, film, photography) can reveal valuable truths that elude the sciences.

12. Jared Dubin, "WATCH: C. J. Anderson's Jump-Cut Is an Absolute Thing of Beauty," *CBSSports.com*, November 30, 2015, https://www.cbssports.com/nfl/news/watch-cj-andersons-jump-cut-is-an-absolute-thing-of-beauty/.

13. For fans of the other football, the great Lionel Messi's inability to win a World Cup for Argentina despite some impressive goals may come to mind.

14. David F. Labaree, *How to Succeed in School without Really Learning: The Credentials Race in American Education* (New Haven, CT: Yale University Press, 1997).

15. Other examples of students bringing glory to the school through academic performances are in spelling bees, debate team competitions, Model UN, or math Olympiads, to name a few. However, student participation in these is not uniform across schools or as institutionalized as the graduation ceremony.

16. *Stand and Deliver*, directed by Ramón Menéndez (Burbank, CA: Warner Brothers Pictures, 1988).

17. See note 9 for reference, 21.

About the Editors

Ian Parker Renga is assistant professor of education in the education department at Western State Colorado University. His current work examines the intersection of practice, identity, and community in teaching and teacher education. He has published in *Educational Studies* and *Science Education*, and recently edited a collection of scholarly essays on education in popular film titled *Teaching, Learning, and Schooling in Film: Reel Education* (2015). Prior to becoming a professor, Dr. Renga was a secondary science, math, and art teacher, as well as a paraeducator serving students with autism. He rowed crew in high school and is an avid naturalist.

Christopher Benedetti is assistant professor of educational leadership, learning, and curriculum at Plymouth State University. His research interests include leader and group psychology, organizational systems, and leader preparation and development. Dr. Benedetti has presented nationally and internationally on organizational chaos in schools, teacher burnout and satisfaction, parent-teacher role conflict, and leader succession. His recent work has been published in the *Journal of College Teaching and Learning* and *Kappan*. He is a former middle school language arts teacher, basketball coach, and elementary principal.

About the Contributors

Crystal L. Beach is a high school English teacher with a PhD from the University of Georgia in the department of language and literacy education. Her research interests include new literacies, identity/ies, multimodalities, popular culture, and technologies in the secondary English classroom. A former collegiate softball player, Dr. Beach currently coaches a variety of sports and has helped lead the young women on her teams to several state championship titles.

Alan Brown is assistant professor of English education in the department of education at Wake Forest University. He is a former high school English teacher and basketball coach who now serves as the secondary education program director at Wake Forest. His scholarly interests include aspects of secondary teacher education, young adult literature, and adolescent literacy as well as various intersections of sport, education, culture, and society. His research focuses on the socialization of classroom teachers and athletic coaches in secondary schools, and he is the coeditor of the book *Developing Contemporary Literacies through Sports: A Guide for the English Classroom* (2016). For more information, visit his sports literacy blog at https://sportsliteracy.org.

Megan M. Buning is assistant professor of research at Augusta University. Her research interests include coach-athlete relationships and the use of sports technology in the classroom. Dr. Buning is a former Division I softball athlete from the University of South Carolina, where she holds numerous collegiate records and a spot in the university's Hall of Fame. She was recently named to the 2017 SEC Women's Legends class and serves as a color analyst for the SECNetwork+ station. She also played professionally for the New England Riptide and coached softball at Florida State, Coastal Carolina, and the University of Mississippi.

Michael Domínguez is assistant professor in the department of Chicana and Chicano studies at San Diego State University. His research interests focus on the schooling experiences of Chicana/o youth, as well as decolonial theory, teacher education, and the development of culturally sustaining pedagogies and ethnic studies curriculum. Formerly a middle school English and ESL teacher in North Las Vegas, Nevada, Dr. Domínguez was an NCAA D-I conference champion in the three-thousand-meter steeplechase, and has posted numerous top-three finishes in ultra and mountain races. He continues to coach youth track and spends most of his summers preparing high school athletes for the fall cross-country season. He has numerous publications, including a piece in *The Urban Review*, and a chapter on de-colonial teacher education in *Culturally Sustaining Pedagogies*.

Katie S. Dredger is assistant professor of adolescent literacy at James Madison University in Harrisonburg, Virginia. Her research interests include new literacies, multimodality, and social justice in text access for marginalized adolescents. Dr. Dredger spent thirteen years in Calvert County, Maryland, as a secondary English language arts teacher and department chair, Advanced Placement teacher consultant, and literacy coach. She has coached high school varsity tennis, varsity cheer, and is a travel soccer mom.

Robert D. Greim is assistant director of athletics for compliance and eligibility at Southeast Missouri State University. A frequent contributor in national college athletics policy discussions, he has presented multiple times at national conventions, is a past participant in the NCAA Regional Rules Seminar Advanced Track Program, is a recipient of N4A's Shining Star Award, and currently serves on the Division I Eligibility Center Advisory Group. Dr. Greim has written articles published in *Inside Higher Ed*, *The Journal of NCAA Compliance*, and *Legal Issues in College Athletics*.

Halley Gruber is a fourth grade ELA teacher in Denver Public Schools. She earned her teaching certificate through the competitive Denver Teacher Residency program and holds an MA from the University of Denver. Mrs. Gruber is a former NCAA athlete who played basketball at the University of Hawaii at Hilo.

Heather Rogers Haverback is associate professor in the department of secondary and middle school education at Towson University. Her research focuses on literacy, middle school, and teacher education. She has been an avid sports fan all of her life. Her work has been published in a number of highly regarded journals, including *Teacher and Teacher Education*, *Journal of Experimental Education*, *Educational Psychology Review*, and *Teacher Educator*.

Mark A. Lewis is associate professor of literacy education at Loyola University Maryland, where he teaches courses in children's and young adult literature, content area literacy, and English methods. His research includes examinations of conceptions of youth within English language arts curriculum, critical analyses of young adult literature, and supporting linguistically diverse learners. His favorite sports memories include attending soccer World Cups in South Korea and Germany.

Antonio E. Naula-Rodríguez specializes in pedagogical linguistics and language acquisition, and his interests lie in social equity in areas that are often overlooked by other scholars, such as youth athletics. His research focuses on how students organize and express themselves in groups and with teachers, parents, coaches, and other adults. Dr. Naula-Rodríguez has taught elementary school, Spanish, and theater in inner-city Atlanta, Boston, and Denver, and earned a PhD in educational equity and cultural diversity from the University of Colorado at Boulder.

K. Jamil Northcutt is the assistant director of enforcement, football development, at the National Collegiate Athletic Association (NCAA). He has held numerous roles in professional and collegiate athletics, including director of football administration at the National Football League (NFL), consultant and director of player engagement for the Cleveland Browns, player development coordinator for the Kansas City Chiefs, and assistant athletics director for internal operations at the University of Mississippi. Dr. Northcutt played football at Ole Miss, where he earned the Chucky Mullins Courage Award and helped the Rebels to four straight bowl games, including a win in the Cotton Bowl. He holds a PhD in higher education administration from Ole Miss and an executive education certificate from the Wharton School. His research interests focus on the intersection between sports, race, education, culture, and the student-athlete experience.

Luke Rodesiler is assistant professor of secondary education at Purdue University Fort Wayne. His scholarship exploring sports culture in the classroom has been published through various academic outlets, including *English Journal*, *Talking Points*, *The Clearing House*, and *SIGNAL Journal*. A former high school English teacher and coach, Dr. Rodesiler coedited *Developing Contemporary Literacies through Sports: A Guide for the English Classroom*, published by the National Council of Teachers of English (NCTE).

De'Andre L. Shepard is assistant professor in the education department at the University of Michigan, Flint. Along with a PhD in educational leadership from Oakland University, Dr. Shepard holds a school leadership certificate from Harvard Graduate School of Education. His research projects include the professional development needs of practicing teachers in inclusive settings, the changing role of school systems operating in a global environment, examining the impact of the *Sit with Us* app on bullying and social emotional experiences of middle school students, and exploring teaching and leadership through the lens of athletics and sports.